COMING CLEAN

With the compliments of the

Author

COMING CLEAN

*A Postscript after Retirement
from Unilever*

Andrew M. Knox

HEINEMANN : LONDON

William Heinemann Ltd.
15 Queen Street, Mayfair, London W1X 8BE

LONDON   MELBOURNE   TORONTO
JOHANNESBURG   AUCKLAND

First published 1976
© Unilever Limited 1976
SBN 434 91066 X

Printed in Great Britain by
Cox & Wyman Ltd
London, Fakenham and Reading

To Mary with love

Contents

Illustrations

Acknowledgements

I have had much encouragement and help in the writing of this book for which I am profoundly grateful, but I limit my specific acknowledgements to those who activated and guided me at important stages of what has turned out to be a longer process than I had expected. I am specially grateful to:

Professor Charles Wilson, author of the *History of Unilever*, who first suggested to me that I should write about my career and who subsequently suggested to Unilever that what I had written could be made into a publishable book.

Mr Maurice Zinkin, also an author, who supported the suggestion and put at my disposal the resources of the Economics and Statistics Department of Unilever, of which he was then head.

Miss Dawn Stageman, my secretary, who got me started. When, before my retirement, I confided to her that I was going to try to write something she said that she would like to type my draft for me—an exercise of which she had had much experience. It was an offer I could not resist. I had to start writing.

The late Lord Heyworth and my brother, Sir Malcolm Knox, who were the first to read my draft and who both gave it the seal of their approval. No seal could have carried greater authority.

Sir Ernest Woodroofe, then Chairman of Unilever, and Mr David Orr, the present Chairman, who agreed that, subject to skilled editing, Unilever would sponsor publication.

Dr W. J. Reader, author, *inter-alia*, of the *History of I.C.I.*, who did the editing. He not only had the skill but also understanding and deep knowledge of my subject as he had been a research assistant to Professor Wilson on the *History of Unilever*. I confess that when he started to cut up my draft I felt a bit cut up too and I am specially grateful to him for his good-humoured patience.

Miss Florence Dace, who with great skill and promptitude did the typing, re-typing, and re-re-typing involved in the editing. She too knew what I was writing about as she had, at an early age, jumped overnight from being a typist in the Lever Brothers London Branch Office to being secretary to John McDowell, Vice-Chairman, in the newly established Lever headquarters in London.

Mary, my wife, who gave me firm and unquestioning support in all my business activities and smiled in patient understanding when, after retirement, I spent many selfish but happy hours writing.

Crieff
1975

1

Port Sunlight

———•———

When I was about four or five years old I was taken for a walk on the road that runs beside the Mersey on the Cheshire bank between what were then Rock Ferry and New Ferry piers. When we reached New Ferry pier the lady who took me for the walk pointed along the road and told me that up there was the beautiful new village of Port Sunlight.

My father and mother had come from Scotland in 1900 to my father's first charge as a Congregational minister. We lived in Rock Ferry which was no doubt officially part of Birkenhead but was actually one of the more fashionable residential suburbs of Liverpool to which it was linked by underground railway and a regular ferry service. The people living in Rock Ferry then would no more have relished being considered as residents of Birkenhead than their contemporaries in Hampstead would have liked to be referred to as Londoners.

Our church was in Tranmere, which was in Birkenhead, but was linked to the main Congregational church in Rock Ferry. Thus, in my earliest years, I found myself equally welcome to take tea in the drawing-room of a merchant's home with all the gracious elaboration of doily-covered plates, India or China tea, and heated silver dishes filled with toasted tea cakes and muffins, or in the docker's kitchen with tea straight from the hob and a freshly made doughnut. Each occasion was a happy one but tea from the hob and doughnuts tended to be the more boisterous.

It was a young lady from the drawing-room who told me about Port Sunlight. At the time Mr W. H. Lever, founder of Port

Sunlight and Chairman of Lever Brothers, was already a wealthy and influential industrialist. He was also a wealthy and influential Congregationalist, and it was under his auspices that my father became minister of the new church built by Mr Lever in Neston on the opposite side of the Wirral peninsula from Rock Ferry. From then on Mr Lever, Sir William, Lord Leverhulme, became a familiar name and a familiar figure in our family. He attended special ceremonies at the church, particularly if they had any connection with children in whom he always took a genuine delight and interest, and on such occasions frequently called with his wife at the Manse for a cup of tea. Father and mother were on his guest list—he was a most generous and thoughtful host—and my brother and sisters and I were on his Christmas present list. We looked in lively expectation at Christmas time for the present from Mr and Mrs Lever as it was sure to be grander than anything we could expect from other sources.

In 1912 father accepted a call to New Road Congregational Church in Bury and although that was in Lancashire it was outside the Lever orbit. It was, however, inside a most warm and friendly community where, as a young boy, I made many lifetime friends including my future wife.

Altogether I went to seven schools but I don't think this did me much harm. I did not enjoy any of them very much except for Bury Grammar School where I spent two very happy years. This may only be nostalgia as I look back; it is not difficult for people of my age to think of the two years before the First World War as happy ones.

The headmaster of Bury Grammar School was a member of the Headmasters' Conference and, *ipso facto*, the school was classed as a Public School—a school for gentlemen. I don't know whether the sons of Lancashire millowners, doctors, tradesmen and ministers in 1914 could be classed as gentlemen or not. Our woodwork/clay modelling/scripture master once addressed us as 'snivelling jackasses'.

It was not a big school, about 200 boys, and I suppose about the same number of girls, though we never saw them unless by peering through the chink between the hall doors when the girls had their morning prayers before us. In the lower forms, at any rate, we were not under any great pressure to work though we were exhorted from time to time by the headmaster to work hard in order to achieve life's most worthy ambition: the senior ranks of the Civil Service. Classes were small, about fifteen pupils, and as most boys came from within a radius of five miles one tended to be on friendly terms not only with class mates, but with most boys in the school; it was a friendly atmosphere. None of the masters was frightening, though most had no difficulty with discipline. There was one great exception who for a term or two was our form master, teaching, or trying to teach us, French and Latin. The form's theme song, to the appropriate tune, was 'There is a happy land, not far away, It is in Lammy's room three times a day'.

The Rev. E. J. S. Lamburn was very kindly and generous, but he had no idea how to discipline small boys. His only punishment was to cancel marks. He used to shout in apparent wrath, 'Sir, your marks are cancelled' and with suitable relish he drew a firm line across his marks' book. But we all knew that he was too kind-hearted to stick to it and that our marks would be reinstated after the lesson. It has subsequently become evident to me whence his daughter, Richmal Crompton, got the knowledge, understanding and love of small boys that enabled her to write *Just William*.

The most austere master was Jimmy Norton, senior language master. Within the school I only viewed him from a great distance, but he was also our next-door neighbour. My brother and I frequently walked up to school with him when I found that he was not so stern as he looked, and indeed he was instrumental in conferring on me the only distinction which I attained at the school. He put me, presumably as the smallest boy present, to lead the torchlight procession with which the school greeted its hero, William Morris, on return from his triumph at the Public Schools' Annual Sports Competition in 1914. (He had won the long jump with a record of 21 ft 1¼ in.) I was proud of my position but my mother was distressed by the ruin of my overcoat from the molten wax dropped from the torch.

From the beginning of our stay in Bury father had been under continuous pressure from Lever to return to his sphere of activity.

Lever foresaw, as his business grew to worldwide proportions, the necessity to put staff relations and training on a wider footing and more enlightened plane than mere paternalism no matter how generous, and he evidently believed that my father's training in and experience of human relations as a minister would fit him to do pioneer work in the field of activities now commonly grouped under the general title of personnel. Lever had great personal magnetism and I am sure would paint a vivid and imaginative picture of the value and scope of the work he had in mind, but it could not have been easy for my father and mother to decide to leave the ministry to which they were both dedicated and within which they were honoured and beloved. Father, aged forty-four, was probably attracted by the possibility of fresh fields to conquer, and so we found ourselves living in Port Sunlight just as war broke out in August 1914.

I remember feeling at the time that although we moved to a very fine house—quite the best and biggest in Port Sunlight—our prestige as a family had received a knock. As the son of a minister in those days I was outside class distinctions (though I would not have put it in those words at the time). As the son of a manager I was 'classed' and, as it turned out, I was classed in a community which became disastrously class conscious.

I have often wondered whether father ever regretted leaving the ministry but I always thought that it would have hurt him if I had asked. He may have done so, especially in the early days at Port Sunlight. The grim wartime atmosphere was not conducive to the developments he had been appointed to effect: there were other priorities and other duties. (Many years later he wrote in a letter to me, 'I chose the betterment of my fellow man as my career and from year to year my opportunities increased.') He influenced the personnel policies of the business very considerably, especially through educational work. He pioneered the movement towards 'Education within Industry' and founded and was the first principal of the Staff Training College at Port Sunlight which was started in 1917. He was also active in the recruitment of university graduate trainees. In my subsequent travels throughout the world I have often been told by Unilever managers that they 'owed everything to my father'.

The canvas, perhaps, did not turn out so wide nor the colours so vivid as Lever had described them, for many dreams were shattered between 1914 and 1918. Lever himself died in 1925 when his own fortunes and those of the Company were at a low ebb. But the foundations were laid and laid firmly on the two corner stones: first, people work better if they are dealt with as individuals, not units; secondly, management does not just grow, it has to be developed. One of the contributions made by Lever Brothers to Unilever was its experience of and belief in management development and its tradition of and skill in preserving human relationships.

In outward appearance Port Sunlight has changed very little since 1914. Lever built it as a 'village' with the aim of creating a happy integrated community, and in providing social facilities he was splendidly generous. For a population of about 2,000, including children, he established:

Church—with graveyard	
Hospital	Men's club with bowling green
Two schools	Girls' club
Technical institute	Hotel (with licence)
Museum	Three public halls of varying sizes
Library	equipped with theatrical and
Gymnasium	catering facilities
Open air swimming pool	Co-operative shop
Tennis courts	Post office
Football field	Band stand

He even provided a station, but the London North Western and Great Western Joint Railway Authority in control of the line between Chester and Birkenhead would only give it the status of a 'halt' to be used only by Workmen's Specials. No scheduled service could stop there.

He had an argument about the church, which although Nonconformist was built of stone in all the splendour of traditional Perpendicular Gothic ecclesiastical architecture. It had the nave, transepts and chancel, choir stalls, communion rail and altar table of a typical Anglican church. It also had a tower with a belfry complete with a peal of bells. The Bishop of Chester took exception to this on the grounds that only parish churches have a peal of bells

—chapels could only have one bell, so would Mr Lever kindly remove the peal? But Mr Lever stuck to his guns and asked by what law he was prohibited from having the bells. The Bishop found that he was depending on tradition, not law, so Mr Lever stuck to his bells too and they have pealed merrily ever since.

Lever certainly did his best for the village, and the inhabitants of modern new towns might justifiably be jealous of such lavish provision. In addition, efforts were made from the very beginning to build up a community. There was a village council, of which the Chairman was J. L. Ferguson (Lever's nephew who became a director of the Company in 1907), other members being residents of the village. This council was responsible for running Port Sunlight, through a series of committees, for example: Finance; Hall (clubs etc.); Provident; Musical; Athletics; Grounds; Shop; Girls' Institute.

Regular reports of council and committee meetings were published in the *Port Sunlight Monthly Journal* (written and edited entirely by amateurs but printed in the works)—yearly subscription one shilling (5p), payable in advance. The Journal recorded all the events in the village and provided a wide miscellany of articles and jottings, ranging, in the bound volume I have for the year 1897, from a graphic account of an extremely uncomfortable journey from Auckland to Raratonga in the Cook Islands, to notes on Sir Walter Scott and his works. Running through the whole volume in twelve parts is the libretto of an opera *The Squire of Burleigh* by Fred H. Seddon, who was choir master when I came to Port Sunlight. There was a regular letter from the London branch office, and a vivid account of a visit to London by 2,300 employees from Port Sunlight in commemoration of Queen Victoria's Diamond Jubilee. It must have been a strenuous day as the first of the six special trains left the Port Sunlight halt at 4.00 a.m. and the last train home left London at 8.30 p.m. It is noted with satisfaction that members of the party would receive their full wages though absent from work. It was a Saturday.

The accounts of the village shop were also published, for example:

December Quarter 1896

TRADING ACCOUNT

Dr.

	£	s	d		£	s	d
To stock Quarter ending				By Sales during Qtr.	722	9	9
September 29th	274	0	0	,, Stock at December			
,, Purchases	770	8	2	24th	392	5	10
,, Balance carried dn.	70	7	5				
	1,114	15	7		1,114	15	7
To Wages	40	15	0	By Balance c/d	70	7	5
,, Rent	5	0	0				
,, Travelling Exes	1	19	0				
,, Postages		7	6				
,, Sundry Exes.	20	17	5				
,, Balance, being net profit for Quarter	1	8	6				
	£70	7	5		£70	7	5

Between 1914 and 1918 neighbours were drawn together for mutual support in the anxieties and bitter sorrows of the casualty lists, and by the great and varied voluntary activities, which started early in Port Sunlight when the Hulme Hall was transformed overnight from a museum to a reception centre for Belgian refugees. Subsequently it became a military hospital, thus providing a focal point for unselfish effort of all sorts.

From the very beginning Lever was the inspirer, the guide and often the leader in village activities. He was a familiar figure, known to everyone. Even in later years when he had vast international interests and many public calls on his energies, Port Sunlight remained close to his heart: he attended church there frequently and was present at all special occasions. All this generosity, this pouring out both of money and of spirit, produced for Lever as loyal and enthusiastic a group of workpeople as any man has ever had, but it did not make Port Sunlight into a happy and lively community.

Why not? The people were living at a standard at least a generation ahead of the times. The houses were of greatly varied but harmonious and pleasant architecture, built seven to the acre, compared with the then officially permitted maximum of forty-five. They all had baths and a private lavatory—though neither was

standard in industrial building at that time. In the interests of the
architectural façade the baths sometimes found themselves in
strange places, and many of the lavatories were outside in the
private walled yard at the back of each house. The houses and the
plots of formal garden in front of each group were maintained,
admittedly on a standard pattern, free of charge and rents were
modest. There was plenty of open space for children to play in and
allotments available for those who were interested in gardening.

Treatment in the hospital was free and to cover general medical
expenses there was a voluntary scheme appropriately if somewhat
abruptly called the Sick Club (and colloquially referred to by a
more vivid word). The schools were free, being recognized by the
local education authority, but the head teachers were appointed and
paid by Mr Lever and were at the top of their profession.

Creature comforts, amusements, sporting facilities were provided very cheaply or for nothing. Help was available in life's
difficulties and anxieties. Employment was virtually guaranteed.
Port Sunlight offered complete social security. Nevertheless as an
experiment in welfare it failed, and it failed because it was too
closely self-contained and it developed a sense of being isolated.

For many years Port Sunlight had no public transport. My
brother and I walked twenty-five minutes every morning and
evening to and from New Ferry pier to take the boat to and from
school in Liverpool. It was ten minutes' walk to the New Ferry
tram for Rock Ferry and Birkenhead, the same distance to
Bebington station for Birkenhead or Chester, and about half an
hour's walk to the nearest 'respectable' cinema or to the dancing
class. The centre of Bebington, then an urban district, subsequently a borough, of which Port Sunlight was a part, was only
ten minutes away. All these distances were quite short at a time
when Shanks's pony was still a normal means of transport, and
Port Sunlight's isolation was not physical but psychological.

Those living in the village found themselves almost completely
ostracized by the immediately surrounding communities, who
regarded it as a sort of tied housing estate for workmen. The fact
that it was particularly comfortable probably added envy to
snobbery. But in Liverpool, at any rate at school, Port Sunlight
was remote, and the fact that you lived there meant nothing. If you

tried to get into Rock Ferry Tennis Club, though, it was a different matter altogether. You lived in Port Sunlight and so you must be the son of a workman—a second-class workman, moreover, because he lived under patronage in a tied and subsidized house. Some people in Port Sunlight felt this second-class status so acutely that they gave their postal address as Bebington. It delayed their letters but no doubt it gave them a feeling of respectability. On the telephone you had a Rock Ferry number and that was acceptable, but very few people had a phone.

This sense of inferiority was not felt by everyone, and in the early days probably not at all. It grew only gradually, and as long as Lever himself was alive it had a strong antidote in loyalty and genuine personal affection. Old and young cheered him when he visited the village and were proud to be Port Sunlighters.

It is true that Port Sunlight was built for workpeople. There were only five or six 'big houses', occupied by those concerned with social rather than business matters. Senior managers and directors lived in Rock Ferry or the nearby countryside. It was not this factor, however, which caused Port Sunlight to fail as a social experiment. The mistake lay in housing people together who also worked together and in limiting the residents of Port Sunlight to employees of Lever Brothers.

Lever—generous, far-seeing, in thought and action on social matters a long way ahead of his time—knew in the end that a mistake had been made. Nevertheless the generation who came to Port Sunlight when it was founded had cause to be grateful to him for thirty years of security, comfort and a standard of living which may never be equalled in our present-day Welfare State. And their children look back on the happy days when Port Sunlight was their world and Mr Lever the smiling and exciting godfather of them all. The failure arose out of the changing social circumstances of the times, perhaps accentuated or accelerated by the rapid growth of Lever Brothers Limited.

When he started making soap in Warrington Lever would certainly have known every one of his workmen by name: even in the much bigger works in Port Sunlight he would know most of his regular employees, as distinct from casuals, and certainly if they actually lived in Port Sunlight. And in those days they would look

up to him as the boss, but he would not have looked down upon
them. This was the tradition of the day, at any rate amongst the
emerging family manufacturing businesses in the North of England. There was a direct link and usually a bond of mutual respect
between the boss and his workpeople. He knew them and they
knew him. But as the business grew, the boss had to appoint a
manager, who, to begin with, might be able to take over and maintain this direct link and the bond of respect. But the manager later
had to have deputies. The direct link weakened, the bond of respect
was questioned and there arose the ghastly spectre of status which
caused and still causes more unhappiness than any other social
factor within industry, or outside it.

In Port Sunlight it had a double action and was damaging to the
happiness of the community and ultimately fatal to its continued
existence.

Clear but unhappy indications of status such as

Directors' dining-room	Directors
Senior managers' dining-room	Private
Managers' mess	Managers
Staff canteen	Gentlemen
Works' canteen	Men

are familiar to most people in industry. It is still usual for workers
to 'clock on', whereas even time sheets have long disappeared for
office staff, though when I was young there was a subtle difference
between signing on a general time sheet and having a weekly time
sheet of one's own. There are other distinctions which ought to
be more important, but are not so for the simple reason that they
are not so obvious, such as length of holiday, though this difference
is rapidly disappearing.

It is difficult to maintain the full intimacy of a friendship if your
friend is promoted from the staff canteen to the managers' mess and
you are not. It is difficult also to explain the situation to your wife
even if she does not know the friend, except by name. But what if
you and your friend are neighbours? And what, worse still, if the
promotion of your friend means, as it did in Port Sunlight, that on
future public occasions he and his wife would receive an invitation
ticket of a different colour from yours, thus advertising the fact

that he had gone up and you had not? It meant, quite often, that you and your wife did not attend the function.

Not infrequently this sort of thing happened to people who had been happy neighbours for years and an unbreakable, if silly, estrangement developed. It could penetrate into family life when the daughter or son of the house achieved a higher status than the parents and might even attain a gilt-edged card instead of the parents' lowly red one. The height, or depth, of this kind of thing was reached, once, when guests above a certain grade not only sat on a dais but were served with chicken and white wine whereas their more lowly fellow guests had hot-pot and beer. Lever himself would certainly never have thought of making a distinction between his guests, and while he was alive the virulence of the status disease did not develop. Nevertheless the infection was there and he knew it.

His own habit, at lunch-time, was to have a light meal in his office. He had a private lavatory attached to it, as the other directors had, but away from Port Sunlight he used the one labelled Gentlemen, not only because he was democratic, but also because he probably wanted to see that it was properly cleaned.

By the time status became a real menace in Port Sunlight, there was a safety valve. In the late '20s and '30s it became possible, feasible and ultimately fashionable to get out of the village both temporarily and permanently. Birkenhead buses came to Port Sunlight, the station was recognized and scheduled trains were available. Motor-bikes with sidecars—even cars—began to come within the range of the popular purse and week-end visits to the Loggerheads and other resorts in North Wales and elsewhere came as a welcome relief. At the same time it was beginning to be possible to find houses in pleasant surroundings within easy reach of the office and factory. Lever himself opened up an estate and made plots available equally to employees and non-employees of Lever Brothers. It became almost a status symbol to move from the village.

Other forces, about the same time, were opening the situation up and making the name Port Sunlight stand for a good deal more than just the village. In particular, the creation of the Port Sunlight recreation ground and the establishment of the Staff Training

College, about the time when transport into and out of Port Sunlight began to improve, made facilities under the Port Sunlight banner available to everyone who worked at Port Sunlight rather than just to those who lived in the village.

The recreation ground was in Bebington. Until Lever bought it, at my father's suggestion, it had been the show ground of the Birkenhead and Wirral Agricultural Society—a magnificent site of 120 acres with a show arena and grandstand which added dignity to the Rugby Club and was used for field days and parades of all sorts. There was ample room for subsidiary football and hockey pitches, tennis courts and so on. Later Port Sunlight Golf Club was established, also in Bebington.

These fine facilities brought together the young people and some of the older ones too who were interested in all forms of sport and athletics. Club members were drawn from all ranks in office and works and from within and without the village itself, but the village provided the rooms where the committee meetings could be held at night, and in the Hulme Hall, a place where Rugby Club, Tennis Club, Hockey Club or any other similar association could have an annual ball or monthly dance in accommodation unmatched for convenience, size and facilities by any other hall in the vicinity.

The Staff Training College was a day continuation school such as is now provided by public authorities. It was a new idea for businessmen to allow employees time off in working hours to continue their education, and also to provide the educational facilities. The College was in the village so it brought both students and masters, from works and office into the village both during the day for classes and in the evening for adult evening classes and for the social activities which arose round the S.T.C. as focal point.*

The Lever business, meanwhile, was growing all the time. As it expanded, the relative significance of living in Port Sunlight or not greatly diminished, and gradually it became less and less likely that

---

* To this day there is a lady who was a pupil of my father's at the Staff Training College and who, following his instruction, forbids her husband ever to refer to 'humans' instead of 'human beings'. By a curious coincidence her husband was a pupil of my brother's in Oxford. He is Sir Harold Wilson, K.G.

one's colleague in factory or office would also be one's neighbour. The feeling of claustrophobia lessened and Port Sunlight came to mean something more than the village. That it did so was partly due to the circumstances but partly also to the leadership and drive of C. W. (Billy) Barnish who, when the Board of Lever Brothers Limited moved to London in 1921, remained behind as a Board member in charge of Port Sunlight. Charles Wilson in *The History of Unilever* records:

The care of Lever's favourite creation was entrusted to C. W. Barnish. It could not have been in better hands. Barnish, like so many of Lever's closest colleagues, was a Lancashire man, a son of Lever's doctor, born and bred in Wigan. To the direction of Port Sunlight he brought all his superabundant energies, an innate democratic sense and a complete fidelity to the aims and principles of his Chief.

He certainly understood, believed in and tried to continue the paternalistic attitude towards employees which was a natural and always a notable feature of his Chief's character. Like him he was democratic in the sense of being able to talk easily with anyone. Through having worked in Port Sunlight in earlier years he knew many of the people there and always showed personal interest in them and their families. He was generous and thoughtful in doing many private acts of kindness. His vitality sometimes led him to try to deal with matters of which he really had little knowledge, and he did not suffer gladly those whom he did not understand or who wanted to think before answering a question. These characteristics led to clashes with his colleagues which his sharp tongue made uncomfortable and sometimes most hurtful.

But no one who knew him doubted the sincerity of his motives or his devotion to the business, and his superabundant energy found full scope in Port Sunlight. During his lifetime he took part in practically every form of sport that came within his grasp. He was game for any game, though his favourites were cricket, tennis, golf and fishing. Fishing was about the only sport for which Port Sunlight did not provide facilities, but I am sure that if the contours of the Wirral had been suitable he would somehow or other have got a trout stream organized.

Billy Barnish was in on everything, usually taking a leading part, whether it was reading the lesson in church or captaining a cricket team. Through him Port Sunlight became the focal point of a large community of people who found in it their work, their sport and a large part of their social life. After the Board transferred to London, and even more after the formation of Unilever, Port Sunlight could not remain the heart of the business, but so long as Billy Barnish was there it remained the heart of the soap business and many people who knew it then, as I did, look back on those years as the Golden Age of Port Sunlight.

I went to London in 1922, but my parents continued to live in Port Sunlight until my father retired in 1935. During those years I was mainly concerned with export, largely of products made in Port Sunlight, so I had both personal and official reasons for maintaining my close links, and indeed continued to regard it as home. I only actually worked there for a year or so at the beginning of the Second World War.

In more recent years the village itself has become an increasingly serious problem. In planning and layout, in variety and pleasantness of aspect, Port Sunlight has never been bettered and possibly never equalled. But, as W. H. Lever told the Architectural Association in 1902:

> The changing life of our citizens, the necessity that is laid upon them to follow their employment wherever it may lead them, and the fact that our experience teaches us that in fifty or sixty years the sites of cottages may in all probability be wanted for other purposes—all point to the present-day requirements in cottages being not for cottages to stand hundreds of years, but tens.

Port Sunlight cottages were built before 1914 and although they were brought up to date in such matters as electricity supply in other ways they remained static at a time of great social change. A beautiful copper with a fire underneath, in an outside washhouse, is no substitute for a Hoovermatic. Moreover, family houses with four bedrooms and a substantial kitchen do not reflect the age of family planning. And as the young people left, an increasing proportion of the houses came to be occupied by retired people.

There were problems both architectural and social. It took the courage and vision of Alex Walker, who became Chairman of Unilever (Merseyside) Limited in 1960 to grasp this nettle. Under his auspices a survey was undertaken of the fabric of the houses. This showed that they were soundly built, would stand for at least another forty years, and would stand up to major internal reconstruction. Detailed plans for one or two blocks of houses were prepared to show how it would be possible to rearrange them internally so as to give a wide variety of modern accommodation, ranging within one block from a one-room flat to a self-contained family house, all to be provided with completely new plumbing, new drains and sanitary arrangements, and equipped with all modern domestic appliances.

This process, applied to the whole village, involved considerable capital expenditure upon which there would be virtually no monetary return. An obvious alternative would have been to redevelop the whole site, with lucrative possibilities in an area of great industrial development, thus obliterating one of the greatest memorials to a great man. I am proud to have been a member of the Board of Unilever when, on the proposal of its Chairman, Lord Heyworth, it accepted Walker's plan and thus ensured that Port Sunlight will continue to exist as a living and worthy memorial to its founder.

2

Introduction to 'Export and Overseas': 1919—1924

From the ease, peace and comparative splendour of Bury Grammar School I went to the Park Road Elementary School in Port Sunlight where from the scholastic point of view, I marked time for a year. Then my brother, who was at Liverpool Institute High School, won a scholarship, which meant that I could fill the place which my parents were paying for. Under H. V. Whitehouse, Liverpool Institute became one of the top secondary schools in the country. Presumably because of my brother's record I was placed in an 'X' form with the scholarship boys. 'X' was for express, set to cover the normal three years of third, fourth and fifth forms in two and to this end we were taught by the senior masters. It was hard going, but with my brother's record before me I felt that I must not fail. If you dropped to the lower end of the class, you were moved out to let another boy get a chance. It at least taught me to work hard, a lesson that is best learned early in life. We left home at 8.00 a.m. prompt to walk to New Ferry to catch the 8.25 boat, then walked through the main streets of Liverpool arriving at school about 9.10. We got home by the same route at 6.00 p.m. with at least two hours homework to do. Anyway it took me two hours. I hated it.

Ryan taught us French. Rather, he battered it into us. He was 6 ft 7 in. tall and, having taken up boxing in his youth, was very powerful. He could and frequently did pick up boys by the scruff of the neck at arm's length—as when there happened to be a particularly tight 'ruck' outside his door when forms were moving from one classroom to another. He had a voice as strong as his physique which he could use equally effectively. He terrified me and no doubt other weaker brethren, but at the end of four years I could read French as easily as English and could spell it a sight better. We did not learn French conversation.

Baxter taught maths, sarcastically and unfairly as he gave marks according to the number of sums you did correctly in the period, with top marks for the greatest number done by any one boy. As we had two mathematical geniuses in the class, I did not stand much chance, and was always pretty near the bottom. When I finally passed the maths papers in the Matriculation with first-class marks, Baxter asked me how I had done it. I told him that they had given me enough time.

Groom frequently exhorted us to 'Learn your Latin, boys', and used to stamp loudly to the rhythm of our Virgil as he paraded up and down his platform:

Dum variis tumulo referunt sollemnia ludis,
Irim de caelo misit Saturnia Juno.

I still recall the rhythm, and even the words, but I no longer know what it means.

We were well entrenched on these three subjects and got a grounding also in English, History, Geography, German and elementary Chemistry, Physics and Scripture.

Over all presided the great 'Vic', the Head. Almost a god to be feared. His judgments were certainly held to be 'righteous altogether'. If a boy was expelled or otherwise punished severely the school was called together and told and it was generally held that he got what he deserved; and if one of the 'sports' rather overdid it, the immediate retribution which followed was noted with general approval. Shepherd III strode into hall one morning proudly displaying the most Oxford of all Oxford bags, and had a moment of glory. After prayers Vic said, 'Shepherd III will see me in my study immediately.' Fair enough! But though Vic's frown could make you tremble, his smile made you raise your head a bit higher and to those amongst the senior boys who could attain his intellectual level he was a lifelong inspiration.

All this added up to as good an education as could be had for the years from age twelve to sixteen. It may not have been as gentle or as gentlemanly as might be available elsewhere, but it got me through matriculation, which had to be passed in six subjects simultaneously. Fail one and you failed the lot.

Before I move on from schooldays I feel I should give an account of the affairs of the Liverpool Jewellers' League, a game devised by my brother and his friend Eric Robinson (subsequently my brother-in-law) to occupy the school lunch hours. The league was run on the lines of the football league with two divisions, pro-motions, relegations and a cup tie. The weekly matches for the season were arranged in advance and they were played week by week by the managers, my brother and friend, inspecting the windows of all the jewellers concerned, usually during the lunch hour, and noting the highest priced item in each. The jeweller with the higher price during that week beat his allotted opponent for that week. There were sometimes drawn games. No jeweller could 'play' the same item twice and the skill and interest for the managers was knowing where to look for the high priced items and remembering which items in the window had already been played. I was not one of the managers and was never invited to the weekly meetings which issued the league table, but I was permitted to accompany them on their sometimes strenuous rounds of the jewellers' shops to note down the various 'scores', and was even able sometimes to point out an item which had evaded the eye of the professionals. I was also very useful when it came to the cup when all 'teams' had to be covered quickly including known pawn-brokers in some of the side streets. It was an interesting and some-times exciting game:

> Boodle and Dunthorn   v   Elkington and Batty
> Bagshaw   v   Russell

At the beginning of the season the team with the really expensive items easily won, but towards the end it was the team with a steady high standard and frequent change of window display that drew ahead. Similarly in a long-drawn-out cup tie the really expensive shops did not necessarily win as some of their best scores might be used up against second division teams. The highest priced item had to be played no matter what the opposition score might be. However, an item which had already been played in a league game could be played again in the cup.

Walking along Bold Street, Church Street and Lord Street now it is difficult to imagine that there were so many jewellers' shops there in my boyhood, but they were there all right and provided what must have been a unique form of entertainment and exercise for three schoolboys during the First World War.

Passing the matriculation would have enabled me to apply for admission to one of the Northern universities. I thought of taking a Bachelor of Commerce degree, but decided that that would be a waste of time, a decision the wisdom of which my subsequent experience has given me no grounds to doubt. In any case I had no wish to continue the ghastly process of learning and had a natural desire to start earning instead. As to learning, I got a nasty shock soon after I started work when my father asked me what I was going to study at night school! My father and brother were scholars, and I knew the difference between their learning and mine. This, together with the pressure under which I was put during the last four years of my schooldays, gave me an inferiority complex towards all educational matters which has been with me until very recent years, and I have never been able to enter any educational establishment, not even the prep school attended by my sons, without mentally trembling at the knees. None the less it was a great advantage to have been brought up in a scholarly atmosphere. The study, lined with books, was the centre of our home—the warmest room in the house, and during the war the only warm one. Also the quietest. 'Background music' had fortunately not been invented. As I look back I realize what a great debt I owe to my father and brother for the example they set me and the encouragement they gave me towards keeping my mind alive during the years when my daily work did not require great mental effort. Without this stimulus my mind might have gone dead, just as, after doing nothing but use a typewriter for a couple of years, I found myself almost unable to write.

I left school in July 1919, aged sixteen, with relief and pleasure and I have never regretted doing so. The Knox family and many others had been invited by Lord Leverhulme (known by this time to those in personal contact with him as the 'Old Man') to have a holiday in the Island of Lewis and we proceeded on a very exciting journey north as soon as the school term ended. The programme was a few days in Lews Castle, Stornoway, then ten days or so in one or other of the shooting/fishing lodges and then a day or two at the castle to round the holiday off.

One afternoon while still at Lews Castle I was sitting with other youngsters having tea and our host had joined us, when a telegram was delivered to me causing general interest as well as great excitement on my part. What did it say? It was from a friend of mine telling me I had passed the Matriculation examination. The Old Man seemed as happy as I was and told his admiring audience that although he had never passed this exam or been to a university he had had many degrees conferred upon him. To me it was not a passport to the university but to the business and, striking while the iron was hot, I asked and received permission to quote the Old Man as one of my referees when I applied for a job.

My application was to the Export Department of Lever Brothers then established in the Royal Liver Buildings, Liverpool. I had crossed the Mersey by ferry day after day for four years and knew the names and house flags of the main shipping lines and the ports they served, so I felt that export must be more interesting than the home trade. I was right, and I had chosen better than I knew.

In 1919 Export (known as A.I.F. Department—accounts, imperial and foreign) was at the very height of its prestige and standing within the Company. A director at its head, a record of successful pioneering all over the world and profits which certainly must have constituted a more notable proportion of the total profits of the Company than has ever happened since.

Speeches made on the occasion of the opening by the Lord Mayor of London of a new export sales room in Coleman Street were no more hyperbolic than the era demanded and the occasion warranted. Contrast was drawn between normal British export practice on the one hand ('Markets were not properly studied, representatives were untrained and ill chosen' . . . it was 'too readily assumed that even necessary goods would sell by their own impetus'), and on the other, the way business was conducted by

Lord Leverhulme who had demonstrated his 'complete mastery of the problems of export'. There was a side-swipe too at Germany where businessmen 'with less original genius and inventiveness' had 'a greater readiness to face new business problems in a practical spirit'. This was a hardy annual in the Board of Trade commercial counsellor's reports together with what seemed to be the standard example of German adaptability—that they sold egg-cups to fit the size of the local egg, whereas British egg-cups were always the size of the British egg.

'Complete mastery' may have been an exaggeration but certainly there was amongst the men in Export a feeling of professionalism that was based on skill, experience and genuine enthusiasm for the job. There may have been a better export organization in the United Kingdom at that time but I doubt it, though the Singer Sewing Machine Company and British American Tobacco may have run it pretty close.

Post-war ebullience played a part in the confident optimism of the day, and with booming sales to every part of the world, the prospects looked glorious.

In addition to Lever products, Export had responsibility for:

Vinolia (a range of some ninety toilet soaps and preparations)
Miscellaneous bar soaps, toilet soaps and preparations of
    about half a dozen other associated companies
Sanitas Ltd (disinfectants and Woodwards Gripe Water)
Trufood Ltd (baby food)
Sparklets Syphons
Delecta Chocolates
Angus Watson (skippers, brisling and other canned foods)
Wall's (tinned sausages)
Mac Fisheries (Kilty Kippers)
Kenneth McKenzie Harris Tweed

The soap trade was by far the most interesting, largest and most profitable part of the department's work. Vinolia at that time had an international business of some significance and of course the bar soaps had to maintain 'their share of the market'. The foods were of some value as they gave early experience of a business which

became more important later. Sanitas, Delecta Chocolates, Harris
Tweed and the Sparklets business were disposed of in the 1920s:
Trufood remained until it was sold by Unilever in the 1950s.

Trade was predominantly on C.I.F. (cost, insurance and
freight) terms with payment as near 'cash' as possible, usually a
D/P draft (documents against payment) which was immediately
discounted: thus cash was received within a day or two of the ship
leaving Liverpool. The agent took the risk of the customer not
taking up the documents, for which he received extra commission.
In normal times, the only bad debts were from ships' barbers, a
tiny trade maintained as a useful training ground for an embryo
representative and no doubt also to ensure that the barber's shop
on a ship on which there might be an important Lever passenger
would be well stocked with the appropriate Lever (and Vinolia)
products.

Prices of proprietary products (as distinct from bar soaps) were
quoted per case, the F.O.B. (free on board) price being that
current in the home trade plus the dock charges. The addition of
freight and marine insurance gave the C.I.F. prices and a 'C.I.F.
Addition' list was kept up to date for practically every port in the
world. I can still recall some of the now unfamiliar yet never-to-be
forgotten names such as Bonny, Brass, Degama, Cocanada, Am-
boina, Zamboanga, and Bagansi Api Api.

Packs were the same as for the home trade, with one or two
smaller sizes for Sunlight soap itself—down to 2 oz. Text was
translated into the appropriate language, again mainly for Sunlight, but the name Sunlight was retained in European translations,
and rendered phonetically into languages not using the Latin
script. Sunlight was to be known as Sunlight everywhere, even
though the nearest a Chinese could get to 'sunlight soap' might be
'isunli-iso'. Correspondence with customers in Europe and South
America was in their own language. The packaging of the toilet
preparations had been described (at the Coleman Street opening)
as 'dainty and exquisite for the satisfaction of the luxurious circles
in Paris, Buenos Aires, New York, Petrograd and Bombay'.

Linking world markets with the home office were between
twenty and thirty overseas representatives whose normal schedule
was eight months travelling and four months at home. They were

paid a salary plus commission and expenses (accounts rendered weekly).

It was claimed that a Lever man had been the first commercial representative in Peking after the Boxer Rebellion, in Khartoum after the Battle of Omdurman, and in Port Sudan when the railway was opened. I never knew these heroes but there were still some of the pioneers about. Among them were Sam Hirst (India) who once shouted across the bar of one of the Calcutta hotels to his new junior, 'Remember Mr So and So, all the gins and bitters Lever Brothers pay for, I can drink'; H. George Roberts (Argentine), whose son, Sir Frank Roberts, after a distinguished career in the Foreign Office became an advisory director of Unilever; A. E. Perkins who represented the Company in the West Indies arrayed in a frock coat and top hat; Lionel Reid, Eastern Europe, who fruitlessly followed the White Russian Army from Vladivostok to Irkutsk.

These and others like them, and their successors after the First World War, created the personal links which have served the Company well whether the trade has remained export or has been developed by locally established companies.

So, with virtually no advertising, selling expenses mainly tied to sales' value by the 3–5 per cent agents' commission, no bad debts, practically no working capital and a competent staff, it was a profitable business. No wonder there was enthusiasm in Export in 1919.

Within a couple of days of my application to this large and important department I was summoned for an interview in Liverpool with Mr E. V. Salaman, the Director. Having ascertained that I knew some French, he proceeded to conduct the rest of the interview in that language, but as his pronunciation and general style were much along my own schoolboy line, I was able to cope with the situation, and was told that I could report for duty in the near future, which turned out to be Monday, September 1 1919. I would be paid twenty-five shillings (£1.25) a week.

I duly reported at a few minutes before nine o'clock and cooled my heels and my excitement for a couple of hours in a small cubby-hole just by the commissionaire's desk, containing only a hard seat and a time-clock which loudly but slowly marked the

passing minutes. Then I was ushered again into the presence of
E.V.S. and rapidly was passed down from his level to the next and
so on, until I found myself sitting at a table between two young
men who noisily operated two heavily built, double-keyboard
Barlock typewriters. I was an embryo order typist and junior in the
India section of A.I.F. department. My neighbour showed me
what to do, and I gradually found my way over the double-
keyboard. Which fingers I used, and how, was a matter entirely of
my own immediate convenience. The only suggestion was that I
might usefully practise 'Now is the time for all good men to come
to the aid of the party'. As I have had to use a typewriter a great
deal since I have regretted that some attention was not given to
basic training, though whether I would have welcomed it at the
time I doubt.

The section—all male with the exception of two female shorthand
typists in a corner in front of the invoice/order typists—consisted of
four invoice/order typists who sat at tables, four invoice/order
clerks at high clerks' desks, a correspondence clerk and the head of
the section or, in common parlance, the 'backbencher', who worked
at a real desk on a six-inch-high platform surrounded by a mahog-
any partition about five feet high.

Up to and including the correspondence clerk surnames were the
accepted mode of address. The backbencher got a 'Mr' from below
and from above. Above him it was 'Sir' from below and 'Mr' from
above. Above senior clerk only equals could drop the 'Mr' and
never under any circumstances were Christian names used, though
nicknames were allowed amongst intimates. This formal approach
was used throughout business and I was later amused to note the
nuances of inter-directorial and senior correspondence. 'Dear Mr'
was safe and ninety per cent of letters were so addressed. Dropping
the 'Mr' showed that the writer regarded himself as being at the
level of the recipient and 'My dear' indicated that he was proud of
the fact.

Our backbencher, Muldoon, was a disciplinarian and wanted his
section to be the best. After all, it was 'A' section, to differentiate
it from 'B', 'C', 'D', statistics, filing, accounts and legal. He used to
visit us in front and exhort us to 'keep down to it' even during slack
periods. One of his jobs was to sign bills of lading. Sign them, yes,

but blot them, no; this was the job for one of the juniors who stood by, blotted the signature and turned over to the next bill. During these interludes he used to philosophize, or in other ways give you the benefit of his advice. Once he said to me, 'Don't make education your god'. My brother and I laughed at this but I think it might now be not inappropriate advice. On another occasion he told me that the only way to ensure that I did not spend the rest of my life as a typist was to make myself the best typist in his section, and therefore, of course, in the office. I did not find this very difficult as competition was not fierce and, although the immediate result was that I got all the difficult and intricate statements to type, it did lead to my promotion to invoice clerk in reasonable time.

The confident enthusiasm of 1919 did not last long. The bubble burst with the great slump of 1920. The effect on the soap export industry was shattering:

			Value *£, million*
Total United Kingdom household soap exports	1919	108,000 tons	7
	1920	82,000 ,,	$5\frac{1}{2}$
	1921	40,000 ,,	2

A lot of the 1920 shipments were either not paid for at all or only after long delay at reduced prices, so the year was more catastrophic for the participants than for the statisticians. I saw and felt the demoralizing effects of idleness, and my colleagues and I did not need to be accountants to understand that no orders must soon mean no pay, and no job. One Friday night everyone in the office got an envelope—it was either the sack or a reduction in pay. I got the reduction.

With reduced prices and expenses the business gradually got going again though, as one representative reported, 'Every order was hard fought for'. Another who found it easier to write reports than book orders was told by the great E. V. Salaman that his reports were interesting but 'What we wants is orders'. Still another who at least believed in brevity wrote: 'BENARES: Benares is the Mecca of the Hindus but not of much interest to the Commercial man. I enclose my expenses sheet for the week.' He did not render many more weekly expenses to Lever Brothers!

Though perhaps not in Benares, the business in India as a whole recovered particularly quickly from the slump as it was practically all in Sunlight soap—a proprietary brand with a long established and firm consumer goodwill.

After three years in Export I felt that I had gained a valuable knowledge and experience of what the night school prospectus called 'The Theory and Practice of Commerce'. I had also gained (though I did not realize it at the time) an equally valuable experience of slump and recovery. It began to occur to me that while the scope of Export was worldwide it did not include a number of most important countries which, I had learned, were looked after by Overseas. I thought I ought to try to expand my knowledge and experience and wrote to C. W. Barnish to ask him if he could help me. Barnish was then (1922) Director in charge of Port Sunlight but I knew that he had a long connection with Overseas. This was not the reason I wrote to him; I felt able to do so because, during the war when I was a schoolboy, he had kept his Sunbeam motor-bike and sidecar in our garage in Port Sunlight (the only private garage available) and my admiration of his motor bike had established a friendly relationship between us.

A few weeks after my letter I was summoned to one of the private offices in Liver Building to see C. E. Tatlow, a Director in charge of D.O.C./A department (p 27 below). He said he had heard that I wanted to join the Overseas side of the business but did I know that the Overseas department had recently been moved from Port Sunlight to London? I said I did not know but that that did not make any difference to me. It did however make a difference to Tatlow who said that although his department did need a junior, there were no doubt many young men in London equally or even better qualified, who would not perhaps expect the same wage that I might require to enable me to live in lodgings, and for whom no transfer costs would be involved. However, if I was prepared to take the job on the basis of paying my own fare to and initial expenses in London and continuing on my current salary, he would be prepared to consider me along with the London applicants. I said I still wished to be considered, but left the interview somewhat downcast.

I was, therefore, surprised a few weeks later to be told by my immediate boss that I was to be transferred immediately to London. He made it clear that this was none of his doing and was angry that he had not even been consulted. I asked him if I could have the Saturday morning off before the Monday on which I was to report in London and he said, 'No, you can get time off from your new department'. This was awkward as there were things to be bought to set me up for living away from home. However, I did have time to get in touch with someone who had recently been transferred to London to seek help in the matter of lodgings, with the result that on Monday, 10th July 1922, when I presented myself in Central Buildings (as the ex-De Keyser's Hotel was called before it was re-named Lever House) I was greeted by a welcome north country voice saying, 'Are you Knox? I'm Atherton and there's room for you in my digs if you are interested.'

My mother had accompanied me to London and after assuring herself that lodgings in the house of Mrs Hooper of Herne Hill would be suitable and presenting me with a three-months' season ticket Herne Hill/Blackfriars/Victoria, she went off to stay with some friends in Hampstead, and I was on my own. I did not feel it at first but I remember that when I had to provide myself with a tube of toothpaste I really did realize that I was away from home.

Tatlow's assistant was J. Laurence Heyworth who in turn was assisted by I. B. Hutcheson and I was the fourth member of D.O.C./A department.

D.O.C. stood for Director Overseas Companies. D.O.C./A looked after Australia, South Africa, France and Belgium (and, when established, the soap companies in Nigeria and Congo). D.O.C./B with A. C. Knight at the head of it and Charles Cole as assistant dealt with China, Japan and India. There should have been a D.O.C./C but H. G. Hart, the Director who headed this department, was not going to be either 'B' or 'C' to Tatlow's 'A', and so coined the initials D.A.S.H. (Director of America, Scandinavia and Holland) and later donated the DASH golf cup. It was a dashing departmental reference and had some dashing personalities associated with it, most of whose careers with the concern were even shorter lived than the department itself.

An eavesdropper at my first interview with Laurence Heyworth might reasonably have concluded that it was somewhat depressing for me. It went something like this:

J.L.H. 'Do you know anything about accounts?'

A.M.K. 'No.'

J.L.H. 'Do you know anything about sales?'

A.M.K. 'No.'

J.L.H. 'Do you know anything about advertising?'

A.M.K. 'No.'

J.L.H. 'Do you know anything about pro formas?'

A.M.K. 'No.'

J.H.L. 'What do you know about?'

A.M.K. 'Packing slips and shipping documents.'

J.L.H. 'We don't do packing slips in this department.'

But I knew from the glint in his eye that I was not being rejected and that I was to be working for a man of an altogether different calibre from those with whom I had previously worked. Laurence was a very shy man and I was shy too, but our eyes must have penetrated the barrier which absence of ready words can create, because, from that first interview, we seemed to understand each other completely. This was very necessary as he was frequently either too preoccupied or too uninterested to answer a question by other than a look or the Scottish 'uh-huh'.

For me he was a great boss and much later became a close and affectionate friend. In the two years I was with him in D.O.C./A he transformed me from a junior clerk to a junior manager and after the Second World War he put me on the track which led me to the Board. He had one outstanding attribute. He was indomitable in his support of anyone in whom he had put his trust.

Many years after we had first met we reached the stage when it became seemly to be on Christian name terms. In mutual shyness this was not an easy step but it was managed over lunch one day when I told him that I had always had a sneaking affection for him. With that glint in his eye, that I knew so well and will never forget, he said, 'Only sneaking?'

I became P.A. to Laurence on all general matters, particularly figures and the writing of memoranda. As a basis for the figure work he told me on my second day in the office to get to know about accounts, and suggested that I did so by studying the Lille accounts. Companies were known by the name of the town from which they operated and 'Lille' meant Savonneries Lever, France.

I duly got the latest set of Lille accounts and pored over them in miserable incomprehension. Balance sheet, profit and loss account, establishment charges, selling expenses, soap making account, etc. Then I noticed a figure on one page that I was sure I had seen on another. I traced it back and wondered why it should appear twice, till it dawned on me that a lot of the figures must come from somewhere and go somewhere else in the process of collection and allocation. Encouraged by this flash of insight I pursued my studies somewhat more hopefully and eventually traced through the whole structure which, after all, turned out to be straightforward and logical. I subsequently underpinned this somewhat brief initial study by a night school course of bookkeeping at the Regent Street Polytechnic.

Overseas companies then reported their operations in considerable detail, but the detail was restricted to what were then considered to be the essential operations.

Sales figures, the most important of all, were cabled in total for each main product every week to be followed by monthly figures giving detailed sales by areas with full comparisons. They also forwarded information about cash position actual and forward estimates; raw material purchase and cover; pan charge returns weekly showing exactly what raw materials had been used for each boil of soap; full commercial details such as bad debts, extension of credit, packed stock levels, etc.

This was carefully scrutinized and a good deal of it was recorded in black books. This description had no derogatory connotation but derived from the fact that loose-leaf books were only then available in black covers.

One of my steady jobs was to keep the black books up to date. It taught me a lot about the type of information required to manage a business and the salutary lesson that to keep black books up to date was a hopeless task, thus steering me clear of all the card index systems which became popular when SYSTEM reigned in the business world. The most spectacular card index system I saw was one devised by or for L. H. Hartland-Swann, a Director who,

having been Chairman of the Icilma Company when it was bought
by the Old Man, was known to specialize in selling and advertising.
One of the difficulties about an advertising campaign is to keep its
preparatory stages up to schedule. A card index to demonstrate the
current state of all campaigns likely to interest H.S. was erected
along the wall of the room occupied by his personal assistant. It
consisted of a series of hooks on which coloured discs were hung,
each colour denoting a specific stage of the preparation and each
disc recording some detail of that particular stage. A special disc
was hung, masking the others, if the job had fallen behind schedule
—a black disc probably, though it might have been red—for
danger. I forget.

On the few occasions when I was permitted to admire this
wonderful manifestation of SYSTEM, it seemed that the girl had
not got round to adjusting the discs that day, but I am sure that,
on the occasions when H.S. himself paid an official visit, the P.A.
had done any necessary stage management to ensure complete
success. As showmanship it was magnificent while it lasted, but it
must have been a poor progress chaser.

Our black books were never up to date either. They suffered
from being a steady and usually rather dull job, though I was
fascinated to record, from the returns of Lever's Pacific Plantations
activities in the Solomon Islands, the current number of 'nuts in
nursery'.

The Black Books were valuable if one wanted to make a historical
survey of some aspects of an overseas company's operations. Even
here there were pitfalls because managements have a strong
propensity to change the basis of their records from time to time,
thus vitiating, or at least making difficult, long term comparisons.

For the purpose for which we always understood they were
intended, namely as figure briefs for discussions with the management concerned, the books were useless. First, the management
would obviously have more up-to-date figures; but second and
more important, was the operation of a strange but, in my observation, absolute rule, namely that head office records of an operating
company's activities will never agree with those of the company
concerned. The difference may be marginal and irrelevant but will
always exist. Many years after my experience in D.O.C./A

department I learned never to take any head office figures on a visit to an overseas company. There is no easier way to trip the visitor up at the beginning of a discussion than by casting doubt on his figures and no more valuable waste of a visitor's time than an elaborate and earnest effort to achieve reconciliation across the table.

So black books were apt to be put aside for more interesting jobs such as the translation of a detailed specification for work required on the building in Rue Royale, Brussels, to transform it into a head office for Savonneries Lever Frères. This took me beyond my knowledge of both French and English into such things as jambs, splays, lintels and joists and I remember being embarrassed to hand out for typing detailed descriptions of the sanitary arrangements.

With guidance from Laurence Heyworth and appropriate technical help I drafted a report which recommended the building of a Rinso plant in Sydney. It is interesting that the initiative for such a project lay with head office, and my examination started from the question whether such a plant would pay. Many years later I was asked by Sidney van den Bergh to make a 'nice calculation to show that a margarine plant in Batavia will make a profit'. Both projects were successful.

Visits both to and from overseas companies were rare and only undertaken by directors, or the Old Man himself accompanied by one or two senior people. 'Boston' (the American company) or companies on the Continent might be inspected once a year but remoter companies would not expect to be visited more than once every three or four years.

How quiet it must have been for overseas companies such as Australia, where nowadays they would be lucky to have a single week in the year (except perhaps at Christmas and New Year) without someone from head office about the place. How peaceful also for head office, now receiving 400–500 visitors a year from overseas.

Preparations for overseas visits were elaborate. First, suitable steamer accommodation had to be secured, then the agenda had to be planned. All facets of the business were covered, and the finished agenda consisted of ponderous foolscap-size volumes (beautifully bound by the Port Sunlight printing department) containing suitably indexed copies of all memoranda and correspondence exchanged with the company concerned over the previous year or so. Donald Baker (a colleague of mine in D.O.C./A and later a stalwart of our South African business) and I prepared three such volumes for the Old Man's visit to Australasia in 1923. We took the precaution of gumming up one or two of what we regarded as the less interesting parts of those volumes, and were rewarded by finding on the return of the expedition that the gum had been undisturbed. The agenda was annotated with decisions and comments as the discussions proceeded so that on its return everyone could be advised of the results of the discussions without any necessity for a report.

Correspondence on all matters of importance (which meant everything except pure routine) was carried on solely between the chairman of the company and the home director, though sometimes the Old Man intervened. Routine correspondence had to be conducted in memo form with no individual reference either to recipient or sender. The memo could be initialled only, not signed, and Donald Baker was reproved because his initials were too legible.

One instance I remember where the Old Man intervened. The pan charge returns from Balmain (Australia) revealed that some red (low quality) palm oil had been put into Sunlight soap. This could not be tolerated and Mr Meek, the Chairman of the Lever company in Australia, was so informed. He replied that he thought the red palm oil improved the appearance of the soap, but this did not impress head office and Mr Meek was asked to think again. He did so in a particularly long letter which came to the notice of the Old Man who wrote to Mr Meek reminding him that he was, by trade, a printer (he had been Head of the Port Sunlight printing works before his appointment as Head of the Lever company in Sydney) and that he was therefore not in a position to argue with a real soapmaker (the Old Man himself) about what went into Sunlight soap. Red palm oil disappeared from the pan charge returns and it was not long thereafter that Mr Meek relinquished the chairmanship of Lever Brothers, Sydney, which was taken over by Laurence Heyworth. He took I. B. Hutcheson who was mainly occupied with advertising matters with him to Australia and left me with a sound grounding in the administrative techniques of business management.

While I was in D.O.C./A department I had quite an exceptional opportunity to get to know the Old Man. It was his custom to pay a visit every August to some of his interests on the Continent, accompanied by a couple of directors, two or three senior managers, and a young man to act as a sort of equerry—to look after the tickets and the luggage, to pay all out-of-pocket expenses, to take notes of meetings if called upon to do so, and generally to act as secretary to the whole party.

The young man was chosen from the overseas side of the business but not necessarily with reference to his previous experience of foreign travel. When I was chosen in 1924 I had had no such experience; the two previous appointees had, but were no longer in the business. My immediate predecessor had distinguished himself by leaving the Old Man's battered but precious black brief-case on the Bergen/Newcastle boat. The captain of the boat was radioed to enquire if His Lordship's black brief-case containing important papers had been found. The reply came that a black brief-case had been found but it contained only a clean shirt and two lemons: was this the one? It was.

At least this taught me not to lose sight of the Old Man's brief-case and in fact I carried it everywhere, to the chagrin, occasionally, of earnest local managers who sought the honour of holding it. I have subsequently always carried my own brief-case on foreign travel no matter what the weight or content of either the case itself or the reception committee at the airport.

In 1924 the fish trade was much in the Old Man's mind. Mac Fisheries, through its subsidiary Bloomfields, had a share in the important exports to the Baltic ports of salted herrings in barrels, in the days when every year the daily papers used to carry photos of the fishwives from Scotland gutting the freshly landed herrings in the East Coast fishing ports. Thus the Old Man's interests included visits to the fish markets in Hamburg, Stettin and Danzig (then an independent state). The itinerary was Hamburg, Berlin, Danzig, Stettin, Hamburg, Copenhagen, Stockholm, Christiania (Oslo), Bergen, Newcastle. The basic party for the whole trip was six people but there were always two or three part-time members in addition, and in a fortnight I dealt with seven different currencies, paying all sundry expenses, tips, etc., and also providing pocket money in the local currency for each member of the party as we went from place to place.

Up to that time I had never had more than £5 in my pocket and before setting out I went to Mr D'Arcy Cooper, the Vice-Chairman, who was to be a 'permanent' member of the party, with a cash voucher for £50, which seemed to me rather a lot of money. 'Good God, Knox,' he said, 'that won't get us to Hamburg. Take £200 to start with.' The cash office could only provide £1 notes so when I reached Liverpool Street Station it seemed to me that every international thief must see my pockets bulging, and I did not feel very secure.

However, all went well. I was not robbed. I was not sacked at the end of it, and I learned a lot. I could not say that I enjoyed it (I was too much on tenter-hooks for that), and it is perhaps as well I did not say so. One of the permanent members, new to the business, said just this to the Old Man at the end of the trip, and the Old Man replied, 'I didn't take you to enjoy yourself, I took you to learn something.'

He was in fact very kind to me throughout the journey and although I got one severe telling off it did not affect his general attitude towards me, which was almost avuncular. I looked after his luggage, passport and tickets and saw to it that arrangements were made for his various requirements in the hotels. He usually had guests for lunch and dinner and I counted them as he issued his invitations and arranged a table accordingly. I usually travelled in the same car as he did, sat next to him in trains, next but one to him at table, so that I could translate his wishes to the waiters who almost always spoke English anyway, and I usually shared his hotel suite. At one fairly small luncheon, my hair stood on end when I realized that we had already run up a bill of £5 at the hors-d'oeuvre stage. Five pounds then might be the equivalent of seven to ten times as much now.

He did not eat a lot himself and certainly not elaborately. In Stockholm, where he had invited a large number of businessmen for lunch, he said goodbye to his guests after the smörgåsbord as he thought the meal was finished. I explained that the real lunch was about to start in an adjoining room but he said he had had all he wanted—in fact an excellent lunch—and was going up to his room to do his private mail. I and his colleagues could see that his guests were further attended to as might be necessary, and off he marched.

He 'attended to his private mail' every afternoon when he was free to do so, and, privately, I was to make sure he was awake at 4.00 p.m. I was thankful for an hour or two off to attend to my own private mail and to my intricate cash accounts.

He did not in fact have much private post, but mail as such was an important factor in his day. He seemed almost to need a pile of envelopes to get him started. In Nyköping (Sweden) he got no letters at all and this was too much for him. As we walked down the street he stopped and turned to me, to the evident amusement of the rest of the party, and told me that my mailing list must have been wrong. 'I know, Knox, that you've never been further than Blackpool in your life before, but you should know that it takes longer for a letter to get to Sweden than to Blackpool.' Actually I had not been responsible for compiling the mailing list nor had I ever been to Blackpool, but I did not think that an argument on the question would mend matters. He got letters that afternoon so his face lit up again and I heard no more about it.

Another of his basic requirements was two lemons and a bottle of soda water in his bedroom at night. I don't know how he dealt with this requirement, but it was absolute. One of my first anxieties on arrival at a hotel was to find out what 'two lemons and a bottle of soda water' were in the local language, and I did not fail to have them supplied. One night after he had retired, which he usually did fairly early, and I was sitting in the hotel lounge with the rest of the party, I was astonished to see the Old Man coming down the stairs, looking round, and on seeing me marching towards me. He was a notable figure with his old-fashioned grey worsted 'morning-coat' and head of curly white hair, so that by the time he reached me everyone in the place was looking at him. He placed in front of me eight quarters of lemon and said in his best Lancashire accent, 'They're no good to me, they're cut,' and marched off again, leaving broad smiles on the faces of the rest of the party, but not on mine. So I had to add 'uncut' to my vocabulary and go off in search of two whole lemons.

Apart from these simple needs, he was easy-going and most interesting to travel with. He did as he was told without question. If I said his bags were to be ready packed and he was to be downstairs at a certain time, he just smiled and nodded—and, of course, he was never late. Once our suite had only one bathroom. He said he would use it first in the morning and the next day he came prancing into my room at 6.45 a.m. and told me the bathroom was ready.

In Danzig he was the guest of the President and there was an enormous official luncheon of welcome, which, as I remember it, lasted from about 2.00 p.m. to 6.00 p.m., and took place in a very large banqueting hall. There were numerous courses interspersed with interminable speeches all of which had to be translated immediately after delivery. So you got two speeches for the price of one.

I had never heard of caviare, let alone tasted it, and had to watch my neighbour to see how to tackle the large soup plate full which was put before me. I am sure I ate too much and felt ill next morning. The Old Man sent me back to bed after breakfast with a large dose of salts and a lecture about eating when abroad, especially on the Continent. 'I have noticed you have a large English breakfast every morning and I thought something like this would happen. You should note and follow local customs in eating when abroad and you will see that on the Continent they have very light breakfasts—you do the same in future.'

On train journeys, after he had read any mail, reports, etc., he often went to sleep, telling me to wake him at a certain time. He could at any time just put his head back and go to sleep immediately. When he was awake he was alert and most interesting about what he saw. I remember him giving us a lecture on the relative agricultural economics of North Germany and England as we passed through the farmlands on our way to Hamburg. He had a wide knowledge, indeed a worldwide knowledge, of commercial and industrial affairs so there was always something to catch his eye upon which he could make an enlivening comment.

On one occasion in the train he was going through his mail and he passed one letter over to me. A new chief accountant, Mr

Locking, had introduced a system whereby all departments would have 'location numbers' which would be debited with all costs pertaining thereto. The offending communication was from the chief accountant enclosing a debit note for rent, etc., of the chairman's room in Lever House and asking that it should be signed, as being accepted, and returned.

'Have you ever seen such a silly thing as that? Fancy debiting me with the rent of a room in a building I already own!' With that he tore up the letter and debit note and threw them on the floor.

During the second half of his life the Old Man was very rich and firmly believed that money was for use, not for hoarding. He was most generous privately and publicly, but being a true Lancashireman he did not believe in wasting money. In the Adlon Hotel in Berlin I shared with him what must have been the most splendid corner suite. As he walked up and down the sitting-room, examining the furniture, his eye was drawn to a notice just by the door. He asked me what it said and I replied that it indicated the cost of the suite. 'How much?' he asked, and I told him. He was not very pleased. Just then the *maître d'hotel* came in and bowed to him.

'What do you want?' Lever asked.

'I have come to welcome your Lordship.'

The Old Man, with a glare at the offending notice, replied, 'I've 'ad all the welcome I want thank you.'

One day, after he had ordered his simple lunch, probably tomato soup followed by biscuits and cheese ('Cheshire if they've got it'), he said he would like an apple. A basket of fruit was put in front of him.

'How much is it for an apple, Knox?'

'Five shillings, sir.'

'What will it be if I take more than one?'

'Still five shillings, sir.'

'Right, then I'll eat one now and put two in my pocket, and you can put two in your pocket and we'll be all right.' And that was what was done.

It was decided one evening to fill in the time between dinner and the departure of the night train by going to the cinema. It was not far from the hotel but it was raining so we had to go by taxi. One was hailed and the Old Man and I got into it. Three or four members of the party were accompanying us, but held back to hail another taxi. The Old Man opened our cab door and shouted at them, 'What are you doing? Do you think you are all millionaires?' So I did the journey more or less sitting on the Old Man's knee.

There was usually a scene of considerable animation when we left an hotel. The party was anything from six to twelve people, and in the days of Continental travel by train there was no serious need to restrict the amount of luggage. Thus there would be plenty of porters and other attendants to tip. Leaving an hotel in Stockholm at the height of the season, and with the easily recognizable figure of a rich English milord at the head of the party, there was a particularly formidable array of such attendants extending from the hotel door to the car. As we were about to move off, a scuffle broke out and the Old Man asked me what was the matter. I said I could only assume that my tipping had not been up to expectations. He asked me how much I had given and I told him. He assured me that I had done well and, unperturbed, gave the signal for us to move off.

It was well known on the railway between Liverpool and London, which he used frequently, that the Old Man was a generous tipper, but somebody acting for him was a different matter.

I think the best instance of his sharp tongue occurred when we were looking over a soap works near Berlin which the owners were anxious to sell to him. As we passed through the panroom the works manager, a German doctor of science, told the Old Man that the production capacity was a certain tonnage per year. The Old Man stopped, looked up and said he did not agree—the capacity was considerably less, and named a figure. The Herr Doctor got a bit excited and started to justify his own estimate. The Old Man turned to him and said, 'Ay nay, we won't argue—you're wrong.' In the car afterwards he told me why the Doctor was wrong. The Doctor was going on theory, not practice. He knew that it takes a week to put through a pan of soap and he multiplied his weekly pan capacity by fifty to give the annual total. 'He should have known that in practice you never get more than thirty-six pans through in a year.' I have always remembered that and also what followed. One of the attractions of the soap works, which he did not buy, was that it had a lot of vacant land nearby on which, it was suggested, he could build a second Port Sunlight. 'I'd never build a second Port Sunlight,' he said. 'It was a mistake. People who work and live together always quarrel.'

I was fortunate in having as members of the party on that trip in 1924 Mr D'Arcy Cooper, already vice-chairman of Lever Brothers Limited, and Mr Ned Quin who had at that time just been transferred from the factory at Lille to the newly created central technical department at head office. Ned Quin, an experienced Continental traveller, never left a station or an hotel without asking me if everything was under control, and D'Arcy Cooper created one, and reported another, incident which no doubt put me in a favourable light in the Old Man's eyes. I had had little experience of alcohol drinking at that time and decided that it would be better for me to declare myself teetotal for the trip. I shared the Old Man's mineral water at meals. One night in Germany, after the Old Man had gone off to bed, the party was sitting in the lounge having a night-cap when D'Arcy Cooper suggested that I really ought to have some beer. After all we were in Germany where beer was the national drink and I had heard the Old Man's views about adopting the customs of the country. So I had my glass of beer. Next morning at the breakfast-table D'Arcy Cooper started pulling my leg about being drunk the night before and others joined in. Finally Cooper said, 'It would not have been so bad if you had not insisted on going upstairs to kiss the Old Man goodnight.' That brought the house down and the Old Man, usually unaware of breakfast-table talk, asked what the joke was. He enjoyed it too.

The reported incident was on a sleeper. We were to pass over a frontier during the night and I had taken the Old Man's passport so that he would not be disturbed. The frontier official was rather more officious than usual and insisted on seeing the Old Man. I opened his compartment door and all that could be seen was a head of curly white hair. 'How do I know it is not a woman?' asked the official. I pointed to the Old Man's trousers hanging up by the braces—smiles and satisfaction all round. I did not know till afterwards that Cooper was witness to this pantomime and the Old Man was delighted with the story the following morning.

All this was a great experience for a young man of twenty-one. I learned a lot about the Old Man, something about the business and a valuable lesson about foreign travel: you can get on fine anywhere if you have enough money and a smile, and the one will not do without the other.

It is small wonder that the Old Man was and has remained the hero of my life and that fifty years later I can recall so clearly a brief fortnight's experience.

I did not know till many years afterwards that on the boat home from Bergen to Newcastle he had written to my father, 'to tell Mrs Knox and yourself how well your son Andrew has done his duties. He has been of the greatest help and promises well for the future.'

3

The Old Man

———◆———

My first five years certainly gave me a firm foundation for my future career, but inspiration arose from my admiration of the Old Man and I step aside from the main theme of my story to pay an entirely personal tribute to him. This is based on my own and my brother's recollections of him, upon a re-reading of published matter and upon a small collection of personal papers which his grandson, the third Viscount Leverhulme, discovered in an old safe and asked me to look through and from which he has permitted me to quote.

William Hesketh Lever was born in Bolton, Lancashire, on September 19, 1851. He was made a baronet in the Coronation Honours of 1911. He was raised to the peerage as Baron Leverhulme of Bolton-le-Moors on June 4, 1917, and became Viscount Leverhulme of the Western Isles on November 11, 1920. As the honours mounted he was known to Port Sunlighters as Mr Lever, Sir William, Lord Lever, and within the business as 'Chief', the Chairman, and, after his death, the Founder. To those who knew him and worked with him in his later years he was known, with affection and respect, as the Old Man.

The liveliness of his interests and the extent of his influence within and outside the world of business are set out in the biography by the second Lord Leverhulme published within a year or two of his father's death. His strength of mind and force of character are equally clearly discernible in *The History of Unilever*, Professor Charles Wilson's account of Lever's battles with competitors, rivals and detractors who, like himself, were individualists.

Mr Nigel Nicolson in his *Lord of the Isles* gives a sympathetic, understanding and true account of the Old Man's last great adventure, a scheme for the development of the Outer Hebrides. So far as the island of Lewis was concerned it was a spectacular failure, and as it took place in the dawning light of modern publicity it tends to be recalled more readily, in association with the Old Man's name, than are the great achievements of his life. One of his schemes for Lewis was to bring together sufficient land under one management to create a dairy farm so that the island could have its own supply of milk instead of importing it from 'the mainland'. What he would have done at his own expense has, forty years later, been done at considerable public expense by the Highlands and Islands Development Board.

In *Men of Stress* the late Dr Harley Williams emphasized the dynamic, almost demonic, energy which drove the Old Man on, ever restless to tackle something new, looking always to the future for opportunities to grasp. He was never satisfied with what he had, even with his own houses and gardens, which were constantly being replanned, extended or improved in some way. Through all this he kept a close eye on a vast business which he had developed in thirty-five years from an investment of £27,000 to a capital employed of £60,000,000, with wider geographical ramifications than any other business in the world. And 'a close eye' is right. On his last visit to the Lever soap company in Norway, he was greeted by its excited Chairman with a large sales sheet and the proud announcement, 'You will be glad to hear, your Lordship, that the sales of our company last month were an all-time record.' The Old Man replied, 'I've no doubt about that, Mr Brown, but what about the staff lavatories I complained about when I was here a year ago?'

With dynamic energy and great strength of mind, he had complete confidence in himself and in his ability to carry through any project of his imagination no matter how vast, how remote, how novel or adventurous. He was a stern master, quick to blame but quick and more apt to praise. A generous host, he frequently gave what he called 'an Irish toast', though, as he said it, its origins seemed to be more Lancastrian:

> Come in the evening, come in the morning,
> Come when you're asked or come without warning,

Thousands of welcomes you'll find 'ere before you,
The oftener you come the more we'll adore you.

If there were some personable young ladies present he would add, with a twinkle in his eye, 'Of course if I were a younger and handsomer man I'd say "thousands of kisses".'

Both he and his wife had a great love of children, and he never looked as radiantly happy as he did when surrounded by them on such occasions as the annual Sunday school outing to Thornton Manor, his home near Port Sunlight. To this great treat were invited the children from Port Sunlight and from Sunday schools in other parts of Wirral too. So there converged on Thornton Manor wagonettes, decorated farm carts, traps and other horse-drawn vehicles loaded with excited children in their Sunday best all out for a grand picnic. Everyone was given a bundle of tickets enabling them to get a free go on everything there was for their entertainment: merry-go-rounds, swings, donkey rides, boats on the lake, coconut shies and all the fun of the fair. There was miles of grass to run and roll on and the afternoon ended with a generous bag of buns, cakes, and tea and lemonade. The Old Man enjoyed it as much as the children. A photograph survives of him on the back of a donkey vainly trying to ride through the crowd.

There is a record of an incident much later in his life when the Old Man was happy in a crowd of children. In 1924 he visited the mission school in Leverville, Belgian Congo:

Perhaps nothing during the whole tour in the Congo gave him so much pleasure as the greeting he got from these Leverville children. They crowded round him, smiling, laughing and shouting. 'You can see that they really mean it,' he said, 'they really are happy: you can tell by their eyes. Children can never disguise their real feelings.'

At one of the Thornton Manor parties he saw a small boy crying and picked him up. He tried to comfort the boy by asking, 'Why don't you call me Uncle?' The small boy through his tears replied, 'Because you never asked me to.' The boy's mother was there to enjoy the retort as much as the Old Man did, and some years later recounted the incident to her son, J. L. Cregeen, for many years a distinguished engineer on the overseas side of Unilever.

On another occasion his eye fell upon my small twin-sisters. He told them, greatly to their chagrin, that they were really taps because they were little Knox. It was subsequently said that the idea that children should be represented on the Port Sunlight War Memorial by twin girls sprang from this incident.

I was in Port Sunlight early enough and was young enough to experience and enjoy the thrill of living within the immediate orbit of a man we knew to be a great national figure, deeply respected and even held in awe by our seniors but who to us was a kindly and friendly man when we saw him.

Lady Lever is specially remembered by the fact that on her return from a visit to America about 1911 or 1912 she went to the day schools to tell the children about her trip. She handed a parcel to the headmaster of the boys' school and said that every boy was to have a piece of what was in it. I don't suppose that either the headmaster or the boys' mothers thought much of this generous gesture but what glory for the boys of Port Sunlight who, in one fell swoop, were all introduced to the everlasting joys of chewing gum.

My mother used to organize kinderspiels in the winter. (I don't find the word in my dictionary now but they were popular before the First World War though I have never heard of them since.) They were light operas for children and how my mother or anyone else had the skill and patience to train fifty or sixty young children to sing and act part-songs, both chorus and solos from the tonic sol-fa notation, I have never been able to understand. But it was done and the performances were great occasions. One, at Neston, particularly took the Old Man's fancy and he insisted on repeat performances both in Port Sunlight and in the Manor at Thornton Hough. What the invited audience at the Manor thought of a performance of *Squire Goodfellow's Famous Hunt* by some unknown children from Neston dressed up in probably ill-fitting theatrical costumes I do not know, but I, as a very small member of the chorus, was entranced to see my mother conducting the performance with a gold mounted baton presented for the occasion.

Afterwards in the drawing-room where I went with the family party I noticed that one of the sofas was badly in need of repair. I drew Mrs Lever's attention to this and suggested that she ought to get it re-covered. My poor mother was embarrassed by this uninvited comment and threw me a black look, but Mrs Lever thought it a joke and explained that that was the first sofa that she and her husband had bought when they were married and they had never wanted to alter its appearance. Mrs Lever was asked once, after the Old Man had bought The Hill, a large house in Hampstead, how she liked it. She replied, 'It's very nice, but it is like having two houses and no home.'

Lady Lever, as she was from 1911 till her death in 1913, was a gracious, kindly and gentle little woman who supported her husband closely in all his activities. She was indefatigable in her personal interest in everything to do with Port Sunlight and the business of Lever Brothers Limited. She used to drive down to Port Sunlight from the Manor to take the Old Man home at the end of the office day and accompanied him on all his major expeditions from his first voyage round the world in 1892 to what must have been a gruelling five-months' journey to the depths of the Congo forests in the winter of 1912–13. She died shortly after their return from the Congo and the loss of an understanding, calm and constant companionship which stretched fifty years back to childhood left a yawning gap which, either wittingly or unwittingly, the Old Man filled by an acceleration in the pace and an increase in the pressure of his constant and unremitting activity of mind and body. He never had played games though he was assiduous in his early morning exercises and he never took a holiday after his wife's death. If there was a demon it was probably loneliness.

The Lady Lever Art Gallery at Port Sunlight, a gift to the Nation, was, like the Taj Mahal, as perfect as the donor could make it. It contained most of the Old Man's collection of pictures, pottery, sculpture and furniture, the latter still remaining one of the finest in the country. Included in the collection are two Derby biscuit-ware figures of a shepherd and shepherdess bought to adorn his first home, a little house in Upper Dickinson Street, Wigan. Amongst the personal papers there was a large envelope on which the Old Man had written:

Items relating to Sunlight Soap
found amongst wife's papers
Aug. 1913
W. H. Lever

There is no more of interest in this small collection of photographs, advertisements, invitation cards and scraps of paper than there would be in any long-forgotten scrap-book; but the fact that they were treasured shows how close his wife was to his business activities from the very earliest days. One can almost sense the shared excitement of the occasion from the handwritten notes evidently passed out from the Court during his first action in protection of the Sunlight trademark in 1886.

Most of what has been written about the Old Man concerns the affairs of Lever Brothers Limited, the company he founded and built up to a dominant position in the soap trade of the world. It is possible however to get a glimpse of him before he became a captain of industry and public figure—a glimpse, I think, of what sort of man he was—and I think it appropriate to give it here.

In 1892, when he was forty-one, he travelled round the world accompanied by his wife and four-and-a-half-year-old son, a journey lasting six months. He wrote letters to the *Birkenhead News* giving an account of his journeyings together with his thoughts on what he had observed. The letters were reprinted and issued in a small book under the title *Following the Flag*. This not only gives an interesting record of travelling conditions at the time but is also a revelation of the Old Man's mental and physical vigour and the breadth of his knowledge and interests. Nothing worth seeing was too remote or too difficult of access. Not a social, economic or political problem escapes examination and usually trenchant comment.

I give some, I hope not too many, abbreviated or summarized extracts from this truly entertaining record.

On arrival in New York we were detained by quarantine regulations for about 12 hours though there had been no case of sickness on board. We were told that this was absolutely necessary and that we had to be sacrificed to encourage implicit faith in the completeness of the arrangements made for preventing the introduction of cholera.

We took a cab to the hotel, paying three dollars (12s 6d) for a distance for which we should pay 2s or 2s 6d in England.

Of a visit to church in Toronto he wrote,

. . . I had to rub my eyes to see whether we were really in the Toronto Cathedral of the English Church, or at some Radical meeting. If a dis-established and dis-endowed church can be so strong and robust, so in touch with the life of the people . . . it is as clear as noonday that should it ever happen that the Church of England is dis-established it will not, in consequence . . . suffer loss in any way on that account.

A third of the whole book is devoted to his visit to the Sandwich Islands where he spent eighteen days, presumably as a sort of holiday though he did not spare himself in the matter of studying 'these remote islands where there was no telegraphic news and mails arrived only at fortnightly intervals'. During the course of his investigations he failed for once in his imaginative grasp of the potentialities of a site.

The great question in the Sandwich Islands now is, can the United States Government be induced to take over a site as a naval coaling station. This project has to me the appearance of being merely a gigantic piece of jobbery promoted by land speculators. . . . Pretentious plans are displayed at all the public resorts. These show a fine city with broad handsome avenues with high-sounding names, hotel, railway station, park, etc., all looking very attractive on paper. In the flowery words of the prospectus it is a desired haven of the artist and author. . . . And then the promoters, coming down to business, state that the capital is 5,000,000 dollars limited liability, that the property offers an opportunity to net a handsome profit on a small amount of money invested.

We went by train to see this wonderful place and we could not find it. Nothing daunted, we decided to try again and this time we drove there so as to have the driver with us to show us where it was. Then we found how it was that we did not discover it on our first visit. The place does not exist except on paper. No hotel, no railway station or park is there and the only inhabitant we saw was a Chinaman who was acting as caretaker. True, the streets and avenues were all marked out with stumps, more or less perpendicular, which were more suggestive of tombstones over the dead hopes of the shareholders than the origin of a fine city.

Just at present it seems more likely that the whole thing will fall flat.

The name of the site was Pearl Harbor and the Sandwich Islands are now known as the Hawaiian Islands.

He got it right about the place as a whole however: 'What appears to me most probable is that the United States will take over the whole of the Sandwich Islands and annex them,' and his description of the situation in the Islands reads like a brief sketch of the idea on which James A. Michener's great novel *Hawaii* is based.

He notes the separation of the various communities, natives, Chinese, Japanese, Portuguese, Americans, and deplores the fact that the native population has decreased so alarmingly,

notwithstanding all the efforts of the missionaries. It appears from the American Mission Report that in 1835 they had 900 schools in the Sandwich Islands and 50,000 scholars. Today the native population is barely 35,000 men, women and children. It is hardly possible to believe that had the same amount of money, time and labour been devoted to teaching such of the arts and sciences of civilization as would enable the natives themselves to make the most of their country and to raise themselves in the social scale, the native population would have sunk from 400,000 at the time of their discovery by Captain Cook to 35,000 today.

To hold the contrary opinion would be to admit that nothing can be done for the material well-being of native races and missionary effort becomes merely a prayer for the souls of the dying, a sending of the Chaplain previous to the execution.

Still on the subject of missionary work he notes that though the natives profess to be Christians, they are still very superstitious. 'We must not forget that even after a thousand years of Christian teaching we, in England, still believed in the power of witches and enacted laws for their punishment and death by burning.'

He deals with many other interesting matters: The growing of taro root and the making of poi, a paste of the fermented root, which formed the staple diet of the natives—'The flavour is exactly like what one would expect to find would be the taste of bill-stickers' paste gone sour, but it is extremely nourishing and wholesome and the natives are very fond of it'; the problem of leprosy; the economics of sugar growing; and the Monarchy.

Everything interested him. He became so fascinated by what he heard of the volcano Kilauea and the crater Halemaumau that he, and presumably those with him, undertook a strenuous expedition to see them. It took two days on a small boat to sail from Honolulu to the south coast of the Island of Hawaii itself and there they landed by surf-boat at a place called Panaluu, which I cannot find on the map. Thence they travelled six miles on a plantation-style light railway and a further twenty-three miles, rising 4,000 feet, on an extremely rough track in a wagonette drawn by six horses— a journey of some eight hours in tropical heat. The accommodation when they got there was comfortable but the following two days of crater and lava walking ruined their boots. Then there was the long return journey. Then, on their way south, they went ashore at Kealakekua Bay to see the Captain Cook monument marking the scene of his first arrival and murder.

The Old Man gave a particularly lively description of the surf-boat landing at Panaluu.

At one moment the surf boat would rise high above our ship as if trying to see if there was not a way over the top deck, the next it would go suddenly down as if to try for a way underneath. The advice given us was the same as is given to would-be operators on the Stock Exchange or Cotton Market 'catch it on the rise and mind you don't get caught on the drop'.

En route from Honolulu to Auckland the party spent three hours in Samoa of which he tells this story:

The missionaries who first landed at Samoa came via Australia and forgot to add a day on passing the 180th degree and consequently were observing Sunday on Saturday. The setting right of this matter caused a struggle, the missionaries offering the strongest resistance . . . as they feared that the change would destroy native faith in Sunday altogether. However, the merchants insisted and, the missionaries giving way, the mistake was rectified last year by holding two Fourth of July celebrations.

In New Zealand he was again attracted by a volcano and describes the eruption of Tarawera which, six years previously, had obliterated what had been 'the busiest tourist headquarters in New Zealand' with two hotels, a church and a prosperous village. They undertook another strenuous journey to see this desolation of erupted lava. A long day's drive from Rotorua to Waiotapu and then, on the following day, 'what, to our town and city muscles, was a hard day's work of 22 miles in saddle, 16 miles in open boat and 6 or 7 miles walking and climbing.'

But in both New Zealand and Australia his attention was mainly drawn to political matters and he comments thereon as a true Radical.

The first ever Labour Government had come to New Zealand and his comments are robust:

These and other measures passed by the present Government tend to prove that it is a competent, capable, and sound Government, and also that the fears of those who are alarmed for the future of the English race, because of the probability that there will be in the future a greater share of political power in the hands of the Labour Party than has been wielded by them in the past, are utterly without foundation. If these nervous people would only carefully study history they would come to the conclusion that just as all the revolutions that the world has ever seen have been brought about by the accumulation of wealth in the hands of the few, accompanied by the political serfdom of the people, so the best guarantee for the progress, development, and prosperity of a nation, is only to be found in the granting of full political power and liberty to the people, than whom no portion of a nation sooner feel the effects of good or bad legislation; and, consequently, than whom no portion of a nation can be so safely relied on to uphold the one and reject the other.

I would not have it thought to be my opinion that there is any form of government that can be devised that will be free from faults and imperfections. I have not the slightest doubt that had I stayed longer in New Zealand I should have found that the present Government have been guilty of as much fruitless, silly, and even, perhaps, pernicious, legislation as could be produced by our Government at home with the approval of our lords, temporal and spiritual. It would hardly be possible for them to be guilty of more. All that we can say at present is, that considering this is the first opportunity the Labour Party have had of using their power, they have used it with singular moderation, and have shown the desire and capacity to govern wisely and in a statesmanlike manner.

In both countries he deals with the question of land ownership and taxation. He advocates free trade for Australia and comments on a proposal made by the Upper House in New South Wales during the debate on a bill passed by the Lower House to give 'one man one vote' that it is a 'question which will shortly come before our own Parliament at home.'

The Upper House felt that 'one man one vote' would discourage thrift and proposed that the virtue of thrift should be rewarded by an extra vote. To this idea, Lever reacted strongly:

We know that we are only a slow-going lot at home, otherwise we should be at a loss to tell how it is that our social reformers have been so far behind the age as not to have made the discovery of how great a power for good may be made of that much abused custodian of our liberties—the Ballot Box. But, now that the discovery has been given to the world, surely such a power for good will not be confined to the Colonies. Let England enjoy her share of the blessing. Now that we know that an extra vote will encourage virtue, it should not be long before someone, eager for a rallying cry—perhaps Mr. Chamberlain—will come forward with a complete scheme. In this easy and simple way we may yet find a short cut to the realization of the Millennium. Do we wish to encourage sobriety, we must give a vote for sobriety; bravery, a vote for bravery; unselfishness, a vote for unselfishness . . . we must give a vote for each virtue taught and preached by our Saviour; and one for keeping each of the Ten Commandments. It would be little less than a crime if the blessings of this beautiful and simple system were confined to the encouragement of only one solitary virtue, and especially so when that is a virtue which many think is not even one of the most exalted for a man to aspire to. . . . In short, the so-called vote for thrift is only a colonial development of the old Tory dodge, tersely described by Mr. Gladstone as 'deck loading'. The Upper House, knowing that it dare not refuse passage to the good ship 'one man one vote' hopes that by deck loading her with a so-called 'vote for thrift' it may either sink the ship or deprive the owners of any profit should she reach port in safety.

It is strange to notice what a strong family likeness there is in the proceedings of Upper Houses of Parliament the world over.

He has some interesting thoughts on the Australian Railways, commenting adversely of course on the inter-State jealousies which caused the railways to be built on three different gauges.

But if three gauges are bad the rates and charges are worse. They seem to have been specially designed to discourage the use of railways as much as possible: they must simply kill any farming industry upcountry. I heard of one case where all that a farmer got for 3000 sheep was an account for £60 which he had to pay, the sheep not having realised by that sum the amount of carriage and expenses.

Now the object of railways in a huge continent like Australia, as elsewhere, is to annihilate distance so as to connect all parts of the country with the centres of population. And it is clear that, where the railways belong to the people themselves, it is directly against their interests to make railway rates so high that a monopoly is given to those who, by their situation as regards the markets, are protected from competition with those whose produce can only be brought to market by payment of heavy railway rates. This is not the system on which Government railway rates ought to be based. There is only one way to make the railways pay the nation properly, and at the same time place every part of the country on an equal footing, and that is to annihilate distance in fixing rates. Just as there is one uniform rate for postage within a kingdom, regardless of distance, so there ought to be one uniform rate per ton for carriage on the railways, regardless of distance. It will all work out right on the basis of the average carriage per ton, as, with goods, it is not the haulage of the greater or less number of miles that is costly, but the terminal charges. If there were any loss, which there could be in the initiation of the system, it would fall with lightness on the whole nation, who would gain more than they lost thereby, as they would have command of every market and centre of production in the kingdom, and break up monopoly in any one district.'

He advocates a similar system for passenger trains on the grounds that the cost of running passenger trains is not the distance but the number of empty seats.

Though, as a child, I had often seen him, my own personal contact with the Old Man started in 1919 in Lewis as I have already recorded.

After joining the business I used to see him from time to time in the Liver Buildings office in Liverpool, or, later, in the London office, as well as at various Port Sunlight functions. On one occasion I met him at Rock Ferry Station on his way via the Mersey Railway (before the Mersey Road Tunnel) to Liverpool. He joined me in the third class to continue his questioning as to what I was doing and how I was getting on. When we got to Liverpool I carried his bag for him from Central to Lime Street Station, a valuable service which was then normally performed by one of a band of casual but official out-porters distinguished by a red band on their caps, which I have never seen elsewhere than in Liverpool.

My closer and more regular contacts with him began after he had appointed my brother his private secretary in 1923. He informed my brother, just down from Oxford with a first in Greats, that he would not be as much use to Lever Brothers as his younger brother —myself—who had already had nearly four years' experience in the business, but that, nevertheless, he would pay him the same salary and would give him any increase that his brother might get at Christmas. After that, he would be on his own. I am happy to say that I got an increase at Christmas.

My brother and I were from to time to time summoned to The Hill, his house in Hampstead, to attend dances of which the Old Man was very fond especially after he became too deaf to enjoy going to the theatre which had been a favourite relaxation. He was an assiduous dancer, partly because it was exercise and partly because he loved the company of young people. He usually chose the wallflowers to dance with and it is recalled that at Port Sunlight he always had a dance with Ethel Williams, the hunchback.

On one occasion I was asked to attend on both Tuesday and Wednesday nights, and on the Monday afternoon received a book on the grocery trade with a request from the Old Man for a précis on two sheets of paper 'by Thursday morning'. I am a slow reader and was fully occupied with my work during office hours so I had to do my best for the grocery trade in the small hours of the morning after walking from The Hill to my lodgings in Golders Green.

Though the Old Man did not write much for publication he was an assiduous, lively and articulate correspondent. As I learned in Sweden, mail was a prime factor in his daily routine. In his letters from the Congo in 1924 he frequently bemoaned the fact that there was no mail. At home his mail was voluminous and he dealt with it all himself—there was no prior sorting. To help him he had a number of small stick-on labels in different colours and carrying varying instructions—each member of his staff having a different colour label. Altogether there were twenty-seven different instructions on the full set of labels but many appeared on more than one label. As he went through his correspondence he set aside those to which he wished to dictate a reply and on the others he licked and stuck on the appropriate label, ticking the instructions he wished carried out.

The most frequently ticked instructions were probably 'O', 'Suitably', 'Unable', which have been a by-word between my brother and me ever since. They meant that a suitable letter was to be written indicating that he was unable, e.g. to open a bazaar, and that the letter was to be signed by the rubber stamp of his signature.

But it was not in correspondence but in speaking that he best revealed himself and his thoughts. He made himself into an excellent and practised public speaker, not unaware that his Lancashire accent might add spice to his discourse, which was usually enlivened by apt simile and a ready wit. 'His voice,' says his biographer, 'was clear and resonant. He spoke with every evidence of physical as well as mental energy.' He was in great demand for all sorts of occasions and was equally at home opening a church bazaar or delivering a lecture to a learned society. He did not find himself so comfortable in either the House of Commons or the House of Lords, though he was active in each. In 1906 he quoted in the Commons an eighteenth-century precedent for payment for M.P.s and in 1907 he brought in a Private Member's Bill to provide old age pensions of which a second reading was carried. The measure was taken over by Government and hence Lloyd George's name rather than his became associated with the granting of old age pensions. In the Lords, in 1918, he advocated a system of decimal coinage, characteristically working up from the penny rather than downwards from the pound, because his business experience was based on catering for housewives in the grocer's shop not on the predilections of bankers. 'Convenience in money is essential,' he urged. The penny, he claimed, had stood the test of twelve centuries whereas 'the parvenu sovereign' had only been in use since 1817. 'Most of the leading Nations have based their decimal systems on the British penny. . . . The American dollar, for instance, is based on our halfpenny; the Latin franc on tenpence. We do not want to make an embalmed mummy of the sovereign.'

He was most at home in the auditorium at Port Sunlight, a large and draughty building, capable of seating 3,000 people, and originally planned as an open-air amphitheatre—subsequently roofed in and now demolished. The acoustics were not good, but he could hold audiences there, whether of co-partners, Sunday school children, visiting grocers or shareholders, without the aid of any

microphone. He must have been one of very few company chairmen whose speeches at annual general meetings were given
extempore.

These speeches followed a fairly set pattern. He started by con-
gratulating the shareholders on the record profits of the year under
review, usually having sound reason for doing so. He dealt with any
specific developments during the year such as the opening of new
ventures overseas, new acquisitions, and directorial appointments,
but said very little about the real progress of the business—in those
days not even the value of total sales was given in the annual
accounts. Expenditure on advertising, as awkward a point in 1909
as it has remained since, was covered, or covered up, by the proud
announcement that the business had been further strengthened
during the year by an expenditure of X pounds on 'repairs,
renewals, depreciation and advertising.'

Reading these speeches from about 1909 onwards one cannot
perceive the difficulties, even dangers, through which the business
passed and there is no hint that the capital employed had increased
from £6·5 million in 1910 to £65 million by 1924 and that the
share capital structure had altered practically every year during
that period.

Difficulties were mentioned but only against the background of
absolute confidence that they would be overcome. In 1911 at the
beginning of one of his most adventurous schemes he told the
shareholders: 'In the Congo we are like a bunch of blind puppies—
all our problems are to come.' A year later, however, he was able to
report that the first palm oil from Lever's mill had been exported
from the Congo!

After dealing thus very generally with the affairs of the Company and giving a much fuller account of the affairs of the village, he
usually finished by giving his views on some current topic. In 1919
he called Excess Profit Tax 'an assassin's blow at business'. The
following year he remarked: 'It is said the optimist is the man who
can buy from a Jew and sell to a Scotsman at a profit but the super-
optimist is the man who tries to conduct his business efficiently . . .
under Government control.' In 1925 he returned to this theme:
'Governments are very like fire and water—good servants but bad
masters.' His strictures on the 'blundering policy' of the Nigerian

Government were taken personally by the Governor-General, Sir Hugh Clifford, but the Old Man refused to withdraw: 'It is too high a price to pay,' he said in 1925, 'when he asks your Chairman to withdraw remarks which he cannot truthfully withdraw, honestly modify or conscientiously regret having uttered.'

He answered questions just as crisply. To a query regarding solicitors' costs he replied, 'We usually get these from an opponent'; to another about rates, 'Can't give the exact figure but they are too high and we pay 40 per cent of the total in this district.' He enjoyed himself at the annual general meetings and so did the shareholders.

On one occasion, at the end of the meeting, he said, 'Time is getting on and I see on the agenda there is a vote of thanks to myself. With your kind permission we will leave that out.'

A lot has been written about what he did in the building up of Lever Brothers Limited but little if anything about how he did it. What was his style of management? I cannot attempt any technical analysis of this but perhaps by picking out one or two examples of how he worked I may be able to indicate something at least of the flavour of his management style. I arrange my examples under the modern headings of Personnel, Marketing and Administration.

Personnel

The Old Man was a stern master. He was the boss and nobody could question it. He was said to have in his safe the signed, but undated, resignations of all his directors. The story may not have been literally true, but it certainly expressed the truth: that the directors held their appointments at his pleasure. When some of the directors questioned major expenditure on one of his schemes he said, 'Well, gentlemen, I don't think the ordinary shareholders will raise any objection.' He held all the ordinary shares.

It was frightening to be told off by him but he was no more severe and certainly more enlightened and generous than the majority of his contemporaries in industrial and commercial life.

In Port Sunlight there was a special bell link between the Old

Man's office and those of the directors, and if this rang the Director concerned would jump to answer and hasten along the corridor to the Old Man's office, no doubt wondering en route if it was going to be thunder or sunshine. As a boy in the Liverpool office, I was amused to see directors straightening their ties as they went into his room, just as I had done a few months previously when entering the headmaster's study. When my father joined the business he was summoned for 11.00 a.m. but was two minutes late. The Old Man spent the first two minutes calculating exactly how much the wasted two minutes of the chairman's time had cost the business. My father was not unduly impressed as it seemed to him that the Old Man had wasted the second two minutes too.

The Port Sunlight office hours were from 8.30 a.m. to 5.00 p.m., which meant that people were supposed to be, and were, at their desks at work at 8.30 a.m. The Old Man certainly was. As the business grew and the directors began to arrive in chauffeur-driven (at their own expense!) cars it occurred to them that it would be more in keeping with their dignity if they arrived a little later than the general staff. They managed to summon up enough courage to persuade one of their number, an Irishman, to suggest this to the Old Man. His reply was, 'Yes, that's a very good idea, Mr Mc-Dowell—but I will be here as usual at 8.30.' And so were the directors, one of whom had a small mirror fixed outside the window of his office at such an angle as to give him a view of the main entrance—thus enabling him to be on the alert after he had seen the Old Man arrive and no doubt relax, or even depart, after he had seen him safely off the premises. I have always looked up at the wooden plugs still in the brick when I have passed that window.

Everyone had to be on hand when the Old Man was about, or have a cast-iron reason why not. One day, at Lever House in London he wanted to see one of the head men in the engineering department. He was told by the man's secretary that he had gone to A. & F. Pears' factory at Isleworth. Enquiries at Pears disclosed that he was not there, nor was he expected. He left the Company the following day, not for taking a day off without leave but for instructing his secretary to tell a lie.

The Old Man certainly got rid of people quickly if they had not measured up to his expectations, but he usually did it generously—

a lump sum, or sometimes even a pension, and directors of Lever Brothers who erred usually only suffered the ignominy of being promoted to chairmanship of an associated company.

On his fifth and last journey round the world he paid his only visit to India, travelling up by train from Colombo to Calcutta, a journey I have done myself, involving four nights and three dusty and hot days in the train when air conditioning had not even been thought of. A party of senior Lever officials in India straight from their morning showers and in nice clean ducks were at the station early in the morning to greet him in the expectation that they would be able to return to the hotel for a quick breakfast while the Old Man bathed and changed. They were shocked when he walked off the station, somewhat crushed as to clothes but otherwise sparkling, and said, 'Well I think we'll just go straight to the factory.' It shocked the factory manager too who evidently did not perform to the Old Man's satisfaction. After the tour of the factory the following dialogue took place:

Old Man: 'Well, Mr Spencer, where did you come from?'

Mr Spencer (with some pride): 'From Lille, sir' (the Lever factory in France).

Old Man: 'I've no doubt they'll be glad to 'ave you back.'

Instances like these were, of course, talked about at the time and are remembered. Just after the First World War especially, when the business was expanding greatly and quickly, people came and went with considerable rapidity. The general feeling at my level was that one could understand better why they went than why they came.

But essentially the Old Man was a builder of men not a destroyer. Fiercely critical letters were sometimes torn up and re-dictated more calmly and for every letter of criticism there would be many of congratulation and encouragement. But it must have taken a good deal of encouragement to counter this handwritten blast addressed to his nephew, J. L. Ferguson, one of his senior directors, who was at the time (just after the First World War) chairman of the Control Board responsible for the home associated companies:

What steps is the Control Board taking with Associated Companies that are either making losses or below datum profits?

If merely 'noting' same, then where does control come in? If you are not taking action then tell me and I shall take hold myself. I feel very hurt at the 'placid calmness' of nerve shown under circumstances that mean ruin.

He knew how to criticize, certainly, but he knew also how to make a fuss of people. There were splendid dinner parties at Thornton Manor as well as great social occasions in Port Sunlight. Senior managers with their wives and members of their families were sometimes invited for a few days to The Hill in Hampstead whence cars would take them sightseeing during the day and theatre parties would be arranged at night. When someone was appointed from Port Sunlight to an important job overseas there would be a special banquet in his honour, with speeches of congratulations and good wishes to him and to his wife.

He had never heard of 'Management Development', but latterly he wrote every year to his directors and senior managers asking them for particulars of any young men in their departments who had outstanding capacity. From there onwards his idea of management development was summed up in what he had said as long ago as 1909: 'I put the ladder against the wall but no one can push you up. If I tried, you and the ladder would fall.' Thus he kept close to his management and they felt close to him.

He also paid his staff well. In *Progress*, Lever Brothers' house magazine, he wrote in 1909: 'A salary should be as large as, or more than, the man could get under any other circumstances that I could possibly imagine.'

Amongst the private papers to which I have already referred were his private lists of salaries for 1910 to 1913, covering the directors, chairmen of overseas companies and other officials whom he obviously regarded as important. To have your salary on 'The Chairman's List', whatever the actual amount of the salary, was a significant status symbol—equivalent to what became later senior manager. The range of salary on the list was from £300 per year to £3,000. That was at the time when £1,000 a year was considered affluence. Directors were paid between £2,000 and £3,000. As a matter of interest I asked an economist friend to work out for me what would be the pre-tax income now that would give the purchasing power of the extremes in 1910 of the Old Man's list. He gave me the following figures which I believe reasonably reflect the position:

Salary 1911	Equivalent gross salary now (1974) to give equivalent purchasing power:
£ 300	£ 3,230
£3,000	£110,000

As inflation had never been heard of, in 1910–13 it was not customary to give annual increases but there were year-end bonuses for those who had distinguished themselves. Many of those in important positions, such as export salesmen, received commission in addition to salary which could be substantial if the man was successful.

His interest in the wellbeing of people at the lower end of the scale was great.

He had been brought up in a Northcountry manufacturing town where in a closely-knit community strongly influenced by liberal non-conformity he had every opportunity to know of the conditions in which many ordinary people worked and lived. All his life he sought ways and means of improving their lot and generally led the way by his own example. He once said: 'You can overwork and kill any machine and that is sound policy but to be lacking in consideration in any way for the life, health and happiness of the employee is the most short-sighted policy a firm can adopt.'

In Port Sunlight he built what is probably the best housing estate for workers ever built. He was amongst the first to adopt the eight-hour and subsequently the seven-hour day. He worked hard to try to launch a six-hour day (two shifts), for general acceptance throughout industry and commerce, but the Unions did not like the idea for industry and the Post Office were not prepared to change the rhythm of their activities to link up with offices starting at 6.00 a.m.

He was a pioneer in granting paid holidays to workers, arranging for pensions on retirement and half pay for periods of sickness or unemployment. He provided canteens and proper washing, locker-room and toilet and First Aid facilities long before this was common practice. This sort of provision and general attitude was not confined to Port Sunlight, but was mirrored wherever a factory was established overseas, though, except on plantations, he never repeated the experiment in workers' housing. But when housing was being provided in the Congo plantations he was insistent that it should be well done and was annoyed on seeing the plans that the houses were arranged on the usual 'coolie lines' pattern with fronts of one row facing the backs of the next. He changed it to what he considered the better arrangement of front facing front.

For a man who did so much by precept and example to improve the conditions and better the status of the employee, it is difficult to say which of all his schemes was the most important. He would I think have said 'co-partnership'. To make people feel part of the business, and also to share in its fortunes, good or bad, was a problem which exercised his mind from the very earliest days. The principles he had in mind were set out in a paper he read on the subject in 1900:

> If prosperity-sharing or profit-sharing do not have a beneficial effect in relation to workshop management then they are charity, and, as such, would be properly resented by every true workman. If, on the other hand, prosperity-sharing or profit-sharing give the employee a greater interest in his work and make him a better man, then their practice becomes a sound business system.

The meeting in the auditorium when the first co-partnership certificates were distributed in 1909 must have been one of the greatest occasions of his life, and incidentally provided an example of his care in treating people equally and as individuals. The programme for the occasion including photographs, all of the same size, of every one of the recipients of whatsoever status—arranged alphabetically with name and occupation underneath. These 1,000 photographs must have been specially taken for the occasion. People like to see their photograph 'in print', but what must have been the gratification sixty years ago when to have your photo taken at all was something special!

The scheme started with a distribution of co-partnership certificates with a nominal value of £113,650 to 1,041 co-partners, all in the U.K. When the Old Man died there were 18,000 co-partners spread all over the world holding a total of nearly £2,500,000 certificates.

The scheme could not have been fitted in to the Lever/Margarine Union merger which created Unilever and it had to be brought to an end. It is doubtful in any case if it could long have remained meaningful in the age of social security. The graduated pension scheme which Unilever built, on foundations originally laid in Holland, has more than compensated those who may have been disappointed to see 'profit-sharing' disappear.

Profit-sharing and workers' participation remain unsolved problems and, so far as the U.K. is concerned, will continue so while high taxation makes the carrot rotten and the Welfare State blunts the spur.

Marketing

The Old Man has frequently been mentioned as one of the fathers of modern advertising and certainly an interesting account is given in *The History of Unilever* of his personal attention to it in its infancy. He must have devised the very first booklet, *Sunlight Soap and How to Use it*, a copy of which was in the envelope of Lady Lever's 'treasures'.

It contained some pretty hard-hitting copy, for example:

FRAUD!

Certain unscrupulous soap manufacturers, jealous of the great success of the Sunlight Self-Washer Soap, have attempted to obtain a share of our trade by making a soap of similar appearance to ours, and trying to palm it off as the SUNLIGHT. Now the fact that these imitations are similar in appearance does not make them the same by any means. Silk is white and cotton is white, but no one can say that they are one and the same article. No other soap manufacturer can make the Sunlight Self-Washer Soap, and every attempt to do so must result in failure.

This is followed by a graphic account of a lady who finds washing day 'the plague of her life'. She has tried every soap she has heard of and they 'are all one as bad as another or else worse'.

She is an honest woman, however, and at last gives Sunlight Self-Washer Soap a fair trial, and is perfectly astonished at the easy way she can wash with this soap.

Her washing is all over and put away before her husband comes home, and after tea they go out for a walk together, a thing they have never been able to do for thirty years.

It seems like their old 'courting' days, and she never felt so happy before.

She begins to think that life is worth living after all.

(T.V. might do it differently, but it could hardly do it better.)

There follows a brief history of soap, going back to Homer with a mention of Ulysses and Nausicaa and the second half of the booklet consists of 'hints on washing and cleaning', some of which graphically reflect the changes in domestic economy and methods since the booklet was published:

To Clean Silk

Take one-third of a tablet of Sunlight Self-Washer Soap, a teaspoonful of brandy and a pint of gin, and well mix them together; when dissolved, strain through a cloth. With a sponge spread it on each side of the silk; being careful not to crease. Then wash it in two or three waters, and iron on the wrong side. The silk will then look as good as new, and will not be injured, even if of the most delicate colours.

Table Covers

Dissolve four tablets of Sunlight Self-Washer Soap in six gallons of boiling water, and mix it with one pound of pearlash. Have three earthenware pans or tubs that will hold about eight gallons each; into the first of these put three gallons of the

1a William Hesketh Lever, first Viscount Leverhulme of the Western Isles, born 19th September 1851, died 7th May 1925. The founder of Lever Brothers Limited and a major figure in Andrew Knox's early career.

1b Leverhulme arriving at the office in Port Sunlight after a world tour, at the age of 73, in 1924. Leverhulme travelled incessantly, throughout the world, from a very early period in his career until a few weeks before his death, which happened after he came back from a tour of West Africa and the Congo in the winter of 1924-5.

2a Sir Francis D'Arcy Cooper Bt (1882–1941), originally of the firm of Cooper Brothers & Co., which he left to join the Board of Lever Brothers in 1923. He succeeded Leverhulme as Chairman of Lever Brothers after Leverhulme died, and from 1930 to his death in 1941 was Chairman of Unilever. 'One of the type of men,' said Leverhulme, 'that I consider most resemble a warm fire and people naturally seem to come up to him for warmth.'

2b Lord Heyworth (1894–1974). One of three brothers, all of whom became directors of Unilever. He succeeded D'Arcy Cooper as Chairman of Unilever and held the appointment for nearly twenty years, from 1941 to 1960.

3 Andrew Knox.

4 A commercial management conference at Unilever's training centre, Four Acres, Kingston-upon-Thames, in 1956. *Standing, left to right*: A. W. Walker, F. S. Walker, H. R. Odling, R. T. Clack, J. G. Muir, A. D. Bonham-Carter, R. C. McPherson, J. C. Walker, T. L. Fordy, C. E. C. Eastman, F. Davies, A. M. Knox. *Seated, left to right*: J. C. Connor, A. A. Haak, H. G. Pinner, A. Watson, Lord Heyworth, P. H. Shirley, R. D. Cameron, J. Greiner, D. J. Nielson, P. James.

dissolved soap and one pail of cold water; into the second, two gallons of soap and one pail of water; and into the third, one gallon of soap and two pails of water. Well work the cover in each of these three soap liquors, beginning with the strongest, and wring it between each. Stir one tablespoonful of oil of vitriol into a tub containing six pails of cold water. Handle the cover in this spirit water for five minutes then take it out and rinse it in one lot of cold water; this is the proper method for cotton-and-worsted or printed cotton covers.

It was a time of self help and respectability, and such booklets and other more substantial volumes which followed, while carrying direct advertising for Sunlight soap wherever appropriate in the text or on a page that needed filling up, aimed at giving useful information on both public and private affairs to all those who would have regarded themselves as being 'respectable' whatever the income group, thus giving respectability to Sunlight soap. Could modern public relations do better?

From 1895 to 1900 a *Sunlight Almanac* was published. Such publications were popular at the time. *The Sunlight Almanac* after giving a full calendar of the year, with every day celebrated by some event, provided a compendium of information; in 1895 general information 'on all topics of the day', but gradually over the years with ever greater emphasis on information pertaining to the home: home millinery; ribbon embroidery; screaming babies; guide to good and pure food, etc. This led up to the publication in 1901 of a 470-page illustrated book, *Woman's World*, edited by 'A Diplomée of a London Hospital', and a veritable compendium of knowledge and advice on all aspects of domestic life.

I could fill a book with extracts from this admirable work but the following will give the flavour of the advice given:

The House Beautiful
Let a young housewife realise that the most charming ornament of a room is a woman's bright, cheerful and sympathetic face.

Advice to a Young Wife
It is a good thing when the young couple have decided on the division of income before marriage.

Let the young wife show tact in bearing her own burdens, and not begin the subject of small domestic grievances when her husband comes in after a long and perhaps worrying day. The shortcomings of her servants, the amount of the baker's bill, the short weight sent by the grocer, the trouble she has had because the butcher sent the meat late—all belongs to her own department and should never form the principal item of her conversation.

A wife who . . . never 'Nags' . . . will have her reward in the entire trust of her husband; for will he not value her opinion of himself all the more in that she does not allow him to see that she notices his small failings?

In the early years he certainly took a detailed interest in all advertising matters and was a pioneer in what is now known as 'promotions'—schemes for giving away small gifts and awarding big prizes. These were not regarded, in some quarters, as 'respectable' but he overrode prejudice by his own effectiveness in the sphere of public relations. He was constantly in the news, as a successful industrialist, a generous donor to public and private causes, a noted exponent of social ideas and ideals and the chief and usually victorious figure in prominent law cases. Port Sunlight as a 'model village' gained much publicity at a time of awakening interest in 'garden cities'.

Even when he had to pass the detail of his advertising to others he saw to it that it continued to have both vigour and novelty.

Looking back, it would I think be fair to claim that the Old Man was in fact the father of modern marketing, using 'advertising' admittedly to a greater extent and more skilfully than his competitors, but it was only one of the ingredients of his success.

Sunlight soap, the rock on which the business was built, was not just an advertising phenomenon, though its advertising backing was phenomenal, it was a skilled marketing job. It was not only the first soap to be presented in tablet form, wrapped and cartoned, but it was in formulation ahead of its competitors, giving a freer, quicker and more copious lather. It looked nicer than the normal tallow/resin soaps of the time and, the point of genius, it was perfumed, not with just the usual dash of citronella or mirbane but with a blended perfume of many ingredients, one of which, as I remember, was oil of rosemary, which I thought sounded very nice. Lever had been a salesman so he knew how to enthuse and encourage his sales force. He started life as a grocer so he knew 'the trade': he attacked and overcame the stronghold of Watson's (of Leeds) Matchless Cleanser soap in London by establishing a depot there, from which he could deliver to wholesalers 'within the hour' if necessary and six times a week if required. This service to the trade was further developed later into a transport company, S.P.D. He wrote from the Congo to the director in charge of the U.K. trade in 1912:

> The key to our position must be prompt and efficient service to our Customers. The first steps are the organisation of a Motor Service of about 100 motors—more rather than less—at most pressing points . . . We must view the proposition not altogether as a question of so and so much a ton for delivery but as a means of holding the trade. We pay Wholesalers an average of over 15/- per ton on bonus—we spend over 20/- per ton in Advertising and it is penny wise and pound foolish to hesitate at 5/- per ton extra on the average for delivery. Quick delivery is the key to victory.

Further successes with astute advertising included Lifebuoy soap. When the soap boiling process is completed the soap is allowed to settle in the pan and the 'nigres' fall to the bottom. These nigres are perfectly good soap but darker than the main boil and were normally sold off cheap as brown soap. Because of the raw materials used, Sunlight nigres were not as dark as from soaps made mainly from tallow, and by the addition of colour and some phenol could be made into a very nice-looking piece of carbolic soap. Carbolic was at that time the accepted smell of disinfectant with a strong connotation of cleanliness. Lifebuoy meant safety, and advertising created the image of sparkling and vigorous personal cleanliness.

It is fashionable now to claim that the life of even a successful trademark is brief. The Old Man did not believe this. In an address to the Sphinx Club of New York in 1924 he said:

Honesty in advertising, the motto of this great Club, where I was cordially received twenty-two years ago, is a cardinal principle of your country and also in mine. Sooner or later the dishonest advertiser disappears. The advertiser of our times is not working for today only. He is laying his foundation deep. He is building for those who will follow after him.

Let me recount the seventy years of Lux. Many of the hints on washing given in the first Sunlight Self-Washer booklet recommended that Sunlight soap should be flaked for easy dissolving and this was quite common practice in the washhouse. In 1899 Lever put the first soap flakes on the market and a year later they became Lux. But they were not flaked Sunlight soap which would have been comparatively thick and somewhat yellow in appearance, but were flakes from the toilet soap mill, white and paper thin, quickly soluble in warm water and giving the typical creamy lather of toilet soap. The Old Man told his shareholders in 1920, with unusual frankness on such matters, that the profit on laundry soap was 10 per cent, on toilet soap 12 per cent and on Lux 25 per cent.

Lux was first developed as a safe washer for woollens and fine fabrics and then gradually with emphasis on the fact that it was mild on the hands, necessarily used in the 'bowl washing' of such garments. This mildness on the hands was picked up in the U.S.A. and used as the base on which to build up Lux as a dishwasher at a time when woollens and domestic service were both disappearing, leaving dishes as the main use for the 'bowl wash'.

A year or two before the Old Man died my father went with two or three other men from Port Sunlight to the U.S.A. to look for new ideas within their own sphere. My father's was education within industry, but he was struck also by the fact that we had no toilet soap business in the U.S.A. and suggested that success might come by the introduction of a really white piece of soap. The Old Man passed on this idea to Mr Countway, Head of the Lever business in Boston, who in due course produced 'Lux in toilet form', soon, as Lux Toilet Soap, to become the biggest selling toilet soap, not only in the U.S.A. but throughout the world.

Lux (flakes) as a dishwasher was outdated when it became evident that non-soap detergents did the job better than soap, but again in the U.S.A. Lever led with a liquid dishwasher called, of course, Lux.

The Old Man certainly built for those who followed after him.

Administration

D'Arcy Cooper, in an obituary of the Old Man, said, 'His precepts will be our guide,' and, in looking back, I believe his precepts in business management have done as much for the subsequent strength of the Company as did his ideas and example in the spheres of personnel and marketing.

First and foremost he was decisive, which is essential for the head of any organization with any life in it.

He followed closely every aspect of the business even when it was worldwide and diversified into other products than soap. He got up very early in the morning and after his bout of physical exercises he read reports and examined sales statistics and other data prepared weekly or monthly as appropriate, from cabled information where necessary. This insistence by the head (or the head office!) of a business on being kept informed in detail about what is going on can be dangerous if it is used so as to inhibit initiative down the line, but it is an essential element in the mutual trust and confidence which binds a business together and if used properly helps to build that trust and mutual confidence.

I don't suppose that the Old Man thought along these lines—he was not only the boss but the owner of the business and he just wanted to know. His knowledge enabled him to be alert to praise and when necessary to criticize, but, being informed, he left his managements to attend to their business. This is clearly illustrated by letters handwritten while he was on various journeys overseas to J. L. Ferguson, then in charge of home soap sales. These letters refer frequently to his regret that because he was travelling he was without up-to-date information about the business. But when he received news his reaction was normally to praise:

I have had a good look over the Sales Sheet for December for Lever Brothers and H. & S. [an associated company dealing in bar soap] and . . . congratulate you upon them.

I am daily thinking of the soap trade at home and abroad . . . but I never went away more contented and happy in those in command at Home.

I will soon be home but I want to write you how pleased and gratified I have been with your handling of your department during my absence.

I received the telegram of offer Thomas, Exeter, made. I replied I would prefer to leave alone but leaving the matter for my colleagues to decide . . . whatever has been done will be right for me.

But even a nephew could not escape the lash.

I am looking to you as filling one of the most important positions connected with our British Associated Companies. You can fill it but you will have to be a little keener than I have seen yet . . . if the Associated Companies are to progress it will be by *Super* work, not 'jog trot' . . .

Responding however alertly to the results of management's efforts, while undoubtedly tending to keep the managements themselves alert, does not amount to control of the business. One of the most valuable of the Old Man's business innovations was the use by him of forward estimates rather than past data for control purposes.

When he was running the Wigan branch of his father's grocery business he had started the practice of making a detailed estimate in advance of each quarter of what the results of his trading during that quarter would be. He called these estimates his pro forma accounts. His basic control over the ramifications of the wide-ranging business he subsequently built up was as follows. An annual estimate (the pro forma) was prepared by the management of each associated company. This estimate was in full detail giving sales, margin of profit, advertising expenditure, cash flow and so on. The Old Man examined these and then set what he called the datum for the company concerned. If he agreed with the annual estimate the datum was the figure of total profit as shown by the estimate. If he did not agree with the estimate he just set an arbitrary figure as the datum and the management concerned had to do their best to attain that figure.

This basic system has been elaborated by subsequent experience and 'annual estimate', 'pro forma' and 'datum' have become almost hallowed words in Unilever House, Rotterdam and London. Annual estimates became the occasion for and the substance of reviews of each individual company by its management with the appropriate head office control group. An accepted annual estimate became the framework within which the company was authorized to work during the coming year, i.e. the datum.

To emphasize 'framework' I might reasonably insert here a piece of advice given in 1890 on a Sunlight Soap Calendar for Retailers: 'Make plans ahead, but don't make them in cast iron'.

I do not know whether the practice of having internal auditors was an innovation by the Old Man but certainly it was established in Lever Brothers Limited long before it became usual. The auditors are responsible to the parent Board and, travelling all over the world, they supplement the work of the official external auditors and ensure that the accounting practice of all associated companies conforms to the standards set by the Board and that the accounts wherever they come from will be such as to ensure a rapid and accurate consolidation in the final accounts of the Company.

Perhaps I might sum up the management precepts by which the Company has been guided as a firm view of what should be going on—the accepted annual estimate; a steady flow of accurate data about what is going on; and a steady eye on that data.

Two more stories about the Old Man illustrate his decisiveness. Letters to him within the business were written on paper divided down the middle, the right hand side being for his reply, usually written in green ink, and usually brief. One of these was sent in by a director and came back: 'Thanks and noted. I do not agree. L.' The director felt that this was a wrong decision and went to see the Old Man about it, explaining that perhaps he had not put his point clearly enough. The Old Man looked up and said: 'Mr——, if I decided everything twice I would double my work—take it away.'

The last battle in the Old Man's long war with Brunner, Mond took place in private and neither the circumstances nor the result are recorded in either the biography of the Old Man or *The History of Unilever*. A full account of the affair, except the incident which I am about to describe, is given in Volume I of *Imperial Chemical Industries : A History* by W. J. Reader.

Lever's acquisition of a tiny soap-making company in Australia revealed a breach by Brunner, Mond of a wide-ranging alkali agreement under which they supplied alkali to the Lever business which had been part of the 'final settlement' in 1919, when Lever acquired the Gossage and Crosfield businesses. This small breach led to the revelation of a blatant breach of the agreement much nearer home —in fact in the United Kingdom. If it had come into Court it would have ruined Brunner Mond's reputation for fair dealing. Sir Alfred Mond, who was in no way personally implicated, came to Lever House for a private talk with the Old Man only a month or two before the Old Man died. On the spot the Old Man demanded £1,000,000 damages. Sir Alfred Mond agreed, on the understanding that the whole affair would be kept strictly private.

Personal Accounts

Amongst the personal papers to which I have already referred were the Old Man's private accounts for 1897, 1907 and 1912, each set written in immaculate copperplate but by a different hand. They give an interesting picture of what it meant to be a wealthy man in an era when it was possible and respectable to become one. Comparisons between the years are unclouded by inflation.

He was already a millionaire in 1897 with assets of £1¼ million. His main assets were:

	1897	1907	1912
Investments	969,739	1,855,447	2,131,837
Land, houses, etc.	121,866	169,371	439,814
Furniture, pictures, china	55,873	285,342	408,545
Horses, carriages, motors	919	1,650	1,045
Books	1,384	1,828	3,063

Investments

Shares in Lever Brothers, his main investment, were valued at cost.

The only substantial investment outside the Lever business was in the Pacific Phosphate Company Ltd., in which he had become interested through the contacts he made in the Pacific when starting copra plantations in the Solomon Islands. His interest must have been great as his investment in 1912 was nearly £500,000. From the Biography it seems that the venture was a success.

Otherwise his investments were mainly of a 'benevolent' nature, individually small. The 1912 figures were:

Charles Thompson's Poor Children's Mission Hall Ltd	£100
Congregational Publishing Co. Ltd	£550
Hampstead Garden Suburb Trust Ltd	£1,000
Liverpool Repertory Theatre Ltd	£500

A 100 per cent reserve was recorded against all these investments, as against the 1897 items:

Opobo Palm Nut-cracking Co. Ltd	£1,000
Oil Rivers Trading and Exploration Co. Ltd	£1,000

Land, houses, etc.

In 1897 his main property was in and around the Manor at Thornton Hough. He only had one small property in Bolton, 9 and 11 Town Hall Square, valued at £3,868. By 1907 he had acquired the following:

In Hampstead (The Hill, a large house)	£70,000
In Bebington and Birkenhead	£14,124
Near Bolton, eighteen different properties which became his country estate at Rivington Pike.	£23,209

The great increase by 1912 was due to the purchase of two large estates in Cheshire.

His properties were depreciated in the Estate Account and the great sums spent on improvements were continually written off so that his main house, Thornton Manor, was valued at £37,220 in 1897 but at £30,000 in 1912 and The Hill, valued at £70,000 in

1907, was put at £25,300 in 1912, by which time it was much bigger. He had a small zoo at Thornton Manor, which appeared in the 1912 accounts under the heading 'Manor Park Animals, £1'.

Furniture, pictures, china

The considerable and mounting value of these illustrates his great interest in his collection which he dealt with personally, even arranging the furniture to suit his taste and sense of period.

Horses, carriages and motors

It is interesting to record the changeover from carriages to motors in which he took an early and lively interest.

| | Horses & Carriages | | Motor | |
	Capital Value	Current Expenses	Capital Value	Current Expenses
1897	919	604	—	—
1907	150	275	1,500	2,263
1912	45	290	1,000	1,581

Cash

Though recorded in patient detail, including the amounts in Mrs Lever's purse and Master Lever's pocket on 31st December, this was never a big item. The Old Man believed that money was for use not for storing up.

Income and expenditure

His income, mainly from the dividends of Lever Brothers Limited, rose from £92,000 in 1897 to £242,000 in 1912. His current expenditure was about 20 per cent of income recorded in considerable detail under these main headings:

| | £ | | |
	1897	1907	1912
General (household etc.)	6,030	12,296	21,541
Personal	1,230	972	2,555
Political	3,691	773	2,986
Benevolent	12,686	12,589	15,860
Presents	4,059	730	2,837
Legal	112	638	105
Reserves—losses, etc.	5,261	97	316
	33,069	28,095	46,200

There are interesting items in the general category:

	1897	1907	1912
Wines, spirits and cigars	158	51	196
Newspapers	14	41	48
Medical	5	94	39
Electric Lights	—	345	845

Wines, spirits and cigars at less than a quarter of the electric light bill would be considered modest now. The cost of electric light in the Manor alone in 1912 was £599.

Personal expenses consisted of

	1897	1907	1912
Travelling and amusements	1,151	451	552
Clothes and dress	75	101	128
Shooting and gamekeeper	4	2	70
Secretaries and clerks	—	310	688
Clubs and masonic lodges	—	108	986
Heraldry	—	—	131

Political expenses were low in 1907. They had been much higher the previous year when he had been successful Liberal candidate for Parliament.

His benevolence was mainly in connection with churches and schools rather than charities and he built three churches in addition to Christ Church, Port Sunlight, which was paid for by himself and not by Lever Brothers Limited (including a payment to Lever Brothers for the land). In later years he made some munificent public benefactions.

So the Old Man lived in affluence but not, by the standards of his equals or his era, extravagantly. He was generous to the causes in which he believed—Liberalism, Congregationalism, and education. His only 'conspicuous consumption' was in his passion for extending and improving his houses and estates and adding to his collection of furniture, pictures and china, most of which he left to the Nation in the Lady Lever Art Gallery.

Conclusion

I end with the text of two letters, one bubbling over with excitement and joy, the other, thirty years later, expressing heartfelt sympathy.

In 1888, announcing to Lever Brothers' agents the birth of his only child, William Hulme, who became the second Viscount Leverhulme, he wrote:

Sunlight Soap Works,
Warrington.
April 5th 1888.

Dear Sir,

I write to advise you that I have been introduced to a gentleman who I hope will take over my interest and position in this business. It will be a trouble to me to retire from a business I have had to work very hard to build up still I feel that this gentleman has qualifications that pre-eminently fit him for the post. In the short acquaintance I have had with him—only 11 days— I have not failed to notice his natural business instincts not the least of which are that he hears what people have to say but has the prudence to keep his own mouth shut and that he never meddles or interferes with what does not concern him. I have never known him to be 'talked over' from any object he had in view, he forms his own opinions and threats or persuasions are alike useless to turn him from his purpose. He shows great perseverence in attaining his object and is never quiet until he has realized his wishes. Of an unassuming nature he attaches more importance to the solid comforts of this life than to any more outward show. He insists on the strictest attention to their duties in all those who are in a position of trust with him but their duties performed he gives them the fullest liberty to follow their own affairs. He makes no promises and tells no lies and I may add enjoys the most robust health. With these qualifications I trust that W. H. Lever Jnr.—my successor—will have the same hearty and generous support you have always given to

Yours truly,

W. H. Lever

In 1918 he sent a handwritten letter to Rev. Luke Beaumont, one time Minister of Highfield Congregational Church, Rock Ferry, whose elder son had been killed in action.

My dear Beaumont,

I am greatly shocked to hear of the death of your brave boy and I hasten to tender to Mrs. Beaumont and yourself my most heartfelt sympathy. I have been to Lewis for 10 days and only heard the sad news and received your letter yesterday.

Words are very poor expressions at these times and I feel how feeble they are to give you my condolences.

He died a noble death and a few years more or less of life are not what will count in eternity but how a man lived and died and your great comfort will be in the thought that he had nobly lived and well and that he left an example to us all.

The grief and sorrow are now yours and your friends'— the joy of hearing the words 'Well done, good and faithful servant' is now his.

You have done all that parents can do in this war—given your dearest one—and memory will with loving hands heal the wound by thoughts of love.

Yours sincerely,
Leverhulme.

[I am indebted to the Beaumont's second son Cyril, a friend and Unilever colleague, for permission to reproduce this.]

The Old Man was small of stature but a conspicuous figure none the less. Original stoutness of build turned in later years to corpulence which was by no means disguised by his normal dark grey worsted morning coat. His feet and hands were notably small and neat and, to the end, he was light of foot with a quick short step. I cannot testify as to his lightness of foot when dancing for which he usually dressed in Court attire. His head tended to look big by reason of his curly white hair, when not wearing a hat, and by reason of the type of hat when wearing one—a grey hard felt, half-way between a bowler and a top hat.

On becoming a baronet the Old Man adopted as his motto *Mutare vel timere sperno* (To change or to fear I spurn).

A Cartoon of the 'Old Man' from the author's collection.

He certainly rejected fear with disdain but he spent his life changing things for the better. But *Mise en valeur* might better describe his basic motive. He strove to improve: he built Port Sunlight on a marsh; he established plantations in Africa where previously there had been jungle; he made a Japanese garden out of a barren and windswept hill outside Bolton; he had visions of transforming the island of Lewis into a viable community; he enhanced the value of his soap nigres by making them into Lifebuoy Soap; and by his vision, leadership and generosity he enhanced the value of many people's lives.

On the ship coming home from West Africa, a few months before he died in 1925 aged 74, the captain asked him to choose and read the Lesson at the Sunday service.

He read from *Ecclesiastes* (Ch. 2. vv 4):

I made me great works; I builded me houses; I planted me vineyards:

I made me gardens and orchards, and I planted trees in them of all *kinds of* fruits:

I made me pools of water, to water therewith the wood that bringeth forth trees:

I got *me* servants . . .

I gathered me also silver and gold . . .

So I was great . . .

. . . for my heart rejoiced in all my labour . . .

Then I looked on all the works that my hands had wrought, and on the labour that I had laboured to do: and, behold, all *was* vanity and vexation of spirit, and *there was* no profit under the sun.

That was not the choice of an arrogant tycoon. It was the choice of a tired and probably lonely old man. The failure of his visionary schemes for Lewis cost him dearly at a time of general slump, and he found himself under restraint for the first time in his life. He had come to the end of his era. But it was a great era and he was a great man of his era.

He was also a good man. He could, and he did, lift up people's hearts.

4

The Formation of the Overseas Committee: Introduction to two Important Developments: 1925–1935

The years from 1925 to 1935 were important and exciting for the Company and for me. First the Company had to be pulled out of financial difficulties and put on to a sound basis of monetary and policy control. Then it had to play its part in the welding together of the Margarine Union with Lever Brothers which created Unilever.

Only one department survives from those early days under the same name and doing the same job, but there are two important sections of the policy control arrangements which have also survived in name and function.

The department to survive goes back to very early days, registrars department, known by initials (REG.) rather than by its full title, as was the fashion at the time. A boyhood friend of mine who spent his whole working life in REG. told me with great pride just before he retired that the department had never made a mistake. Whether Registrars, now of course computerized, maintains this unique record I do not know.

The two policy control sections which survive are the Special Committee and the Overseas Committee.

The Special Committee was formed in 1921 by the Old Man as an 'inner cabinet' of the Board and consisted originally of himself, his son, and two Directors, H. R. Greenhalgh and John McDowell. D'Arcy Cooper was co-opted on to this Committee even before he became a Director of the Company in 1923. The

Committee was and still remains the top controlling body of the whole Company.

The Overseas Committee was formed in 1926 to take over control of the overseas operations (excluding United Africa Co. hitherto dealt with by three separate departments. With the exception of an interlude from 1938 to 1945, I worked within the orbit of this Committee from its inception until I retired in 1968.

The first Chairman of the Overseas Committee was H. R. Greenhalgh and its first Secretary Charles Cole. The style and pattern of operations which they established guided the Committee through all the changes and development of the next forty years.

Greenhalgh believed in letting people alone. Shortly after the committee was set up he called me in and told me that I was a very young man to have such considerable responsibility as I had in connection with exports to India, but that I must not be frightened of it. If things went well I was not to bother him, but if I was in any difficulty the Committee would see me immediately. My activities would be watched from the weekly sales sheet, the quarterly profits and copies of any important letters I wrote.

Many people say this sort of thing but not everyone abides by it. Greenhalgh did. Weeks went by without my seeing any member of the Committee except by chance in the corridor. Ten years later I was in a different job but I was still getting copies of letters from India and from one of them it seemed to me that a serious mistake was being made. My boss was away and I went to see Greenhalgh. 'You don't keep a dog and bark yourself,' he said. 'If you alter their instructions you take their responsibility away from them and they will rely on you to check everything they do. Leave them alone and they will see in due course that they have made a mistake and that will teach them not to make another.'

On the day before a new soap factory was due to start in Bombay I suggested that the Overseas Committee might send a cable of good wishes to the management. Greenhalgh replied, 'I don't like backscratching.'

Back-scratching he disapproved of. Nor would he tolerate either criticism or instructions (except on routine matters) being sent to overseas managements. He believed that letters of criticism had a much more devastating effect on a recipient far away than on those at home than the writer either intended or could imagine, and such letters, if required, were to be written only by members of the Committee. In policy matters managements were to be guided, not instructed. He was, to all appearance at least, imperturbable. He made up his mind firmly, had a comprehensive knowledge of the business and applied to its problems a great deal of common sense.

In contrast Charles Cole was easily perturbable, but his flashes of irritation and the words that accompanied them were really only mannerisms. They never had anything of malice in them, nor did they disguise his essential courtesy, kindness, understanding and great good humour. They were frequently merely the prologue to a good laugh—a laugh which everyone who worked with him will remember. Pipe removed temporarily but not very far from his mouth, moustache and hair impeccably groomed, his whole face enjoying the joke.

Cole's room was the first port of call for all visitors from overseas and during the Second World War there were many of them. Whoever they were and whatever their problem they were set on their proper course and helped along it.

He was a firm and able administrator being particularly careful to see that correspondence was fully and promptly dealt with, whether by members of the Committee or anyone else concerned, and that all involved with any matters under consideration were fully and promptly informed. No letter could be put on the file without an initialled and dated note of what had been done about it: even a line through it to denote that nothing further need be done had to be initialled and dated. If by chance a letter did get through not so 'marked off' Cole would use his favourite expletive People! to express his exasperated amazement at the incompetence of mankind in general and members of his immediate audience in particular.

Each in his own way Harold Greenhalgh and Charles Cole both understood that their essential job was not dealing with problems but with *people* and I was exceptionally fortunate in being under such enlightened management in my formative years, and being entrusted by them with some responsibility for two developments which were, at the time, regarded as important. I hope that an account of these developments and my part in them will still be of interest. The first is of how and why it became desirable to invest in India and establish Lever Brothers (India) Ltd., now Hindustan Lever Ltd. The second is of how and why United Exporters Ltd., now Unilever Export Ltd., came to be formed.

To explain the significance of these developments I must first give some historical background. (My quotations in this are from *Enterprise in Soap and Chemicals* by A. C. Musson, being the history of Joseph Crosfield & Sons Ltd.)

In 1885, when the Old Man started in the soap trade, exports from the United Kingdom were already at the rate of 20,000 tons per annum, and increased over the next thirty years to 100,000 tons. The United Kingdom in fact supplied the bulk of the soap requirements of the whole of Africa (except French territories), India, Burma and Ceylon, the Far East and most of Central and South America. This was an attractive trade for a man determined to establish a world-wide business. Moreover, like the piece-goods trade (goods or fabric woven in lengths suitable for retail sale by usual linear measure), it was centred on Liverpool with its then unrivalled international shipping facilities both for the import of the necessary raw materials and export of the finished product. Cheap sea freights were an important factor. 'The comparative cheapness of sea transport made it no more costly to send soap to Bombay or Rio de Janiero in 1885–86 than to the other end of England.' (The cost was £1.10 and £1.65 per ton respectively.)

Another factor which gave export special prominence in the affairs of Lever Brothers was that the chief export competitors were their closest and immediate rivals on Merseyside, William Gossage and Sons Ltd. of Widnes and Joseph Crosfield & Sons Ltd. of Warrington. Gossage was the bigger soapmaker, being, it was claimed, 'the largest manufacturers of soap in the kingdom, if not in the world', with output at the time of 25,000 tons per year of which about half was exported. Crosfields, though not making as much soap, was longer established, had an important and growing chemicals business, a leading position in the Soapmakers Association, and family links with other industries in Lancashire. John Crosfield, son of the original Joseph, was the first Chairman of Brunner, Mond & Co., alkali makers of Winnington, with whom

Crosfields continued to have close links. From the very beginning Crosfields had a marked antipathy towards the Lever business and a personal animosity towards the Old Man himself. 'Lever's first factory,' says Musson, 'was established in Warrington in 1885, next door to Crosfield's, who, being an old-established and much bigger firm, tended to regard him as an upstart, using dubious and ungentlemanly marketing methods.'

Crosfield's links with Brunner, Mond Ltd. did not help matters because the Old Man carried on a protracted war with that company on the matter of alkali supplies in which he never thought he got the treatment he deserved. From 1911, when Brunner, Mond bought both Crosfield and Gossage as a move in the war with Lever, till the final settlement, competition from 'B.M.' was countered with particularly watchful vigour.

So export was of special importance to the Old Man—great opportunities for sales expansion and a second battle ground on which to fight his most bitter and eventually his biggest competitors.

But it was not an easy battle ground on which to fight.

Gossages had been the pioneers of this export trade and were mainly responsible for its development. In 1855 William Gossage started soapmaking in Widnes by patenting a process for production of good cheap soap from palm oil and silicate of soda. His company became experts at making all sorts of 'filled soap'.

Pure soap contained 63 per cent fatty acid, or it did when I was a boy, and while it is not technically correct to say that detergency diminishes in inverse relation to the amount of the 'filling', substitution of fatty acid by alkali, it is near enough for my purpose. Certainly the cost of the soap reduces with the reduction of fatty acid content, or it did so in the early days of the trade when alkali, essentially derived from Cheshire salt and produced by Brunner, Mond, was very cheap. Gossages skill was in making filled soap, which necessarily contained a good deal of water, of such texture as enabled it to stand up to the severe conditions of shipment through the Tropics and subsequent exposure for sale on the sunbaked earth of Africa, India and China. If too much evaporation took place the soap was either reduced to a useless crumble of powder or to rock-like hardness from which lather could only be produced with considerable detriment to the cloth on which it was rubbed. Gossages bar soap looked nice, it felt nice, it did not smell rancid. It was cheap and as a detergent was away ahead of the traditional ingredients hitherto in use in the uttermost parts of the earth, namely wood ash and elbow grease. Gossages export enterprise consisted in offering a selection of these soaps on 'on consignment' terms to established U.K. merchants trading to the country concerned. ('On consignment' terms require that the goods are shipped to a foreign agent, or the foreign office of a home-based agent, for sale by the agent as best he can, the sales proceeds being subsequently sent back to the manufacturers.) I am indebted to my late friend and colleague, Mr R. Hinchliffe, for the following account of the Housewife's Friend trade in Mauritius illustrating Gossages early methods and the strength of the business established thereby.

One day in 1886 Mr. H. S. Timmis, Chairman of Gossage's, on one of his regular business visits to London, was walking along a City street when he noticed a nameboard at the entrance to a small block of offices. It read 'Andrew Stein & Co., Agents for Scott & Co., Mauritius'. Apparently Mr. Timmis was not sure where Mauritius was, but he was sure that it was not in the list of countries to which Gossage's exported their soaps. He went into Messrs. Stein's office and asked whether they ever shipped any soap to this place Mauritius. They did not and knew nothing about the soap trade there, but they promised to get in touch with Scott & Co. on the subject. In due course Scott & Co. replied that the soap used in Mauritius was a rather poor quality Blue Mottled imported from the Seychelles and Zanzibar; they, themselves, did not handle soap. Gossage's asked Scott & Co. whether they would be willing to try out on their market a trial shipment, to be sent on consignment, of two or three types of soap, and to this Scott & Co. agreed. One or two small trial shipments were then made and sold by Scott & Co., and they reported that the Brown Soap, 'The Housewife's Friend', seemed likely to prove the most acceptable for their market. Scott & Co. were appointed agents for Gossages in 1887 and regular small shipments of H.W.F. commenced. The shipments, sent on consignment, were entered in Scott & Co.'s books as 'adventures' (as they were in Gossages Accounts till 1928).

When I first became connected with Mauritius as the Gossage representative in 1923 sales of H.W.F. were averaging 43,000 cases a year. It was faced with severe competition from this time up to the outbreak of war in 1939. This competition was always at prices lower, mostly much lower than the price of H.W.F. From 1946 the imported competition gradually lessened, until by the end of 1951 it had stopped altogether and H.W.F. had 100% of the imported trade. The only competition it then faced was from the locally made Bar soap which sold to the extent of about 1,200 cases a year.

In 1954 which was my last full year of responsibility for Mauritius, H.W.F. sales were 104,000 cases, equivalent to 2,650 tons.

Housewife's Friend is hardly the name that modern marketing skills would choose for a soap to be sold in a French- and creole-speaking country. But marketing had not been invented when Housewife's Friend first went to Mauritius. What people knew about then was trading.

And so we got Housewife's Friend in Mauritius, Empress Pale in India, Beehive Honey in Malaya, Fragrant Honey in China. In addition to the name the bars were stamped with a device such as a ship's wheel on Housewife's Friend and a star on Empress Pale. It soon became accepted trading lore that consumer goods should be marked with a symbol recognizable by the consumer. This more or less coincided with the establishment of proprietary ownership of trademarks under trademark law and Gossages and their competitors began selling under brands such as Star and Wheel, Hammer, Footprint, Umbrella, Tiger, Camel and Beehive.

In one instance, at least, Gossages sold soap under a brand name belonging to their agents, Singletons of Liverpool. This was, no doubt, bad marketing but it did enable them to build up a long standing trade in Jacare (alligator) Brown Soap in Iquitos, 2,000 miles up the Amazon to which the Booth Line had a regular direct service from Liverpool.

By these methods and with virtually no direct personal representation on the spot Gossages held 50 per cent of soap exports from the U.K. for over fifty years. They did this by making good products, having good trading agents—and by getting in first.

Crosfields were always keen on the export business too and were Gossage's main competitors in bar soaps and, later, Lever's main competitors on proprietaries. Their technology was undisputed. They made the best blue mottled soap and claimed that their Perfection Soap (a direct competitor of Sunlight Soap) was as good as Sunlight and could be made at a lower cost.

Their method of sale was basically the same as Gossage's 'on consignment' terms, but their philosophy of direct selling at least took them as far as to appoint local agents rather than merchants working from a U.K. base. In 1901 they had 'nearly 60 agents and correspondents for the export all over the world' and by 1911 had five overseas representatives. In 1909 they spent £1,000 on 'developing the export trade to China' and their export manager paid a visit there in 1910. £1,000 was a lot in those days for export advertising but neither the expenditure nor the visit seems to have done much good as in 1912 total exports to China were 10,000 tons of which Gossage did 7,000 and Lever Brothers 3,000.

Crosfields fought hard for 'their share of the trade' but they did not dislodge Gossages from their strongholds nor seriously impede Lever Brothers in the development of their advertised brands. They did establish a good trade for Guardian Carbolic in Egypt (a country listed in the official British export figures for 1919 as a British Possession), and were accorded the honour of being appointed Manufacturers of Soap to the Khedive of Egypt, no doubt balancing the similar appointment of Lever Brothers Limited to the Bey of Tunis.

Lever Brothers were ill-equipped to do battle against the established bar soaps. 'The name Lever on soap is a guarantee of purity and excellence', but by no stretch of even an advertiser's imagination could a 45 per cent fatty acid blue mottled soap be called pure. Moreover, although before leaving the little works in Warrington Lever Brothers had filched from Crosfields the Wainwright family of skilled soapmakers, Port Sunlight's heart was never in the making of filled bar soap. It was not until 1907, when Lever Brothers bought Hodgson & Simpson Ltd. and Hazlehurst & Sons

Ltd., two small makers of bar soaps with a stake in export, that they were able to make a direct attack. Soaps, though made at Port Sunlight, could be sold under these associated company names without any twinge of conscience about the Lever guarantee of purity and excellence, and vigorous direct selling enabled them to gain their share of the market.

But from the very commencement of his soap business the Old Man was determined to build a worldwide trade in the type of soap, and by the selling methods, he knew. He believed in personal representation, so when he wanted to start up in Siam he sent a salesman there. In due course the man returned and made a report to the effect that Siam was a 'blue mottled market' and that yellow soap was not liked; all that had to be done was to give him blue mottled to sell and he would soon produce orders. The Old Man sent for him and said, 'Well, Mr So-and-So, I've read your report and I see that you can't sell Sunlight Soap in Siam.'

'That's right, sir, it is a blue mottled market.'

'All right then, if you can't sell Sunlight Soap in Siam, I'll have to find someone who can.'

It was a long and uphill fight continued in due course through local manufacture, but at last in the mid 1950s Thai Industries Ltd., the Unilever Company, ceased the manufacture of blue mottled soap as Sunlight had captured virtually the whole of the household soap market selling at the rate of over 9,000 tons per annum.

Brand loyalty was considerable—witness the strength of Gossages for over fifty years—but price was a sharp weapon in markets where consumers had limited wants but even more limited means. But prices were strictly controlled from home and the battleground was the Lime Street Station Hotel or other suitable place for meetings where high management from the companies concerned battled to keep prices up while leaving themselves loopholes through which some price advantage might temporarily be gained.

Typical of these meetings is the following account:

On the 7th April 1886, it was reported that Crosfields were selling mottled soaps for export at 1/- per cwt. below the agreed prices 'without giving notice to any of the other parties to the agreement'. Their conduct was strongly condemned, and they agreed to raise the prices, but not on orders already received: at the next meeting on 5th May, therefore, Gossages stated that they would have to reduce their prices accordingly.

There were many such meetings over the next forty years and one of particular significance was in 1913 under the personal auspices of the Old Man and Sir John Brunner, Brunner, Mond then owning both Gossage and Crosfield. The discussion resulted in agreement in principle and much bonhomie all round, but the subsequent detailed agreement never got beyond the draft stage.

All this fighting for 'a share of the trade' did not alter the basic position. Gossages held half the total trade and Lever Brothers gradually but successfully superimposed the concept of brand marketing, mainly with Sunlight and Lifebuoy soaps, on the basic bar soap business.

The position in 1913 was:

Gossage	40,000 tons
Crosfield	13,000 ,,
Lever Brothers	27,000 ,,
Other	2,000 ,,
Total	82,000 tons

The main markets were:

India (inc. Burma)	15,500 tons
Malaya	4,000 ,,
Dutch East Indies	3,000 ,,
China	10,000 ,,
British West Africa	8,000 ,,
South Africa	2,000 ,,
British West Indies	6,000 ,,
Canary Islands	2,000 ,,

and at least on a 'sales per head' basis:

Mauritius	1,200 ,,

India and China stood out as the biggest markets and with their enormous populations the markets of greatest potential.

China was the first to be considered for individual development. It was again visited by Crosfield's Export Manager (C. H. Hamilton, subsequently Chairman of Gossages) in 1912. He recommended the establishment of a factory there, and with support from W. Hulme Lever, the Old Man's son who paid a visit in 1913, a project was put forward for a joint Crosfield/Lever enterprise. The project was abortive and Crosfields subsequently founded with Brunner, Mond and Price's Candle Company, the China Soap and Candle Company in Shanghai, thus stealing a march on the Lever business, because it was cheaper to make soap in Shanghai than to ship it from England. (As a temporary expedient, supplies for China were sent from the Lever factory in Kobe, Japan, thus giving that ill-fated venture a brief period of profitability.)

This incident was one of the sparks which led to the final showdown with Brunner, Mond, the result of which was the purchase in 1919 by Lever Brothers of both Crosfield and Gossage, and incidentally the China Soap and Candle Company.

A new company, the China Soap Company, was formed in 1923, which took over the Soap and Candle Company and acquired, in exchange for shares, the goodwill and trademarks in China of Crosfield, Gossage and Lever. Lever Brothers had control of the whole China business leaving a financial interest, through a shareholding, to Crosfield and Gossage who had had the major part of the trade. A new factory was built in Shanghai to make Lever, Gossage and Crosfield soaps for the China trade.

Having thus brought the important China business more closely under his control, the Old Man's thoughts turned to India. Although there was then no question of manufacture in India, a company, Lever Brothers (India) Ltd., was registered in England to hold the trademark rights in India of the three main exporting companies and to divide the profits as in China. Responsibility for this company was put into the hands of the overseas side but it must be admitted that 'Overseas', by that time in London, had little if any control over the operations of the separate export departments in Liverpool, Widnes and Warrington.

Close on the heels of this move negotiations took place with an entrepreneurial group called Boulton Brothers which was building up interests in India, including the soap and edible oil industries. The plan was to form a joint enterprise with this group and as a focal point for the local management of this enterprise a second Lever Brothers (India) Ltd. was registered in Calcutta. The plans came to nothing when Boulton Brothers went bust leaving large debts but few serviceable assets.

Following the Old Man's only visit to India, in the spring of 1924, he was particularly concerned to bring Lever exports to India, potentially the most profitable part of the trade, more closely under his wing through the overseas department in London.

This was where I came in.

5

Transition in India

While I was with the Old Man on the Continent in August 1924 the following conversation (as far as I can recollect it) took place:

'You were in the export department weren't you, Knox?'

'Yes, sir.'

'Do you know anything about exports to India?'

'Yes, sir, I was in the India section.'

'Well, I want this business run from London under the overseas department but the export management in Liverpool tell me that this cannot be done for reasons connected with shipping documents and catching the mail, etc. What do you think?'

'I think it could be done, sir.'

'Are you sure?'

'Yes, sir.'

'Well, after lunch, while I'm doing my private mail, you sit down and write a note for me setting out in detail how it can be done.'

So I sat down and on Adlon Hotel-Berlin notepaper I wrote out a detailed description of how it would be possible to get signed bills of lading to London for goods shipped from Liverpool, in time to prepare the documents for the banks who could in turn despatch them to India to arrive before the ship carrying the goods.

Within a few days of our return from the Continent I was informed that it had been decided that the handling of the export of Lever lines to India was to be transferred from export department, Liverpool, to D.O.C./B department, London, and that I was to arrange the transfer and be in charge of the operation thereafter. I had an exciting few weeks and the new arrangements came into force on 29th September—about six weeks after my note written in the Adlon Hotel.

I found myself responsible for a trade of some 5,500 tons a year, mainly Sunlight Soap, with a profit of £60–70,000 which was at a rate of about 20 per cent on turnover.

Three men were transferred from Export to D.O.C./B: W. G. J. Shaw (representative in India), A. D. Gourley, and A. J. Bird (both home staff).

So with me, plus a junior clerk/typist and a shorthand typist, the total staff was six. The administration and selling expenses, including agents' commissions, were less than 5 per cent. Shaw, Gourley and Bird were all older than me: they had fought in the War. I had been a schoolboy. During the first few weeks there were some difficulties but we soon settled down to work happily together and became close colleagues and lifetime friends, though in the convention of the times it was twenty years before we used each other's Christian names. I use the word 'happily' with reason. Lever Brothers Limited as a whole was under pressure. No ordinary dividend was paid in 1925 and 1926. Many associated companies were making losses. Cash was short. In an atmosphere of 'rationalization' one was glad to have a job, and to have a good job and to be left alone to do it was happiness indeed. The senior ranks of the overseas management were content to leave alone a small section which was soon producing cash sales of £500,000 a year on no working capital, with profits at the rate of 25 per cent on sales.

In those days it was not the custom to tell 'middle management' anything more about the business than they needed to know for their immediate purposes, and thus my colleagues from Export had never had access to sales figures, knew nothing of profit margins and had never heard of quarterly pro formas and annual estimates, which had been the very essence of my job for two years in overseas department (D.O.C./A). It was a revelation, and I believe an inspiration, for them to have free access to this hitherto secret information and to co-operate in its study for the future guidance of the business.

We were together for three years, during which sales rose to 8,748 tons in 1927, and profits to £142,000. Ninety-five per cent of the trade was in Sunlight Soap: the rest in Lifebuoy, Lux Flakes, Velvet Skin Toilet Soap, and Monkey Brand. As our agent in Ceylon once said: 'Sunlight Soap is like a ship upon the water—it is easily pushed along.' Competitors' soap, by contrast, was like a ship upon the mud. In my first report I wrote, somewhat arrogantly:

> Sunlight Soap holds the premier position in the laundry soap market of India: while there are countless other tablet soaps on the market none of them is of any importance whatever from the point of view of competition with Sunlight Soap. Their prices are such as to put them into competition with the Bar Soap class.

Many attempts were made by local competitors and competitors from the U.K., U.S.A., Australia and France, but none succeeded. In 1927 I reported with evident relish:

> Fels Naptha made an attempt to sell their soap in Bombay; despite advertising and dealer offers they have been unsuccessful . . . their stocks have been taken over by a dealer who specialises in old and dilapidated soap.

Our trade in 1927 was almost entirely with the port wholesalers. There were fifteen to twenty of them in Bombay, our biggest market, about the same number in other main ports, and for some very successful years a 'ring' of three in Colombo. Our customers paid very strictly cash: 'Cash against Documents' with 6 per cent per annum interest charged from the date of drawing in London to the date of meeting the draft on the ship's arrival to cover the cost of our discounting the draft when the shipment was made.

We relied on the strength of the port dealers' credit to his upcountry customers to give us our distribution and on my first visit to India in 1927 I reported:

> That we are right in relying upon the wholesalers for our distribution is not only proved by our freedom from financial trouble but also by the wonderful distribution that has been effected. Our lines are everywhere where they can be expected to sell.

Distribution was cheap and effective and distribution was certainly nine points of the marketing law at that time, but the following sentence from my report in 1925 seems a bit of an understatement:

> In 1925 we spent £1,650 on advertising in India, but we do not consider that expenditure at this level is enough even to maintain our strong position in the large territory we have to cover.

The 1925 advertising had consisted of some enamel iron plates for dealers' premises and a distribution of calendars.

A. D. Gourley was appointed Shaw's assistant in India at this time and this enabled us by extended visits to up-country to gain first-hand knowledge of our business outside the main centres. We soon found that the strength of dealers' credit as a factor in distribution diminished pretty sharply the further you got into the 'mofussil' and that there were areas where Sunlight Soap had hardly penetrated.

Extract from report:

> The port wholesalers are mostly willing and able to extend credit to big dealers within a certain radius of their port, but that this radius is definitely limited is shown by both Mr. Shaw's and Mr. Gourley's reports, for in the former it is clearly demonstrated that the Rangoon merchants refuse to give credit beyond Mandalay and Mr. Gourley shows how the Calcutta wholesalers have practically no connections at all with Eastern Bengal.

This led us to devising various methods of 'up-country propaganda' so that we were able to put forward an advertising programme for the selling season of October 1928/September 1929 costing £22,000 and covering a number of strenuous pioneering schemes. To carry these out J. E. Lloyd joined Shaw and Gourley in India.

The basic concept of this up-country selling and propaganda work has remained the same ever since, though in practice it has been elaborated as it has spread through the years to all underdeveloped countries.

The first tour would comprise two visits at weekly intervals to the main villages. The first of these visits would be made on market day and would be used to distribute propaganda material and samples and get into touch with the main dealers. The second, a week later, also on market day, would be made with the object of selling to the village merchants, then, from their stocks, selling to the itinerant stall holders and then, from their stocks, selling to the consumers.

To begin with this was done using such transport as could be hired, usually bullock carts, but for 1928–9 we proposed to purchase two lorries (for Ceylon and South India) and were going to join a 'bazaar special'—a new feature of railway service in India, pioneered by the Eastern Bengal Railway—and also a 'bazaar boat' on the Irrawaddy. We began using the vernacular press for Sunlight advertising, and £1,000 bought us space in some forty newspapers in eleven languages. For £300 we produced *Chowpat the Dhobi*, a 1,000-ft film which must have been one of the first advertising films made in India.

Crosfield's and Gossage's business during this period did not do as well as Lever's. The table below shows that during the years 1925–27, when Lever's sales were rising, Crosfield's sales fell from 602 tons to 595 and Gossage's from 10,690 to 9,963. Crosfield's were losing money and the long established Gossage bar soap trade was beginning to feel the pressure of local and imported competition on sales and profit margins. Gossage's profits, about £90,000 in 1924, fell to £60,000 in 1927–8.

| | Sales in tons | | | |
	Lever	Crosfield	Gossage	Total
1924	5,459	637	10,688	16,784
1925	6,677	602	10,690	17,269
1926	8,141	687	10,433	19,261
1927	8,748	595	9,963	19,306
1928	9,865	422	9,294	19,581

(These figures covered India, Burma and Ceylon.)

In India and the other export markets where Gossage, Crosfield and Lever competed so fiercely it was well known that the three companies were closely allied at home. It seemed obvious, by 1928, that a united effort against the growing outside competition would further the interests of 'the Family' more effectively than a continued waste of time and ingenuity in a hopeless attempt to limit the effects of mutual mistrust and recrimination by ever more detailed regulation of the way the three companies were allowed to run their separate businesses. The upshot, an account of which I give in the next chapter, was the formation of a joint exporting company, United Exporters Limited.

The Lever, Gossage and Crosfield trade to India thus came to be managed together by United Exporters and as head of the India section of that company I wrote the report on 1929. From the vantage point of the 1970s (if it is a vantage point) it is somewhat sad to read:

A good deal is heard about the depressed conditions of the Indian wage earners. Any really informative figures on this matter must of necessity be relative and there are many such now available indicating that the general standard of living amongst the Indian people has risen enormously during the last decade or so, and for visual proof of this one has only to consider the increasing consumption of simple luxuries such as travel by bus and by train; cigarettes, etc. There is also the evidence provided by the increase in deposits with the various thrift organisations which are becoming an important factor in Indian economic life. Evidence of this general material progress is also furnished by the increase, in comparatively recent years, in both the imports to and the exports from India. The possibilities of further expansion are being widened year by year by the increase in the acreage under irrigation and also by improvements in agricultural methods and stock.

As to the business, I used the standard phraseology to report absence of any increase in sales. 'In general, we may say that 1929 has been a year of consolidation rather than progress.'

Even to maintain the Gossage business, prices had had to be reduced to the extent of halving the rate of profit but a notable and valuable addition was made to the Lever business by the successful

introduction of Lux Toilet Soap. In addition to the Lever, Gossage
and Crosfield trades, the India section had taken over the trades of
other Lever associated companies which had remained since 1924
with the Lever export department in Liverpool: this was mainly in
toilet soap, toilet preparations and foods. I noted that we had
altogether some eighty different packs of toilet soap on sale in
India and that several of these could with benefit be taken off our
list . . . the Toilet Section (D. E. Budgett-Meakin) is examining the
position.

In conclusion I wrote:

We have confidence in the potentialities of our business in
India but this confidence must be tempered meantime by an
appreciation of the immediate difficulties due to temporarily
adverse economic conditions, and to a certain extent to the
uncertainty of the political situation.

A little cloud . . . like a man's hand. But the cloud was not discernible in the excitements of the amalgamation with the Margarine Union. Exports from Holland of hardened fat known as
'vegetable product' were as big as exports of soap from the U.K.
This had the effect of doubling the size of the Indian business.

In the early months of 1930 far-reaching plans for the joint
development of the two trades were actively discussed: they
envisaged complete local control from a head office in Calcutta and
the development of a network of 7 branch offices, 111 salesmen and
1,880 distributors. However, as economic and political conditions
deteriorated, it became obvious that such a major and costly reorganization was out of the question.

India was hit particular badly by the world depression of the
early thirties and this coincided with the disturbed political conditions pinpointed for us by Gandhi's boycott movement which was
most effective in our most important selling area, Bombay.

Sales in India, particularly of Sunlight Soap (the main profit
earner), began to slip in 1930 and by the end of the year the position
was serious. I accompanied J. H. Hansard (one of the joint managing directors of United Exporters Ltd) to examine the position on
the spot and it was clear to us that the first necessity was a reduc-

tion in price—a very unpopular proposal! The current C.I.F. price for the main Indian pack of Sunlight Soap (48 cartons each of 3 × 12-oz tablets) was 51/3d (nearly £2.56). Our proposal was 43/- (£2.15) to effect a reduction from 14 annas to 12 annas in the retail price of the carton. The Overseas Committee suggested that we consider 47/3d/ (nearly £2.36) and we replied that 'our highest' would be 44/- (£2.20).

We got home in the middle of February and I decided to tell the Overseas Committee how very serious the situation was.

Extracts from Report 10th February, 1931

No one who has tried to study the position in India in recent months . . . can help coming to the conclusion that the India we see today is vastly different from the India of even two years ago, and that the India of today is only a chrysalis for yet another India which will develop tomorrow.

We must face the fact that an Independent India, an 'Indianised' India is at hand and we must so adjust our policy as to bring it into line with the new conditions and the fundamental ideas and aspirations that underlie the awakening feeling of Nationalism in India, and thus ensure that no unconsidered tenacity to old plans and ideas stands in the way of the development of our Indian trade. . . . The Boycott movement has captured the imagination of the people to an extent which must, I think, have been a surprise even to those who have spent their whole life studying the Indian problem. I do not think that we can ever hope to return to that happy state of affairs under which British goods could command a premium over those of equal quality from other sources . . . but I do believe that when the hysteria has evaporated it will be found that any article which has had a real standing in the market will return to favour insofar as that article represents real value to the consumer. That part of the goodwill that rested merely on prestige and not on intrinsic value will disappear.

The halo may go, but the virtue will remain.

The fact that Sunlight was predominant in the market was our greatest asset in the past, and the fact that it has undoubtedly lost that predominance now is the most insidious factor in the present depressing situation, and, unless we can restore that pre-dominance, the most pessimistic augury for the future.

After making various recommendations, the memorandum con-cluded:

> Taken as a whole, these recommendations are drastic, they entail
> the consideration of some large sum of Capital Expenditure in
> the not far distant future on a factory, the decrease in the price
> of our biggest profit earner, and the re-orientation of our selling
> force in India. But unless we are prepared so to take the bull by
> the horns, we will find ourselves tossed out of India by the united
> effort of Nationalist sentiment and a growing indigenous soap
> industry.'

'Our highest' was agreed and when, within a week or two, the import duty on soap into India was increased from 15 per cent *ad val.* to 20 per cent it was agreed that we should maintain our Rupee price thus reducing the C.I.F. price to 42/2d (nearly £2.11).

Even this price reduction was not enough to make headway in the prevailing economic conditions in India. Between 1929 and 1931 the general collapse of trade throughout the world carried down with it both the price of India's main exports—all agricul-tural produce—and the value of her imports. Between October 1929 and April 1931 the export price of Indian tea fell 21 per cent; of groundnuts, 43 per cent; of jute, 53 per cent; and of rice, 58 per cent. During the first six months of 1931 the Lancashire cotton trade to India was slaughtered, with a fall in value of 60 to 68 per cent., and the drop in soap imports, though slightly less spec-tacular at 26 per cent, by value, was very unpleasant indeed for Lever Brothers. Total laundry soap trade in India, in all brands belonging to Levers and their associates, fell from 18,830 tons in 1929 to 11,289 tons in 1932.

Sunlight suffered much worse than ordinary bar soaps, being both more expensive and unmistakably British. Bar soap might come from anywhere, but there was nothing more British than Sunlight, and the tonnage sold in India dropped from 7,300 tons in 1929 to 3,300 tons in 1932.

'Stormed at by shot and shell', Sunlight had to stand up against boycott, depressed market conditions, local competition and a further increase in customs duty from 20 per cent to 25 per cent. That rate, though not intended as such, was an almost complete protection of the local manufacturing industry which had in any case been gradually improving its technology and its selling skill.

Crisis point was reached at the end of 1931. Weekly average sales to Bombay, our biggest market, which had been 1,400 cases in 1929, dropped in September/October 1931 to 346, and I well remember one week when the only order was from the Army & Navy Stores for forty-eight cases.

Our assessment was that we could, in the special circumstances of India, just about cover the 25 per cent duty and remain competitive but not profitable. And we were still selling the best soap. But we were not *selling* it. Boycott and 'lack of demand' had silted up our channel of distribution through the port wholesalers whereas our Indian competitors with small 'soapworks' all over the place were in direct touch with their customers.

I noted in a memorandum dated 24th November, 1931:

It is our belief that selling effort must be the essential feature of any policy we lay down for our future in India, and a change in our methods to enable us to use this effort is the first move we must make towards the reconstruction of our business.

We have lost our business in India through no fault of our own. We would, however, be at fault if we did not realise the real cause for our loss, and we would gravely be at fault did we not have the courage to adjust our policy to new conditions, and the confidence in our ability successfully to do so.

Obviously we would have to carry stocks in India and create our own sales force to sell to up-country merchants. This would be a costly operation and we faced not only falling sales but disappearing profit margins. There were 'doubting Thomases' who suggested a less costly half-step forward but Hansard was not one of them and neither was Shaw nor I. A few weeks after writing the memorandum quoted above, I was in India with Hansard to 'do something about it', as Greenhalgh put it to me. Hansard, together with Shaw and myself, made a detailed review of the situation, and then went off farther East, leaving us to make the large step to ex-depot selling.

It was Hansard's courage which saved our Indian business plus a lot of hard and continuous work by Shaw and me. There were no local Lever office facilities and we had to do our own typing, cable coding, calculating and everything else. We worked or travelled morning, noon and night for five months with only Sunday mornings off for personal mail.

We had agreed that if we were to build foundations for the future development of the business we had better build firm ones. Our aims were firstly, to sell only on strictly cash terms and, secondly, to sell at one price F.O.R. to any railway station in India. (Burma and Ceylon were outside the scheme, but our trade there was reorganized on much the same lines.)

Such European commercial opinion as came our way judged that these two intentions were anything from impossible to daft. Our valuable Bombay Indian agent was neutral. In discussing possibilities with him he said (and I can remember his words), 'Mr Knox, you dictate the policy, I carry it out.' In the event he was as good as his word.

We had good reasons for sticking to our policy. We had little knowledge of and less direct contact with up-country dealers. Money was scarce. We had visions of our salesmen spending the first few journeys establishing credit ratings and the rest of their lives collecting debts. Their essential job was to sell.

The strong weapon of a merchant wholesaler is the granting of credit and this can be sharpened by offering a cut price with credit on a fast selling line. In its heyday Sunlight Soap had been in the forefront of fast selling lines and it was not unusual to find it far from Bombay, selling at little if anything more than the net landed cost in Bombay. No up-country dealer would buy C.I.F. the port and take the risk of being undercut by a port wholesaler, let alone the trouble of arranging port clearance and up-country forwarding. Selling F.O.R. any station on the railway at the same price as we sold ex godown at the port made it virtually impossible for a port wholesaler to undercut anywhere outside his immediate delivery area, and incidentally we saved the up-country dealer the trouble and cost of railway forwarding.

Having decided to go ahead with F.O.R. terms the next thing was to estimate the cost. We had no figures on the extent or territorial distribution of our up-country trade. We knew only the sales to each port.

Operating from Bombay as our base we approached the B.B. & C.I. and the G.I.P. Railways to see if they would quote us a standard rate for all stations within their systems, on the understanding that to do so would save them and us a great deal of clerical work. They told us that there was no allowance for such a system of charging in their rate book.

So we set to work to estimate the cost.

Sunlight soap was 90 per cent of the Lever business and all sales were recorded at that time in terms of a standard case of 144 8-oz packages. We calculated the freight per standard case from Bombay to all the main towns in the area we judged to be served by Bombay, and took the average of these figures, which came to 15 annas a case. We then guessed that half the sales ex-Bombay stocks would be to the Bombay trade and hence 'ex godown'—no freight. So the average freight expenses for the Bombay area would be Rs. 0–7–6. We did the same sort of sums for Karachi, Calcutta, Madras (adjusted for Cochin and Calicut).

We then multiplied the resultant figure for each port by the Sunlight sales to that port based on 1931 figures and divided the total result by the total sales. The result gave the estimated cost of freight per case for the whole of India—ten annas, which turned out to be very near the actual cost. We covered 228 'main towns' in our calculations.

This was certainly the first attempt to sell a grocery item at a standard price throughout India and probably the first attempt anywhere to do so over such a large area. It was possible because the shipping companies had the very sensible arrangement of charging the same freight rate from Liverpool to Karachi, Bombay, Madras, Calcutta (and incidentally Colombo and Rangoon).

We thought of covering octroi (local taxation) also in our price but found that this greatly varied and, as we suspected that rates might be susceptible either to official or unofficial negotiation on the spot, we concluded that they were better left to be paid by the recipient of the goods. In our price calculations we allowed half an anna in the rupee for octroi.

This was the first time also in our export practice, when the price of a product which was important in the U.K. (particularly Sunlight Soap) was worked back from an aimed-at retail price on the market, rather than just being the U.K. price plus freight and charges. We had to try for a retail price which would stand against competition and also to offer an attractive proposition to the dealers.

Our selling price was subject to an annual bonus on a sliding scale up to $2\frac{1}{2}$ per cent on total sales of Rs 20,000. This was to encourage the continued support of the port wholesalers and engage the support of the more important up-country dealers.

The total trade margin on our selling price was 11 per cent and we commented at the time:

These trade margins look big when compared with those available on Sunlight Soap in the past but it is necessary now to offer direct inducement in the way of profit on Sunlight Soap.

The cost of free delivery and the cost of the further increase in duty which had taken place in the interim reduced our C.I.F. price from that established about a year previously of 42/3 (about £2.11) per case to 35/3d (about £1.76). Thus in the space of just over one year the price of Sunlight Soap to the Indian market had been reduced, in round figures, from £51 to £35 per ton.

The Bombay wholesalers thought that we might at least give them free delivery to their premises. But Gossage's bar soap had always been sold ex godown and Gossage profit margins had become so frail that they could not stand even a brief bullock-cart journey. To protect their interests we stuck to prices ex godown.

We also maintained cash selling terms. Port dealers gave cash with order and up-country dealers got their railway receipts against payment either through banks or through the post office cash collecting system known as V.P.P. It was music to my ears to hear the individual rupees being rung out at our Bombay agent's cash desk. When I last visited India Hindustan Lever Limited were receiving from some customers batches of signed blank cheques to be filled in when orders were despatched. This foundation has been firm.

Having fixed our terms and methods of sale we got down to the practical side. Our Indian agents in Madras, Bombay and Karachi all agreed to become almost local branch offices. They assumed responsibility for stock-keeping and for ensuring that stocks were maintained at a proper level. They operated our bank accounts and made weekly statistical and accounting returns to London, where the central administration of the business remained. They agreed with us the number of salesmen to be employed and co-operated with our representatives in their training and supervision.

Our scheme was so far from the traditions of the British Merchant House representing us in Calcutta that by mutual agreement they withdrew from the agency and we established our own depot and branch office. We had a fine time buying desks, typewriters and 'horses' for the goods to stand on in the godown we rented. I remember with what relish I sent off a cable to London just before leaving Bombay for Calcutta, 'Please send £1,000 to me in Calcutta next week'.

By the middle of April we had stocks in all ports ready for sale on the new terms and to sell them a staff of five resident Europeans and twenty-nine Indian salesmen, mainly for the Lever business. The Gossage business remained on its established basis of sales mainly by agents from consignment stocks.

We were only just in time. Sunlight sales continued to fall while we were working to save them. In the March quarter of 1932 they were at only half the rate of the previous year and as we surveyed the position from port to port the best we thought we could expect on the old basis of sale was 25 per cent less than we had estimated only four months previously.

It was uncertain whether such a disastrous trend could be reversed but we held to our firm belief that it could and, looking ahead to the reduced price level for Sunlight and our direct selling throughout India, we estimated our future prospects. From 5,116 tons in 1929, India sales had fallen by March 1932 to a yearly rate of 2,064—a fall of about 60 per cent. On the new basis, we hoped to get them back to 3,380 tons a year. (The figures given in this paragraph covered only our immediate sphere of operations—India excluding Burma and Ceylon.)

The Lever business only just made a profit in 1932. Gossages' profits had fallen even more than their sales and the total profit from India, Burma and Ceylon was less than £10,000, against well over £200,000 four years earlier.

Our new foundation held firm but it was 1935 before we got the Sunlight sales over the 3,380 tons mark with somewhat better profits.

On the boat home in May I slept night, morning and afternoon all the way to Port Said. When I got back to the London office all Greenhalgh said was, 'Is it all right, Knox?' 'Yes,' I replied, and I was given two weeks' special holiday and a bonus of one month's pay.

The whole of the export business was, of course, hit by the depression and although by 1933 it had reached a degree of stability it was at a lower level both of sales and profitability than had been expected when United Exporters Limited had been formed. It was obvious that some restructuring of the company was necessary, essentially to reduce the costs of administration.

The Indian situation pointed the way. Here was a business almost entirely managed on the spot but with administration and responsibility still held in London. Shaw was fully capable of carrying responsibility for the whole of the local operation and all that would be needed would be a central administration in India, with quarterly reports and accounts coming to London instead of volumes of weekly data.

Since the formation of United Exporters other senior representatives had been encouraged and taught to take a wider view of their business than that of a salesman pure and simple (if there is such a person), so it was possible to make a major change in the organization of United Exporters by establishing a regional 'head office' in Bombay, Batavia (Indonesia), Singapore and Cairo.

This was to be my task. At the end of 1933 I went off on my

fourth visit to India, accompanied by Bill Rigby, to set up a head office for United Exporters in India and to hand over to Bill Shaw the responsibility for the local management of the soap business in India, Burma and Ceylon.

In May 1933 a capital proposal for £150,000 had been put forward for the building of a soap works in Bombay and extensions to the North West Soap Company factory in Calcutta (a survival from the Boulton Brothers fiasco.) This proposal was passed by the Board in July after some protest on the grounds that no allowance had been made in the profit estimate for the loss the home factories would sustain by the transfer of the quite substantial tonnage to overseas manufacture. The Chairman, D'Arcy Cooper, said he thought that India was too big a gap on the world's surface to leave uncovered.

In anticipation of this factory the third Lever Brothers (India) Ltd was registered in Bombay in October 1933. The documents connected with this registration were signed in my bedroom in the Taj Mahal Hotel by the first directors of the Company—Hansard, Shaw, Gourley and Cocker. I noted in my diary that it was a great day for them but a sad one for me. Although the hand-over of the business from United Exporters to Lever Brothers (India) Ltd did not take place for another year, the absence of my signature pointed clearly towards the end of my ten years' involvement in the Lever soap business in India.

I did not lose contact for a couple of years as from the end of 1933 until 1935 a special section of the Overseas Committee administration was formed called Eastern Executive with Hansard in charge and me as his assistant. Our job was to 'nurse' the new companies being established in India, the Dutch East Indies and Thailand and look after China. This gave me the satisfaction of seeing Lever Brothers (India) Ltd through to full independence and of gaining sufficient knowledge of the sister companies connected with the vegetable product business to enable me to give the following brief account of their origins too.

Ghee (clarified butter) is the traditional cooking fat in India and it has special significance for the Hindu as it is a product of the cow, a sacred animal. It is generally in short supply and is therefore expensive and has in consequence been subjected to adulteration, more particularly by hardened fats since the invention of the hardening process. Holland was the chief supplier of these fats under the general description 'vegetable product'.

In the early 1920s the Dutch margarine manufacturers were fighting for tonnage and profit in Europe. Some of their customers in Bombay suggested that vegetable product would be improved by being made granular in texture like genuine ghee. They were soon on to this and the export of vegetable product to India became a most valuable trade. Van den Berghs and Jurgens led the field till Hartogs, another Dutch firm which eventually became part of Unilever, sent out to India as their representative a young man named Abraham Leser, who knew nothing about India and did not even speak English.

Within a few years Hartogs were selling as much as Van den Berghs and Jurgens together. British oil processors tried to enter the trade but they lacked the flexibility required to cope with the nuances of sentiment and rumour, the mixtures of fact and fiction, which made up Bombay bazaar trading at its most vigorous and in which vegetable product had become a large factor. It soon became known by the Hindi word *vanaspati* and the Dutch trade developed very quickly. It took fifty years for British exports of soap to India to reach a value of £1 million. *Vanaspati* reached that figure in little more than five years.

The development was not only rapid, but rough. Undoubtedly the product was seen initially, at least by the buyers, as an adulterant rather than a substitute, and in the scramble for tonnage, in which at one time the Japanese whale oil processors joined, there was no time for thought about trying to build up an identity for the product as such, let alone a distinctive brand name.

Established Indian industrialists soon began local production from two of India's main oilseed crops—groundnuts and cottonseed—and this coincided with the 1929 slump in India which affected the import trade in *vanaspati*. So when the main Dutch manufacturers came together as Margarine Unie, prior to the formation of Unilever, they took a new look at the trade and decided that it could better be handled by local manufacture. The decision to build a factory in Bombay was taken after the formation of Unilever and when land was bought for the factory in

1913 allowance was made for a possible soap works on the same site.

The Unilever *vanaspati* business in Bombay started in August 1932, under a dual company structure: Hindustan Vanaspati Manufacturing Company (H.V.M.) and Hindustan-Holland Vanaspati Trading Company (H.H.V.T.) The enterprise started well with factory production at full capacity—10,000 tons a year—but soon ran into difficulties partly because of management trouble and partly because of Japanese competition—unscrupulous, naturally.

When in 1934 W. G. J. Shaw became Chairman of Lever Brothers (India) Ltd, A. D. Gourley was appointed to a similar position in H.V.M. and H.H.V.T. (with A. Leser as his chief henchman). The two factories were on the same site but joined only by a steam main. Their head offices in Bombay were separate. Both businesses prospered—as separate as their two managements could make them.

My ten years' close association with India was a great and valuable experience. At an early age I had carried serious responsibility and had had scope for initiative, bringing me into close contact with members of the Board. My self-confidence had been built by having been able to gain the confidence of four men for whom I have had lasting respect and affection: Hansard, Shaw, Gourley, and Lloyd. We worked together in a close bond of complete understanding and abounding good humour.

My debt to those years goes deeper than the foundations laid for a business career. On my first visit to India I had a glimpse of the splendours of the Raj. New Delhi consisted of imposing and lonely-looking buildings in a desert criss-crossed by rows of majestic street-lamp standards. The guide-book told me that the population was 30,000, 'but provision has been made for a population of 70,000'. They had already built residences for the viceroy and his military secretary, private secretary, surgeon and controller, and for the commander-in-chief, as well as quarters for his staff and 'the Lines' for his bodyguard. Residential quarters for clerks looked like a cross between barracks and good-class stables.

In Calcutta I remember a troop of sparkling Bengal Lancers trotting through the gates of Government House with the be-plumed governor following in an open carriage, and I also remember perspiring Scotsmen marching along Chowringhee in the full kilted uniform of the Calcutta Scottish, to the skirl of the pipes, on their way to church parade at St Andrew's Presbyterian Church. In Bombay, on Byculla Cup Day, the governor would arrive at the race course in state with a bodyguard of Indian cavalry. There would be no sound from the second-class enclosure, gentle claps from the first-class and a good reception from the members. Indians and British wore appropriate dress clothes, but grey toppers did not appear until 4 p.m., when they replaced topees.

The P. & O. may not have been part of the Raj but certainly the P. & O. voyage Marseilles–Bombay V.V. reflected aspects of it. Even the departure of the P. & O. Special from Victoria Station created more fuss than any other departure. People going to India seemed to have many more relations and friends than other mortals. The alleyways and concourses on the ship at Marseilles buzzed with anxious murmurs of 'captain's table' as those who thought they should be amongst the elect awaited the verdict. One captain put all the members and entourage of some great Commission and their wives at his table—and went and sat with the chief engineer.

On the whole the chief steward knew his job and efficiently matched people at table, though it must have been difficult. It seemed to me that the more military men looked the more likely they were to be bank-managers.

'Commercials' like me, known as 'boxwallahs', were low in the social scale. Once at the fancy dress ball, which always took place the night before landing in Bombay, about a dozen of us decided to go as boilermakers. We borrowed dungarees from the engineers and suitably smudged our faces. We arranged to have a table all together and the captain came, uninvited, to sit with us. Afterwards when I was sitting on the deck by an open window of the drawing-room I overheard comments. One lady said to the others in the party, 'Of course one must have a common cast of countenance to do that sort of thing.'

On my first voyage out, a lady asked me quietly at the table whether I had heard of Mr Manners in my nursery. I replied that I had not had a nursery. Well,' said she, 'you should always leave something on your plate for Mr Manners.' I was shattered, for I was brought up to 'waste not, want not'.

Travelling by rail in India enabled me to see, hear and almost feel something of the gentle pace of Indian life at the lower end of the scale. I picked my way through the indescribable squalour of Calcutta and walked quietly through the marble corridors of the Fort in Delhi and through the Taj Mahal. It has always seemed to me that unless a tourist attraction is beautiful in itself it cannot have much interest unless you can fit it into its historical, architectural or artistic background. When I saw the Taj Mahal I had read enough about India to give me an adequate background, but I did not need it. The Taj Mahal is beautiful. I just needed to look and wonder at the skill which could produce, over 300 years ago, such perfection of symmetry in outline and beauty of detailed decoration. It is a tomb of peaceful, not sad, beauty. Shah Jahan certainly honoured his favourite wife, Mumtaz Mahal; he achieved perfection as he knew it, like the builders of our cathedrals.

These sights were all very strange and wonderful but it was the people in India who opened my eyes and perhaps my heart. On all visits I dealt mainly with Indians—agents, dealers, shopkeepers, managers, clerks, railway officials, servants and coolies. I saw little of the life of the *koi-hai* and what little I saw I did not much care for, though I must admit that I loved having a personal servant.

In what I write next I must avoid the perils of rash generalization. I remember being in a small group of my colleagues and their wives, one of whom was a Scot who had spent many years in Shanghai. His wife continued the custom of Scots women of an older generation by referring to her husband by his surname. She said with some pride, 'The Chinese like McNicol.' One of the party asked quietly, 'All of them?'

Without being quite so sweeping as Mrs McNicol, I can say that I found Indians with whom I dealt *simpatico*, a Spanish word which means something more than 'sympathetic'. But it was deeper than that. Dealing with Indians means talking with them because they do love talk. They talk with their lips, their eyes and their hands. Even now, many years after my experience in India, my wife occasionally tells me that I use my hands needlessly when I talk. Imitation, even if unconscious, is still flattery. But I cannot imitate, because I have not got the liquid, luminous expressiveness of eyes that have through the ages looked hardship, but not degradation, in the face and have, it seemed to me, thereby developed a look of inner serenity, of patience and trustfulness, a look which readily responds in kindliness to a smile or a friendly word whether the word is understood or not.

It was this responsiveness which gripped me and has continued to hold me in its grip as I have in more recent years come to work closely with my Indian colleagues.

To have sensed so quickly and clearly a mutual but unspoken understanding with a people of different religion, culture, outlook and language, touched my heart and has enlightened my whole life.

6

The Formation of United Exporters Limited

U.K. soap exports increased quite substantially after the shock of the 1919–21 slump, reaching by 1927–8 the pre-1914 level of 80,000 tons. However, it was the Lever proprietary business, mainly Sunlight and Lifebuoy soaps, that was making the running: the bar soap business was being squeezed between these proprietaries and gradually developing local manufacture of cheap bar soaps. This intensified the internecine competition, particularly between Gossage, Crosfield and Lever. Under the Brunner, Mond ownership the export departments of Gossage and Crosfield had been amalgamated, but when the Old Man bought the two businesses he separated them again in line with his belief that inter-company competition expanded the total trade more quickly. So both Gossage and Crosfield increased their export effort; increased overseas representation, increased the number of proprietary brands in direct competition with Lever Brothers and increased their advertising expenditure. But the market was not sufficiently expandable to justify this desperate and mutually defeative effort which the Export Executive in London was powerless to control. The Lime Street Hotel meetings became more and more artificial, merely patching up the surface of agreement and driving the business as a whole into an absurdity of petty regulations.

As responsible to the Overseas Committee for the export of Lever proprietaries in India, I attended these meetings, with a watching brief, when India was on the agenda. It was well known in the markets where Gossage, Crosfield and Lever competed so fiercely with each other, that the three companies were closely allied at home and it seemed obvious that a united effort against the growing outside competition would more effectively further the interests of the Family (as it was sometimes referred to), than to continue to waste time and ingenuity in a hopeless attempt to limit the effects of mutual mistrust and recrimination by ever more detailed regulations.

In January 1928 I wrote to the Overseas Committee giving some examples of these regulations and expressing the view that:

> There is no disguising the fact that in export markets under present arrangements, our three chief companies spend most of their time competing against each other rather than finding new business for the Family as a whole: while we have one united interest, we have no common policy.

I am sure the Overseas Committee did not need me to tell them that the situation was unsatisfactory and that something had to be done about it.

In August 1928, out of the blue, the export managements of Lever Brothers, Gossage and Crosfield, together with representatives of other associated companies having some export trade, received the following letter from Lever House, Blackfriars.

Dear Sir,   1st August 1928.

I am instructed by the Chairman of Lever Brothers Limited to ask you to attend a Meeting at the Derby Room, Midland Adelphi Hotel, Liverpool, on August 8th at 12 noon when intended changes in the organisation of the Export business will be explained.

I shall be glad to hear that you will be able to attend.

Yours faithfully,

J.M.B. Stubbs

F.I. ASSOCIATED COMPANIES.

When they got there they found facing them the Chairman of Lever Brothers Limited and members of the Overseas Committee, plus the Chairmen of all the associated companies concerned.

H. R. Greenhalgh, as Chairman of the Overseas Committee, announced that it had been agreed by the Boards of the companies concerned that the export trade dealt with by those present would be amalgamated and operated by a new company to be called United Exporters Limited to be established in London before Christmas.

The Board of the new Company would consist of D'Arcy Cooper as the Chairman; the chairmen of the companies concerned plus two managing directors; W. P. Scott, a member of the defunct Export Executive; and J. H. Hansard, a recently engaged senior member of the Overseas Committee staff.

Everybody had realized that there was 'something in the air' but this announcement was a bomb-shell.

The sudden submergence of the Company name which had been the focal point of their loyalty hit the Lever people particularly. They felt that, as members of the parent company and in charge of the most progressive part of the export business, they should have emerged as top dog in any reorganization.

Gossages relinquished their export independence for the second and last time, and export by then had become the mainstay of their business. Crosfields felt the first real dent in the armour in which they had fought constantly, sometimes bitterly and hitherto successfully, to preserve inviolate the complete independence of the Crosfield business.

It was not a happy meeting. The presence of the various chairmen on the platform indicated from the start that there would be no argument—just shock, disappointment and anxiety about the future.

I was appointed secretary to the managing directors of United Exporters Limited (with a 50 per cent increase in salary to £600 p.a.) and was given the task of organizing the new company and arranging the transfer to London. I was twenty-five.

I devised the office systems to be used, designed the forms required and wrote descriptive notes and detailed instructions as to their use. This required linking the factories and the service sections, to ensure that instructions issued to the former and information provided by the latter were adequate and clear. Accounts and statistics were to be on the Hollerith machine: this involved devising a code which covered the varied needs of export but came within the limitation of a Hollerith card. All this was very detailed but not difficult as no one questioned my arrangements.

It was less easy to recommend who should be transferred to London and how the organization should be planned to accommodate them. The senior men all had to come, but there was obviously to be some 'rationalization' (the word used then for what is now called redundancy) amongst the staff in general and it was impracticable to transfer juniors. I knew the Lever Brothers men and that made it difficult to compare them with their counterparts, whom I did not know, at Crosfields and Gossages, particularly as I also knew that to lose your job was a terrible blow, no matter how generous the rationalization terms might be. I had some sleepless nights.

I eventually produced my plan and my list. I was asked if the organization I had suggested was the ideal for the work to be done. There was much talk at the time of 'system' and theories as to the ideal number of people who could respond to one boss. I said that my plan was devised to make the best use of the men available and not on some theoretical system, and it was accepted. It was based on what, nearly forty years later, was hallowed within Unilever as co-ordination. I proposed specialists to guide the over-all policy for soaps, toilet soaps and preparations, and foods, with territorial managers to direct groups of countries. Whether the specialist or the territorial manager should have the last say was of course the problem. I came to the same conclusion as did the Special Committee years later, but perhaps on a simpler argument. I wrote:

> In coming to this conclusion I have ultimately been swayed by the thought that had we in our business literally concentrated by territories we would by now have been making soft soap in Sweden, white soap in Canada, dhobie soap in India and profits nowhere.

That settled it: but it also gave excuse for clashes of personality which were inevitable amongst the older men who could not free themselves from the shadow of a lifetime's bitter enmity. The majority, however, who still had a career ahead of them, settled down quickly together and presented a united front to the 'slings and arrows of outrageous fortune' which lay ahead.

United Exporters Limited, known immediately as U.E.L., was not born under a lucky star and its birth pains were longer and more severe than I had hoped. There was bound to be some upset in bringing three different sets of people together and into an environment strange to them all, especially as the move was undertaken with great reluctance. But troubles arose from the very beginning as I had not anticipated the difficulty of training newly recruited junior staff in the intricacies of export documentation. Typing packing slips for instructing the factories and shipping department, and invoices for the customer is 90 per cent copying but 10 per cent creative transcription, and this proved to be beyond the copy typists employed for the job. I wished that I had brought the juniors to London even on a temporary basis. Moreover the central accountancy service in London underestimated the load which the volume and intricacies of export work would put on the Hollerith machines.

With delays and mistakes at one end and bad tempers at the other, it was a trying time, and when, about six months later, things began to run reasonably smoothly the company faced the depression in world trade which followed the financial crash in U.S.A. There was also the minor upset of the temporary move from Lever House while it was being rebuilt as Unilever House.

Soap exports from the U.K. fell from 80,000 tons to 40,000 tons in the ten years 1928–38, but this was partly accounted for by the transfer in the early thirties of the trade in India (then including Pakistan and Burma) and Indonesia (then called the Dutch East Indies) to local manufacturing companies. The loss of these important territories reduced the size of U.E.L. but the thirties were nevertheless a period of steady development of the Company.

The trend away from bar soap trading towards proprietary brand selling had been manifest in the twenties. The depression of the thirties leading as it did to increased customs duties and other protectionist measures, bore heavily on bar soaps. Many of the countries to which they were sold produced soap-making raw materials and soaps of adequate quality were easily and cheaply made from them.

U.E.L.'s business therefore became more and more concentrated on specialized proprietary products. Toilet soaps, led by the successful introduction world-wide of Lux Toilet Soap, and the Toilet Preparations business, began to assume greater importance. By 1939 toilet soap exports were one-third, by value, of total U.K. soap exports, and toilet preparations exports were equal to the *total* soap figure—about £1,000,000.

Thus U.E.L. added advertising to selling and through its success with Lux Toilet Soap in 'native' markets learned two valuable lessons. Firstly, how to do effective advertising at low cost where no normal media exist, and, secondly, that housewives are houseproud wherever they live and are therefore all potential customers.

Thus the Company was drawn on towards the sophisticated techniques which have since been comprehensively called marketing and also towards the realization of the necessity for greater knowledge of and closer contact with the ultimate consumer of the products.

This marketing experience during the strenuous but not unsuccessful years of the late thirties was to stand the company in good stead when it was drawn together again after the interruption of the Second World War.

7

Interlude: 1935–1945

In 1935 I was appointed Head of O.S.C./sales department which acted primarily as a secretariat to the Overseas Committee on everything now known as marketing. In this position it might be assumed that I would have had reasonably close relations with the U.K. soap companies which, after 'Boston' (Lever Brothers company, U.S.A.) were at that time the main fount of selling initiative in its widest sense for the whole business. This was not so, however, for a variety of traditional and personal reasons stemming from jealousy. The home soap companies not only provided valuable initiative but also a large and dependable share of world soap profits and nearly a third of total concern world soap sales. They could well, and did, look down with scorn on the small and comparatively primitive operations in all the overseas companies except those in North America and it was a source of frustration to them that their contacts with 'Boston' were not direct, close and intimate but had to be through the Overseas Committee. So there grew up in the home trade a tradition that people working overseas (other than North America) could not possibly have the necessary sophisticated experience to be of any value in the great U.K. market, and that people trained in the U.K. market could not reach their full potential without direct access to the higher flights of sophistication in U.S.A., and would be wasting their time and talents elsewhere overseas. The tradition dies hard.

So there was no love lost between the home soap companies and overseas operations and any requests to the home companies for information or help by Overseas had to be made at top level in Unilever House.

Geoffrey Heyworth (later Lord Heyworth) of the Home Soap Executive was above these jealousies. He certainly never felt them, nor did he follow in the tradition. He had served the Company overseas, in Canada, and his brothers, Laurence and Roger, were both overseas men.

It was not out of the ordinary therefore when in 1937 I was asked one day to go and see Mr Heyworth, member of the Home Soap Executive responsible for what were known as the Hard Soap Companies, but it was extraordinary to be told by him that I was to succeed David Morrell as secretary of the Executive in a few weeks' time on Morrell's departure to take charge of the Lever company in Australia. I wondered how I, who knew nothing of the home trade, could be of any assistance to Geoffrey Heyworth who knew everything about it and who had as his colleague L. G. Fisher, one of the best commercial men in the business with a powerful reputation for getting straight to the point in as few words as possible. I had evidence subsequently that my view as to my patent inadequacy for the job was shared by some of my hard soap colleagues outside the Executive itself.

Indeed I stepped into a new and unknown world. Hitherto I had dealt almost wholly with the written word—reports, correspondence, minutes—an almost continuous battle to keep down the level of the in-tray. In O.S.C./sales I had regularly spent two or three evenings a week reading, making précis of and drafting replies to reports which were the necessary means of keeping the Overseas Committee informed, before the era of air mail, air travel and regular personal contact at many levels.

But in the home trade there were no reports and no correspondence, not even regular meetings of which I might take the minutes. What was I to do? One day stands out in my mind when all I was asked to do was to provide my boss with a packet of Lux which I was readily able to do from the near-by Overseas Technical Sample Room. On another occasion, soon after I started in the job, some difficulty arose in Bridgwater division which I was asked to sort out. I felt myself fortunate in being able to discuss my instructions without revealing that I had not the faintest idea where the Bridgwater division was, except that it was not in Scotland.

There were of course some co-ordination jobs to do, notably that of trying to ensure that there were no serious clashes between major promotional schemes amongst the operating companies. As there were still nine hard soap companies and seven companies making toilet soap and toilet preparations to deal with, this was a touchy problem. The smaller companies with strong local goodwill did not want to see their pet scheme of the year swamped by a big national operator, nor did the latter want to operate a scheme limited, say, to South Wales. It was in this area particularly that I was sometimes pointedly reminded of my lack of home trade credentials. I was much more at home in statistical comparisons such as the following, for 1939:

	No. of salesmen	Av. cost salary & exp. per salesman £	Total selling expenses % of turnover	Sales routine cost per delivery s. d.	Av. no. accounts per salesman	Av. no. of orders per salesman per day
Lever						
Brothers	167	453	4·59	1.10¼	342	12·0
Crosfield	125	451	5·45	1.11½	289	9·0
Ogston &						
Tennant	16	432	9·28	1.8½	352	5·6
A. & F.						
Pears	32	681	13·67	2·1¾	606	4·8

There was not in fact a great load of day-to-day work but with occasional visits to some of the companies, a steady flow of statistics of all sorts to be studied and frequent opportunities actually to join in discussions of current problems and projects being considered by the Executive I soon gained not only a knowledge of the home soap business but an understanding of the many skills then being developed which have since come together under the umbrella of marketing: skills in which Geoffrey Heyworth and the team he led in the U.K. soap business were outstanding pioneers.

The most notable step in this process while I was Secretary to the Executive was the introduction to the United Kingdom from the U.S.A. of the Nielsen Index. Up till then anyone who had had any connection with selling soap under the Lever auspices had taken his weekly temperature from the weekly sales sheet, and the idea that there could be any other method, let alone a better one, of judging the progress of the business was regarded by many as almost sacrilege. To pay highly for such an unbelievable alternative was surely nonsense.

Geoffrey Heyworth must have used his powers of persuasion to the full to get this new idea accepted by his colleagues on the Board, and to tempt Art Nielsen the founder of the Index, to venture outside the U.S.A. It was Art himself who sold the service to the many sceptical U.K. managers by giving a demonstration of salesmanship which I have not heard equalled, except perhaps by the late Charles Rattray, tobacconist of Perth.

The basic concept of the Nielsen Index was clear, simple and convincing—that a record of retailers' sales over the counter to the consumer would be a better index of sales progress than a record made up of deliveries to wholesalers and retailers. As advertising appropriations began to mount (Rinso and Persil were both at about £350,000 in 1938), and with growing emphasis on promotions, it became increasingly desirable to know accurately not how much a promotion had loaded into the trade but how much the consumer had bought. The difficulty of the Nielsen concept was to gain acceptance from men who knew they were selling to some 130,000 'household trade' shops in 116 territorial divisions that an index based on a three-monthly audit of 600 shops scattered all over the country could give any reliable guidance at all, let alone guidance which would be worth the considerable cost. The carrot was that the index gave details not only of your sales over the counter but those of your competitor too, and the stick was 'supposing your competitor has this information and you haven't?' Anyway the Nielsen Index got started in the United Kingdom and has spread world-wide with many rival indices. Marketing managers have become more glib with indices than with their own sales figures.

Under the wing of the Home Soap Executive a market research service had been developed, market research having already ceased to be regarded as just a bit of fancy work provided by the bigger advertising agencies. Outdoor advertising—house-to-house couponing, demonstrations, etc.—was a major competitive weapon, and into that also a valuable element of professionalism was introduced by Outdoor Advertising Service who provided trained teams nationwide, backed by full data on housing densities, the best routes to follow, and so on. A typical operation of 1937 was a two-for-one coupon offer for Persil: 6,376,000 coupons were distributed and 65 per cent were redeemed at a cost of 1·685d a call and 2·598d per coupon redeemed.

Early in 1940 I was plunged into the practical side of home soap activities. I was appointed Sales Director of R. S. Hudson Limited and after twenty-one years in the business, eighteen of them in London, I found myself for the only time in my life working in Port Sunlight. After many years at the centre of the business, I did not much like working in a backwater—even a comfortable one.

R. S. Hudson manufactured nothing. It was a marketing company—its head was called Marketing Controller—and its products came from three different factories. It earned the biggest profit— over £1 million—in the home soap group. Its main line Rinso, outsold both its 'inside' and 'outside' competitors, Persil and Oxydol. Sales in round figures were:

Rinso	30,000 tons a year
Hudsons Extract (another soap powder)	10,000 ,,
Vim	10,000 ,,

Hudsons also sold the cooking fat Spry (at a loss) until it lost its identity in the wartime fat rationing scheme.

I found myself responsible for five branch offices and some 130 salesmen in conditions which still called for competitive selling. For many years my passport had described me as a salesman but I was well aware that this meant nothing to my new colleagues as I had not come up through their mill. I might know where Wigan was, but did I know Rushtons? I was on trial—at least I thought I was.

The first thing to do was to get to know the people, so I asked all members of the sales staff to send me a passport photo which I put on their staff record file. Before going to a branch meeting (of 25–30 people) I pored over these files and tried to memorize the name and photo. It worked pretty well and I subsequently used the same dodge with senior staff throughout the world. Ultimately in the Overseas Committee all company organization charts were adorned with appropriate photos.

The real test came when I had to address a salesmen's meeting. I had never previously stood up in front of people I did not know with a view to instructing them, encouraging them and, hopefully, even enthusing them; and while salesmen are usually not reluctant to be instructed, encouraged and enthused, they do not suffer bores gladly. Therefore I must speak to them, not just read a speech. I managed quite well but when, after the meeting, I got out of the car in which a friend had driven me home my legs went from under me and I was glad that no one saw me creep up to my front door on hands and knees.

When I had settled into the job I enjoyed it and gained a respect for the men who undertake the job of salesman. They have to be self-starters, even on days when they don't feel like it and must have super-abundant energy and natural resilience. In the end they become realists and imperturbable.

In Hudsons, and probably in other companies, it was the rule that branch managers rendered weekly reports giving their activities in detail with comments on what they had seen and done. One of them, an old hand, was dictating his weekly report to a new secretary.

Monday. I arrived at the office at 9.0 a.m. and after dealing with the mail I caught the 10.15 a.m. from Fenchurch Street to Meet Mr. . . . in Southend . . .
Tuesday. Arrived at the office 9.0 a.m. and after dealing with urgent matters I caught the 10.40 a.m. from Liverpool Street to see Mr. . . . in Colchester . . .
Wednesday. Arrived at the office 9.0 a.m. . . . .

This was too much for the secretary. 'But Mr. . . . you must remember that you did not get to the office on Wednesday till after 11 o'clock.' With a wave of his hand to stop her prattle, he replied, 'They want 9 o'clock—let them have 9 o'clock.'

My immediate predecessor was wont to spend Friday dictating letters to salesmen to cheer them up or spur them on on Monday morning—normally the latter. He showed me one which seemed to me to burn the paper in its virulence. 'That'll make 'im sit up!' he said with evident relish. Sometime later I met the salesman in question and asked how he reacted to such letters. He laughed and said, 'Not at all, I just tear them up and put them in the wastepaper basket.' Realist and imperturbable.

During 1941, supplies gradually became restricted with the probability of soap rationing. There was no longer any need for competitive selling and many salesmen had been called up to the Services. R. S. Hudson was amalgamated with Lever Brothers and the Hudson name disappeared, though it briefly re-appeared in the title of Hudson & Knight, a selling company, after the war. I became a colleague and friend of George Richman who in his day as Sales Director of Lever Brothers had as deep a knowledge and understanding of, and as close a grip on, the U.K. grocery trade as any of his contemporaries. He had originally been promoted by Geoffrey Heyworth, then in charge of the Lever U.K. business, from agent in Hackney to branch manager in Bristol, and was asked to report on the efficiency of the Bristol branch salesmen. Geoffrey Heyworth went to see him and said, 'I see you don't think much of your salesmen here.'

'That's right, sir, there's none of them any real good.'

'Well, Richman, which is easier for me, to find twenty-five new salesmen or one new branch manager?'

'I see what you mean, sir.' A realist.

In 1942 I was called up to join the Royal Ordnance Factories (Filling) Lancashire Region to be Regional Planning and Progress Officer. The R.O.F. was part of the Ministry of Supply, of which Sir Robert Hall (later Lord Roberthall) was a senior official. Some years after the war I was sitting next to Sir Robert at the Unilever directors lunch table and in course of conversation it was revealed that we had both been in the same Ministry. He asked what my job had been and I explained. He turned to me in wonderment and said, 'You've come up quickly since then, haven't you?'

Looked at from the top the job must have seemed very lowly, not even a director or deputy director of something, of which there must have been several hundreds in the Ministry.

At the time it seemed to be a valuable job—a small cog, admittedly, but in a machine which was producing something quite obviously necessary for the war effort: filled ammunition.

The Lancashire region had three of the biggest filling factories in the country: Risley near Warrington, Kirkby near Liverpool, and Chorley, built just before the war to replace Woolwich. We filled practically all the ammunition except small arms ammunition, including detonators, primers and fuses, which the Army and Air Force required. It was really a gigantic filling and assembly job ranging from detonators, very small but highly dangerous through the intricacies of some of the fuses, to the 10,000-lb bombs into which explosive was shovelled like sand.

Tens of thousands of empties of one sort and another and tons of explosives were received at the factories daily (the day was twenty-four hours) and an appropriate number of filled items were despatched. The whole operation depended on stocks which were never more than three days' supply and frequently down to three hours'. I took a bit of convincing later that a soap depot could not work on less than a four-week minimum cover!

There was a competent staff of progress chasers who could command absolute priority in transport and who had direct links by phone to big suppliers, but it was still an object lesson in planning, particularly as the programme for any one factory was continually being altered. As the war developed more and more new types of ammunition were devised, some being required only in quantities of a few thousand. Marker bombs for air raids, eventually, had to be made with codes of colour change which differed from day to day. Our most exciting job was to fill, at Chorley, the bombs and fuses for the Möhne Dam raid—so secret that they were never even mentioned on the official Top Secret Programmes.

My job was to keep these volatile programmes running smoothly. I had to ensure that the various items on the programme could be dealt with at the factory concerned and that the labour force available at each factory was fully used. This involved regular visits to the three factories and frequent visits to the central office at Shell-Mex House, London.

As production units the factories were very flexible. A great deal of the work was manual and, because of the explosive risk, the individual production units (shops) were small and necessarily very little mechanized. The big bomb-filling shops had to have cranes and gantries and the detonator shops had protective shields. But between these extremes there were many shops which, with the provision of the necessary jigs, could be adapted for a wide range of work.

The main problem was how much labour would be required? Here the regional production staff made a major contribution. Under the guidance of a few experienced men a production study (then known as time-study) team was built up which gradually put together a set of 'standards' for the main elements in most jobs and, while actually continuing to study each individual job to set standards for shop and team bonuses, could also give reliable approximations as to the work force required for any given job. I was closely linked with these men and thus gained some insight into the mysteries of time and motion study, planned maintenance and incentive bonus and later training within industry.

The filling factory organization had had to be vastly and quickly expanded for war purposes with the result that there had been a great influx of temporary amateur management. The whole of the regional staff were amateur, many in Lancashire from the textile industry: in the factories, the key personnel were from Woolwich. Most of the people with whom I was working were therefore from industry and on the whole we got on well together. The permanent staff of course understood the necessity for the great influx, but some of them made it clear that they did not welcome it.

Quite soon after I joined I had to ring one of the permanent staff and, after explaining my problem, the answer I got in a somewhat languid voice was, 'Do we speak at like levels?'

One soon got used to the jargon—my glossary had over 100 groups of initials in it—and on the whole, considering we were a scratch team, we worked well together and certainly effectively. The standard of performance of the ammunition we filled was high and very few programmes fell far behind schedule.

The morale of the factory workers, mostly women, was high too. It was a hard job. Practically all workers were on a three-shift basis, six shifts a week. The factories were out in the country and spread out over large areas. People had a long way to go to get to the factories and a long way to walk within the factories to get to work because the shops were widely spread for safety reasons. It was a dangerous job and discipline as to smoking, the wearing of 'danger building' clothing by everyone, the use of guards, etc., was strict. It was a tedious job, where standards of work were exacting.

But there was never an instance where, after even a fatal accident, there was any question of the team not returning to the shop to continue the same operation, and the atmosphere as you went round the shops and the canteens was cheerful. Absenteeism was not a serious problem.

Morale was high, and it was certainly not because of the joint consultation meetings which, on instructions from above, we faithfully created and patiently maintained. Productivity problems never raised any enthusiasm. The only problems which were of real interest were such as 'Why are the chips cold in No. 5 canteen?'

Consultation has become a growing problem since the war and no doubt necessarily so. But it is a rare breeding ground for complaints. Delegates from the shop floor to the boardroom or from students to the council chambers must be seen to be doing something on behalf of their constituents and the easiest way to do so is to look for trouble. Their job is to raise issues, not bring down soft soap from above, and the chips in No. 5 canteen come to mind whenever I think of joint consultation.

The morale was founded on the fact that the job was obviously a direct part of the war effort. You can't fight without ammunition. I remember seeing elderly women screwing fuses into shells with a look on their faces as if they were screwing Hitler's neck. Morale, given this foundation, was maintained I believe by the frequent contact between members of the staff and the workers in the filling shops. The nature, the importance, even the danger of the work called for frequent visits by senior staff.

The filling shops were small (20–30 workers) and few were authorized to enter, so that everyone in the shop could identify any visitor. The time-study staff were mainly men from the textile mills who knew how to deal with Lancashire women workers, and they spent whole days and nights in individual shops and became well known. Canteens were for staff and workers alike. Even the administration had only one canteen, the only concession to seniority being that the superintendent had a table reserved and could ask

5 Directors of Unilever Limited, 1960. Directors of Unilever Limited are also directors of Unilever N.V. and *vice versa*. Miss M. B. Penston, secretary to the Special Committee, is in the foreground.

6 The author at Calcutta airport in 1933. K.L.M.'s Amsterdam to
Batavia flight was one of the first and longest regular air routes in the
world. Unlike today, the crew took the plane right through the route.

7 Mrs Knox talking to Mrs Msimang, the cook at Sunlight Beach –
the sports and social club for African employees and their families near
Durban.

8a and b Two views of Port Sunlight. 'If I were to follow the usual mode of profit sharing I would send my workmen and work girls to the cash office at the end of the year
and say to them: "You are going to receive £8 each; you have earned this money; it
belongs to you. Take it and make whatever use you like of your money." Instead of that
I told them: "£8 is an amount which is soon spent, and it will not do you much good
if you send it down your throats in the form of bottles of whisky, bags of sweets, or fat
geese for Christmas. On the other hand, if you leave this money with me, I shall use it
to provide for you everything which makes life pleasant – viz. nice houses, comfortable
homes, and healthy recreation. Besides, I am disposed to allow profit sharing under no
other than that form." ' W. H. Lever, 1903 – the year of Andrew Knox's birth.

whom he liked to join him—but you ate (or were given) the same food whether at that table or elsewhere.

So although the factories employed thousands of workers there was no cause for them to feel remote and disregarded—they were part of a joint effort. And indeed the Director General of Filling Factories, Mr C. S. Robinson, a Scottish engineer, made a point of coming from time to time to tell them just that. He was not a great speaker, but I am sure that the fact that he came and visited every canteen on every shift so that he could speak even for a few minutes to practically every operative was a definite factor in the maintenance of morale. People need the human touch—and it need only be a touch.

The Royal Ordnance Factory (Filling) certainly did an effective job, and it had to do it economically because the main cost was labour which became increasingly scarce as the war continued. But my observation of Civil Service procedures and attitudes convinced me that I had been right to ignore the advice of the headmaster of Bury Grammar School—not about working hard, but about the desirability of the Civil Service as a career for me. The strait-jacket of necessarily detailed regulation and limitation of authority, where ultimate responsibility is so remote, would take the zest out of a job for me and is probably the reason for what seemed to me to be the somewhat detached attitude of the Civil Servants I dealt with to their job even in wartime. I certainly don't speak at like level.

Victory in Europe immediately released the pressure on ammunition production and the regional staff, mostly temporary civil servants anxious to get back to their ordinary jobs, folded their tents like the Arabs and as silently stole away.

This interlude had been interesting and valuable from the point of view of my work. It had been an exciting and happy time from the personal point of view. I had got married in 1939 and we had had three sons. Soon after the end of the European war I was called to London where my old boss, J. L. Heyworth, asked if I would return to the overseas side of the business to examine the future of Export and of one or two of the smaller overseas companies, a post which would obviously entail a great deal of travel.

On return to the north I had to explain this to my wife with some emphasis on the foreign travel. All she said was, 'Would you like the job?' to which I replied that I thought it was just the job for me. So she said that I had better take it, which I did, and I felt that by rejoining Overseas I was going back home.

Fortunately we were able to share that feeling as, by chance, I found I could buy the house we had lived in when we got married and which we had left with sad hearts when I had been transferred from London to Port Sunlight five years previously.

8

Return to 'Overseas' and Five Problems of an International Business 1945-1955

When I came back to Unilever after the war I found a somewhat different 'overseas', though the overseas companies were recognizably the same.

Originally the Lever companies on the continent of Europe and in North America were classified as 'Overseas'. Under Unilever the European companies were transferred to Continental management and as the business in North America grew in importance it gradually came to have direct links with the Special Committee at the head of Unilever.

In 1938 there were Unilever 'Overseas' companies in Australia, New Zealand, the Philippines, China, Dutch East Indies (Indonesia), Siam (Thailand), India (including Burma and Ceylon), South Africa, Belgian Congo (Zäire), Nigeria, the Argentine (with offshoots in Uruguay and Chile), and Brazil. United Exporters Limited also came under the Overseas Committee.

The total sales were approximately £10 million. The companies, with two exceptions, were soap companies. Australia was the biggest, with sales of £2.75 million, followed by the Philippines (oil-milling), India (half soap, half edible fat) and South Africa, each with £1 million.

During the war contact was lost with the companies in China, the Dutch East Indies and the Philippines, where the oil mills were destroyed by American bombing. The South African business was extended by the purchase of a soap-making company in Rhodesia and the Indian business expanded greatly. In 1946 total overseas sales were £25 million, with India £10 million, Australia and South Africa each £3½ million.

In order that the companies should not feel isolated by the growing difficulties of regular communication in wartime it was arranged that the Board should be represented personally at one or two main centres. Laurence Heyworth, who had joined the Overseas Committee from Australia in 1937, went to Boston to cover the whole of North and South America. C. W. Barnish covered Southern and East Africa from Durban and Geoffrey Rushworth, Chairman of Lever Brothers in Sydney, covered Australasia.

Presumably out of these emergency measures sprang the idea of maintaining contact through regional offices rather than re-centralizing in London after the war. 'Contact Directors' had taken the place of the Overseas Committee and companies overseas were arranged in groups, each with its headquarters: South America (Buenos Aires); Africa—except West Africa (Durban); the East (Bombay); and Australasia (Sydney). Smaller 'ungrouped' territories—Congo, Nigeria, later Trinidad—came under Laurence Heyworth who had returned to London as one of the Contact Directors. Marketing, technical and accounting services were established at each group headquarters and the old Overseas Committee services disappeared, although O.S.C./sales and O.S.C./technical provided the nuclei, respectively, of two departments created for the service of Unilever as a whole—Marketing Advisory Division and Technical Division.

These group arrangements did not last very long. The rapid development of air mail and air travel made possible much closer contacts between overseas companies and London than had existed before the war, and the cost of maintaining regional headquarters with the necessary specialized staff gradually became evident. Equally gradually the contact directors slipped back into a committee form of working and the Overseas Committee became officially re-established in 1954.

I returned in 1945 to Overseas Contact Directors, not Overseas Committee, and gladly accepted the dual assignment, with Laurence Heyworth once again my boss, of rehabilitating export and looking after ungrouped territories.

My main immediate work was in connection with Export, but when Trinidad was added to ungrouped territories I found myself much preoccupied with the complicated local copra controls which were closely intertwined with the intricacies of West Indian politics. I seemed to be required to give by cable a never-ending series of exact answers to an equally never-ending series of hypothetical questions posed by the sharp and exact mind of my friend, J. P. Stubbs, then our Trinidad Managing Director. I was glad when he was promoted to Germany. Many years later he was a colleague on the Overseas Committee subsequently becoming its Chairman. I was equally glad that he was promoted from Germany.

Over the next ten years I visited about forty countries. I wrote many reports and also kept a diary recording minutes of meetings I had attended, a note of people I had met and of what I had seen of interest, and any important set of figures or calculations which had a bearing on the problems discussed. I found this diary valuable as a record and writing it helped to fill in the difficult gap between leaving the office and the usually somewhat late hour for dinner.

Looking back on these reports and diaries in retirement I recall that in their great historical work *1066 and All That* Messrs Sellers and Yeatman recorded that after the First World War History came to a full stop. I must be careful therefore in trying to record happenings after the Second. People are interested in the old days, which can usually be taken to mean before they were born or, in business, before they joined the company, and also, as you get older, you recall the old days better than what happened last week. This is another reason for me to be careful, and I have limited myself to recollection of five problems with which I had to deal, and an account of which I can give mainly from what was written at the time and not just from memory. Three of the problems were just normal problems of an overseas business affecting only the territories concerned Two had rather wider significance.

Unilever Export Limited

My first task on return to Overseas was to review the post-war prospect for export, the review to comprehend all Unilever consumer products from all sources.

Soap exports from the U.K. had been the mainstay of the whole trade before the war, with United Exporters the main operating company.

In contrast to the First World War, the Second brought no boom to U.K. soap exports, though during 1940 and early 1941 special allocations of raw materials were made to enable the trade to be maintained. From the end of 1941 however, exports were severely restricted and subject to Board of Trade quota. The quota for 1945 was only 4,500 tons of which 2,000 went to Malta and Gibraltar and 2,000 to the Middle East.

Many of the Home and practically all the Overseas staff of United Exporters Limited were on National Service and the nucleus of the Company was evacuated from London to Port Sunlight where they were accommodated in an austerity-style conversion of a warehouse. From that homely vantage point a network of alternative supply bases was contrived so that all markets could continue to receive as nearly as possible the type of goods (particularly soaps) to which they were used. Unilever Overseas companies came to the rescue; Canada supplied the West Indies, South Africa supplied the East Coast of Africa and Mauritius, India supplied Ceylon and other Eastern markets. Port Sunlight was maintained as the Principal in the business so that although personal contacts were broken, a continuing link was maintained between U.E.L. and its agents. In the conditions of wartime scarcity, available supplies were readily taken up, and with minimal administrative expenses and no selling expenses at all the company, though a shadow of its former self, continued to draw some profits from its sketchy supply lines.

The equally sketchy sales records for the war period gave no basis for forecasting what might happen in future and it seemed to me that only a detailed examination of the position just before the war would give such a basis. I enlisted the assistance of R. G. Barnshaw, an old export colleague, who was Secretary of the

United Kingdom Soap Trade Export Group, and by dint of a good deal of detailed clerical work and a judicious amount of guesswork we assembled a complete and detailed record of all Unilever exports in 1938. We adjusted the figures where circumstances had clearly changed—the soap trade to Ceylon, for instance, had been taken over by Lever Brothers (Ceylon) Limited in 1943—and concluded that the remaining figures would represent a reasonable initial estimate of the trade for which an export organization should be provided:

Destination	Soap	Margarine and edible oil	Toilet preparations	Foods	Total
Europe and Mediterranean	189,000	149,000	98,000	12,000	448,000
Africa	335,000	41,000	39,000	81,000	496,000
East	212,000	54,000	87,000	64,000	417,000
Australasia	9,000	7,000	—	7,000	23,000
N. & S. America	93,000	19,000	158,000	3,000	273,000
C. America and West Indies	157,000	66,000	8,000	9,000	240,000
Ships stores etc.	38,000	—	5,000	37,000	80,000
Total	1,033,000	336,000	395,000	213,000	1,977,000

Exports of soaps and foods had been predominantly from the United Kingdom; of margarine and edible fats from Holland; toilet preparations had been from a wide variety of sources including the United Kingdom, France and United States of America. It was obvious that a new organization to deal with all exports would have to be centred on United Kingdom and Holland with some links with United States and France.

As, at the time, exports of soap and foods from U.K. were prohibited and exports of margarine and edible fats not possible, our estimate of approximately £2,000,000 as an immediate aim was, to quote the memorandum to the Board, 'necessarily somewhat speculative'. However, the proposals for the organization were accepted and thus came into being early in 1946 two sister companies, Unilever Export Limited and Unilever Export N.V., charged with the overall responsibility for the whole of the export of consumer products. Apart from the name, the essential differences from the pre-war arrangements were that margarine and edible fats were brought within the main export structure, thus drawing the two main exporting managements, Dutch and British, together; that Gibbs' and Pears' exports and those of the recently acquired Pepsodent business were brought into the fold; that the specialists for soaps and edibles, toilet soaps and preparations, and foods, were directors of the Company.

It was quite impossible at the time to move the main export staff back to London nor was it considered necessary. On the other hand it was vital that the top management of export should be in close touch with the contact directors in order to ensure co-operation between export and the developing group structure overseas. So the specialists directors were established in Unilever House and the main organization was built up in Port Sunlight. Laurence Heyworth, the Contact Director concerned with Export, was Chairman and I was Managing Director, though not with that title.

I had never loved the name United Exporters Limited, nor the abbreviation U.E.L., so when Laurence Heyworth told me that my suggestion of Unilever Export had been accepted I was delighted. With his glint in his eye he said, 'Yes, Knox—U.E.L.' The thought had never crossed my mind and I am happy to record that the twin companies rapidly became known by their proper and honoured name—Unilever Export.

The star under which the company was reborn was luckier than the one which flickered on its birth in 1928. People throughout the world were longing for a release from the limitations of austerity and the main problem was to get the goods from the factories and find ships to carry them. As export restrictions eased, sales began to move ahead and when a U.K. Government scheme of bonuses in hard currency for sales to hard currency markets enabled us to buy raw materials from sources outside the sterling area we put our products back to pre-war quality and appearance long before our rivals and long before it could be done for United Kingdom trade. Lux Toilet Soap in particular swept the board, often in defiance of restrictions. It was the biggest seller, for example, in Athens, although the import of toilet soap into Greece was prohibited: sales to Malta were particularly good at the time. In the free market of Hong Kong English Lux Toilet Soap sold at a premium over the same brand imported from Australia, India and even the U.S.A.

It was a grand time for everybody—the older ones who had held the business together during the war, the younger ones back from war service, and the recruits. All worked with a will, frequently seven days a week, and in 1948 we reached our sales target of £2 million. In 1952, when I became Chairman of the Company, sales were £6 million with trading profits just over 10 per cent of sales value.

The first rush of post-war demand was for pre-war, familiar, products, but advances in technology during the war opened new avenues for expansion and completely changed the outlook for what had been the corner stone of Export—soap. Detergents, known originally as non-soapy detergents (N.S.D.s), are certainly not soap and thus, somewhat unexpectedly, avoided the protectionist barriers round the local soap industry in many countries of the world. We, and our competitors, found it possible to sell detergents where we had previously been reduced to a mere trickle of specialized soap products.

Theory was all against it: N.S.D.s were far too expensive; powders had never sold in this market; and powders wouldn't do for river washing.

But housewives everywhere had learned to equate lather with washing powder. A spoonful of N.S.D. powder in a bucket of brackish water seemed like magic to the housewives in the Persian Gulf rubbing their clothes away with a piece of filled bar soap and getting hardly a bubble for their pains.

The United Kingdom was not the cheapest, not the 'natural' supplier of N.S.D.s to world markets as it had been for soap, and had to meet vigorous competition from other industrialized countries, notably the U.S.A. By 1968 exports of hard soap from the U.K. had decreased to 4,000 tons valued at £500,000: N.S.D. exports, nil in 1948, had reached nearly 60,000 tons, valued at £10,000,000. In the same year the U.S.A., never an exporter of soap, also exported N.S.D. to the value of £10,000,000.

So the 100-year story of the British soap export trade came to an end.

Unilever Export had to work hard to gain and retain their share of this quickly expanding detergent market. The experience gained in the thirties of making an effective appeal to unsophisticated consumers was valuable, while advertising media remained unsophisticated; but there was a lot more to learn when the Americans began to set the pace in export markets with radio and television advertising.

At that time Export was responsible for Unilever trade in very many markets, some quite small, scattered all over the world. To plan and execute some 400–500 individual advertising campaigns in the appropriate language for about twenty-five products was a superhuman task even though many of the campaigns were for an expenditure of a few hundred pounds only. It was a job for a juggler rather than an advertising man but H. R. M. Barratt who spent his whole career in Export advertising restarted it all almost single-handed after the war and continued to carry a very heavy burden even when an adequate staff had been assembled and trained. The measure of his success is that Unilever Export hold their share (and sometimes more) wherever they operate.

Another technical development which opened new vistas for Export was deep freezing. U.E.L. had tried to develop a trade in canned goods but not with great success. Personal representation made little headway against 6d a case in a very cut-throat trade which is really that of a produce merchant. So what had been Angus Watson's trade before the war was left by Unilever Export after the war in the skilled hands of John West Foods Limited. Some trade was done amongst nostalgic expatriates in the tropics for Walls' sausages and Mac Fisheries' kippers but this took a severe blow when the British Army left India.

Deep freezing was a different thing. We had great difficulty in persuading the shipping companies that it would be worth while to have special deep freeze accommodation and our trials had to be made virtually by our own inventiveness and certainly at our own risk. I can remember the first trial. The consignment was personally seen off in Liverpool and met in Lagos to ensure quick loading and unloading. I took a personal interest in it because on my first visit to Nigeria, when there were no hotels, my hostesses provided me with tinned peas, which I don't like, eleven times out of my first thirteen cooked meals.

This business too started with expatriates, but while it is one thing to provide an occasional sausage to an expatriate in a tropical country, it is quite another to provide a regular supply of fresh temperate-climate vegetables and Northern-waters fish—to say nothing of ice cream and real cream cakes. The export trade gave a valuable boost to the early beginnings of Birds Eye in the United Kingdom.

A technical development of another sort, initiated in the early fifties, greatly widened the scope of Unilever Export activities.

Export's traditional role was to develop a trade to the point where it was more advantageous to continue from a local factory. But a soap factory adequate for local requirements in the Belgian Congo cost £23,000 in 1922. It was nearer £1,000,000 in Malaya in 1951, and it takes a big soap (and edible fat) trade to support investment of that size. So there began to be a limit to the number of countries to which Export were shipping where the trade would warrant a major investment. There seemed to be no limit however to the number of countries where local enterprise was willing to manufacture, with suitable protection, albeit on a modest scale. Unilever Export were therefore faced with the alternative of making a manufacturing agreement with the local enterprise or finding itself excluded from a useful trade. An agreement inevitably meant technical assistance to ensure the maintenance of quality and the passing on of know-how to people who could theoretically become competitors. A matter of principle was involved and had to be decided at a higher level. I did not think I would improve my case when facing the Special Committee by mentioning that there had been a precedent: Export had had Woodwards Gripe Water made *à façon* in Paris in the 1920s.

Even without this support the proposition was passed with the valuable corollary that such enterprises should continue to be under the administration and for the profit of Unilever Export. This has turned out to be a most valuable adjunct to the export business and now covers the manufacture of soap, margarine, detergents and toilet preparations in many different parts of the world.

The bringing together of the soap and edibles business through the sister export companies, Limited and N.V., did not bring much immediate benefit to either. Soap had found its way into world markets because it was a better product than what had hitherto been available. Margarine in its early stages was a cheap substitute for butter and as such sold readily in butter-consuming countries— the countries of Northern Europe and the United Kingdom. It was virtually prohibited in butter-producing countries (Canada, U.S.A. South Africa, Australia and New Zealand), and was unsaleable in oil-using countries (Mediterranean and tropics). So Dutch exports of margarine which at one time were considerable, reaching 160,000 tons in 1914–15, were confined to the Continent and U.K. and had been transferred to local manufacture in all the main consuming countries by 1939. However, technical development in oil processing, especially hardening, enabled the enterprising Dutch manufacturers to lead world trade in white opaque cooking fat (like lard), refined edible vegetable oil from raw materials less costly than olives, and granular semi-solid vegetable fat that looked and behaved like Indian ghee.

These products were undoubtedly first used as adulterants, but they were valuable, undisguised, at times and in places of scarcity. Subsequent technical development and market effort enabled them to establish their own identity, particularly the granular vegetable *vanaspati* in India.

British firms tried to compete in this edible export trade but never got very far, so that Rotterdam was the trade's Unilever centre and it represented almost the whole of Unilever Export N.V.'s business. The trade in 1946 was still in the bar soap era and the growing marketing skills of Unilever Export Limited could do nothing to move it. In fact it had lacked the essentials for the emergence of a Gossage to found it on a trademark recognizable by the consumer and of a Lever to develop it with proprietary specialities. The trade was highly competitive and, as it depended greatly on price, the products came to be packed mainly in the container which was as big as could be conveniently handled, readily recognized, and was cheaply available—the standard forty-gallon kerosene tin. There might be a picturesque label on the tin but identification ceased when the contents were scooped out on to a palm leaf or poured into the customer's own bottle or empty cigarette tin. Smaller containers meant a much higher price to the consumer and that was out of the question. Nor was there, until recent times, any technical edge on which a proprietary brand could be successfully balanced.

Limited could not give much help to N.V. but the link formed by the establishment of the sister companies developed into a close and steady interchange of ideas and knowledge between people selling different articles by differing methods but to the same sort of consumers. This proved to be so valuable that companies exporting Unilever consumer products from France, Spain, Portugal and Australia were all subsequently linked to the original Limited and N.V. twins by means of a Central Export Division in London the Chairman of which was also the Chairman of Unilever Export Limited.

I was proud of being Chairman of Unilever Export Limited (from 1952 to 1961) and I intensely enjoyed it. I was working with men I knew and who knew their job backwards. Their initiative had been oppressed in the conditions of the thirties and regulated out of existence during the war. All they needed was the opportunity and the confidence to use their own judgment and knowledge. Post-war conditions provided the opportunity and I believe I provided the confidence.

We worked well together, happily and with success. And while they worked with all their strength they also passed on to the next generation the knowledge and experience they had gained in the ups and downs of the twenties and thirties and something of the determination that those hard years had wrought within them.

As Managing Director of Unilever Export Limited I was the spearhead of the discussions with the sister N.V. Company. Just before I went to my first meeting with them, and incidentally my first visit to Rotterdam, Arthur Hartog—then an Overseas Contact Director—sent for me and said that he wanted to advise me on how to deal with my Dutch colleagues. 'You must always agree with them if at all possible, even you must stretch a point to do so—but if you cannot possibly agree, you must say "no", and stick to it.' On my return two days later he sent for me again and asked how I had got on. While we were talking his phone rang and it was obvious that he was talking to Rotterdam. He finished his conversation in English by saying, 'If Mr Knox said "no", he meant "no",' and put the receiver down with a broad smile.

I always greatly enjoyed my visits to Rotterdam and particularly valued in later years the support I had from my Dutch colleagues on the Board. By those with whom I worked closely as fellow members of the Overseas Committee my wife and I were accorded a lasting, affectionate and generous friendship which has given us much happiness. The retirement present I received from my Dutch colleagues could not have been more thoughtfully chosen— a beautifully framed map of Scotland 'Performed by John Speed'.

Malaya

During the 1930s our soap trade to Malaya had been static at about 2–3,000 tons a year, and although this represented nearly 100 per cent of the soap exported from the United Kingdom to Malaya it was obviously becoming an ever decreasing share of the total market which was expanding through local manufacture, based on plentiful supplies of cheap coconut oil. Roger Heyworth, then Chairman of the Company in Shanghai, had visited Malaya in 1941 to examine the situation and recommended the building of a factory for both soap and edible oils in Telok Anson, a small port twenty-five miles up the Perak river and 1½ hours 'pushful driving' from Ipoh. It was the main import and export point for Lower Perak, small coastal boats linking it with Penang and a branch line linking it to the main railway system. The invasion of Malaya prevented the carrying out of this project.

In mid-1946 I was present when contact directors were considering the Malayan situation and it was decided that someone should go out to up-date the Heyworth report in the light of the post-war situation of which little was known. The question was, who could do the job? Ned Quin, Head of Technical Division, who was sitting next to me said, 'Here's somebody who could do it,' and so I got my first post-war overseas assignment. J. D. Buxton, Head of the margarine works in Bromborough, accompanied me for what for both of us was a most interesting and also extremely uncomfortable two months. We travelled there and back by flying boat and on the bus going down to Poole I sat next to a Civil Servant who asked me from what department I came. I told him I did not come from any department but from Unilever. 'But,' he said, 'only top priority people are allowed on this flight.' I replied that I was aware of that and that my colleague and I were top priority. He looked at me in disconsolate wonderment.

But top priority meant nothing to the Singapore hotels and we spent the first night sharing a room in Raffles Hotel with four members of a visiting jazz band. With the fan not working (of course no air conditioning) and large holes in the mosquito net, it was not easy to get to sleep; and it was impossible to stay asleep when our bedroom companions arrived at about 2.00 a.m. and proceeded to drink beer, eat chocolates, and talk about the seamy side of their trade. The following day, with appropriate baksheesh, we were able to arrange a small room in the old part of the hotel for our exclusive use, and though we found that the gutters outside our room served the dual purpose of dealing with the regular rain water and as a race track for the local rats, we did at least not have nocturnal reminiscences of an itinerant jazz band.

Rice, the staple diet of Malaya, was forbidden to Europeans. This was not unreasonable as the rice ration for a male was $1\frac{1}{2}$ catties (2 lb) per week and less for women and children. The normal consumption would be about $1\frac{1}{2}$ catties per day. Hotels were not very earnest in their search for alternatives and the food was frankly awful in Singapore, though a little better in Malaya where the chicken population had evidently survived the Japanese occupation.

In matters other than accommodation and hotel food, we did not suffer greatly from prevailing acute shortages. Our working base was the Singapore office of United Exporters Limited, the only inconvenience of which was that it was on the third or fourth floor of the building and the Japanese had removed the lift ropes. There was a staff of half a dozen Chinese clerks and a broker, all glad to be back in employment after the war. The Head Clerk, Cheong, and the broker, Kho, were towers of strength.

Kho was particularly valuable in the matter of shortages. On our arrival in the office he asked us if we wanted anything. 'Whisky? Gin? Cigarettes?' All these were unobtainable in the shops. I said I was very interested in cigarettes. 'What brand—Players?' This was the scarcest brand. Within the hour I had 1,000 Players on my desk. Later we asked the Chief Government Analyst if he could do some simple tests for us involving the use of beeswax. He said he would have been delighted to do so but that there was no beeswax in Singapore. 'Kho—have you ever heard of beeswax?' Shake of head. 'Can you get some?' Nod. 'How much?' 'About a pound or two.'

Next morning to his utter astonishment we delivered 5 lb of beeswax to the analyst and got our tests done.

The situation in the whole of Malaya had changed fundamentally since the Heyworth report. Before the war, though the area was nominally divided into two, the Straits Settlements— Singapore and Penang, and the Federated and Unfederated Malay States—the mainland, everything in fact radiated from Singapore. The Governor of the Straits Settlements was also High Commissioner for the Malay States. European firms mostly had their head offices in Singapore and branches on the mainland. Singapore was thus the centre of Government, the main port for Malaya and the main trading centre for the whole of South-East Asia. Singapore was a bustling international centre of activity, essentially British but mainly inhabited by Chinese. The mainland was a quiet backwater, essentially agricultural and Malayan. The war disturbed both.

The post-war proposal was that there should be four separate entities within (British) Malaysia under the Governor General: Singapore; Malayan Union, including Penang; British North Borneo; and Sarawak.

Singapore had lost its predominant position but the White Paper recognized that 'Singapore requires separate treatment. It is a centre of entrepôt trade on a very large scale and has economic and social interests distinct from those of the mainland.'

Already in 1946 there were clear signs of the separateness of Singapore and signs also that Malaya (the mainland) would wish to stand on its own feet. We concluded:

From our point of view we must regard Singapore as definitely separated, commercially, from the Union, preserving a separate immediate economic policy and enjoying no favours from the Union that are not accorded to the Empire as a whole.

We studied the economic situation and prospects and, as Government had not got as far as publishing figures, we had to depend on interviews and such Roneo-ed statistics as were available. Everybody from the Governors of Singapore and of the Malayan Union downwards willingly talked to us and of course we had close contacts, through our agents (the main merchant firms), with the business community. Even our soap-making competitors received us hospitably and Mr Ng, the proprietor of Lam Soon, gave us information about what had happened to copra and coconut oil during the Japanese occupation when he had 'gone underground'.

We were particularly interested in the copra position as coconut oil had been the mainstay of the soap (and edible oil) business in Singapore, and the prospects for copra generally were of importance to buyers at home anxious to increase purchases of edible oils. Pre-war exports from Singapore/Malaya had been of the order of 200,000 tons a year, a lot of it from the Singapore entrepôt trade.

The immediate situation was one of shortage.

There had been a notable increase in local consumption partly due to increased population and partly to lack of alternative edible and lighting oils. Copra cake was selling at almost the price of the copra itself as it was the only substitute for rice bran, the standard feed for pigs. We saw no immediate prospect of an exportable surplus and, as we had a strong feeling that Singapore's entrepôt trade would not return in the pre-war volume, we took a fairly bearish long term view too. For our own purposes coconut oil was not so important as it was to our local soap-making competitors. The palm oil prospects were good—little damage had been done by the Japanese to the estates and all we needed to do if we established local manufacture was to ensure that the Malayan Government would, when necessary, allow for our requirements when calculating their 'surplus to local requirements' which they had contracted to sell to the U.K. Ministry of Food.

The fact that Malaya was a source of supply of our main raw material—oil—whereas Singapore could only import, was one of the factors in favour of Malaya for our proposed factory. But what we mainly had in mind was that Malaya was bound to impose customs duties for revenue purposes and such duties would undoubtedly apply to goods made in Singapore, whereas Singapore would wish to remain a free port for everything except its main revenue producers—tobacco, alcohol, and petrol. Also, Malaya would eventually be the bigger market for our goods with a population of 5,000,000 against Singapore's 1,000,000.

So we agreed firmly with Roger Heyworth that Malaya was the right place for the factory in spite of the many obvious immediate advantages of Singapore.

The main reasons for Roger Heyworth's choice of the somewhat remote Telok Anson was that it was the only place in Malaya with both reasonable communications and a supply of water in industrial quantities. No public water scheme in Malaya had ever been dreamed of on the basis of industrial use and most of the towns were short of supply anyway in spite of the enormous rainfall.

A subsidiary reason, and one which had put the balance of costs in favour of Telok Anson against Singapore, was that great logging activities in the area made available large quantities of scrap wood and sawdust as a very cheap fuel. Our enquiries showed that this 1941 logging had been exceptional but that Malayan coal from the mine near Kuala Lumpur would be a not too costly alternative.

The water situation remained critical. In spite of high and low level enquiries it seemed that only Telok Anson could be sure of an adequate supply of water (from the river) which had been found both by analysis and experience to be economically treatable.

Having decided on locations we could then proceed to estimate costs of local manufacture and distribution, and finally an estimate of sales and profits from the proposed venture. We found Telok Anson only marginally cheaper than Singapore as a base of supply for the whole market but much cheaper than the U.K., in spite of the fact that at that time there was no import duty (actually there were no imports from U.K. either, owing to soap rationing).

With local manufacture we would be able to regain the initiative we had lost to Singapore competitors in the late thirties and probably increase our 25 per cent pre-war share of the soap trade to 50 per cent.

The project also included local manufacture of edible oils,

margarine, etc., and our estimate of profit was £70,000 p.a. before tax compared with about £15,000 pre-war. This comparison frightened us a bit so we hedged behind generalization by saying that current shortages made circumstances favourable but that even in 'normal' conditions a local factory would enable us to rebuild our business in a market which was bound to expand and that we would make a normal rate of profit therefrom.

We cabled these findings to London and promised full data in our report. The response I recorded in my diary for 24th October, 1946; 'Cable from London saying we need not delay our departure. Both B. and I most thankful as we have had enough and could not easily have wound ourselves up again.'

It had been a strenuous two months. Apart from the discomforts of climate, travel, and living conditions we had had to assemble and fit together a very large jigsaw, and in view of the almost complete dearth at home of up-to-date statistics about Malaya we felt it desirable to put in order and record all the data we had sifted. Our report had seventy schedules, many of them of double foolscap size. As there was no paper or typewriter of this size available, the job of typing two halves of a statement and gumming them together was laborious to say the least.

Kho, Cheong and their small staff worked day and night (assisted at night, as was not unusual amongst Chinese office staff, by various unpaid brothers and cousins). When it was finished we invited them all, brothers and cousins included, to a Chinese dinner. We asked Kho to arrange it. 'Black market?' 'Yes'.

We enjoyed a convivial evening on whisky, warm champagne and beer and a twelve-course meal which included pig's stomach in groundnuts, shark's fin, bird's nest soup, and Bawal fish.

On a later visit Sidney van den Bergh was able to persuade the authorities that there was a suitable factory site in Kuala Lumpur. During our visit there had been reluctance to see Kuala Lumpur as other than a capital and centre of administration, and also some religious objection to the use of the river water for industrial purposes. But reluctance and objection did not stand against the growing realization of the need to industrialize Malaya, and our decision to invest in the future of Malaya at a time of difficulty was welcomed. The plan to build in Kuala Lumpur instead of in unknown Telok Anson was no doubt well received by the staff concerned, the senior members of which were among the first, if not the first, residents of Bukit Kenny which quickly became a very desirable residential area. The factory started in 1951, and soon became a very successful operation.

Nigeria

Early in 1948 I visited what was then called the West African Soap Company in Apapa near Lagos. It was my first visit to Africa and the first to an overseas company for the purpose of reviewing the business. The Company had been started in the early twenties but had never prospered, even though on the face of it it should have done so with palm oil for soap-making practically on its doorstep. But soap was a valuable staple in the operations of the big West African merchants, mostly based on Merseyside. In the depressed trading conditions of the twenties and thirties merchants, and shipping companies, were prepared to handle it, and U.K soapmakers prepared to make it, at virtually no profit rather than lose the tonnage. The Soap Company, as it became known in Nigeria, might get cheap palm oil, but U.K. makers could call on world supplies of all manner of fats and oils, some of them sure to be cheaper than palm. The Soap Company had to import chemicals, etc., buying them in small quantities: U.K. makers had them in bulk near at hand and cheaply. In addition the merchants had a hold over the channels of distribution in Nigeria which the little Soap Company was powerless to loosen.

The boot moved to the other foot when war conditions put a stop to U.K. soap exports and the Soap Company found itself under Government controls bursting its seams to produce 10,000 tons p.a. to try to satisfy the requirements of the Gold Coast as well as Nigeria. This was still the situation at the time of my visit but the outlook for the Soap Company had fundamentally changed. The greatly increased range and quality of merchandise which would be required to satisfy the post-war Nigerian public made it unlikely that either merchants or shipping companies would be desperate to ship bar soap from the United Kingdom, and competition from other sources was unlikely.

When the merchants had held the trade in their hands they had required soaps of different qualities, different sizes and bearing their own names and marks. This kept soap as a simple trade staple with no distinctive brand. Under Government control a bar of good quality and standard size, stamped with one brand name (Key) had been produced and sold throughout Nigeria and the Gold Coast. Key soap had thus become known to the public, and as Nigerians, like most other peoples in the world, are strongly inclined towards the product they know, Key had acquired consumer goodwill. A classic example of preference for the known make was current while I was in Nigeria on this visit: a second-hand Raleigh bicycle sold at a higher price than a new one of any other make.

As we looked to the future of the West African Soap Company we knew that we now had a business which was on a firm foundation and had an individuality of its own peeping out from under the overshadowing cloak of the big merchants, and that there was scope in Nigeria for the development of something other than just a bar soap business.

Before I could help with plans for that development I had to know something of the pattern of distribution so I went on a 3,000-mile tour of the country, mainly by road, only the first fifty miles of which were metalled. The rest were red dust. A diary entry from that time read: 'The worst day yet. 250 miles of twists, turns, narrow bridges, slides, "drifts", bumps, dust, heat and uncertainty because of lack of a map and poor road signs.'

It was an uncomfortable journey but valuable. These were my necessarily superficial impressions of Nigeria nearly a generation ago:

The most notable impression I got was as to the standard of life. Judged on cash income this is admittedly low, but in fact the people are generally well clad (except on the Plateau where the pagans do not, by custom, dress at all and in the Tiv country on the Benue where the whole standard of life is low) and they are certainly better fed than in other tropical countries I have visited. I know that on strictly dietetic standards the balance of the diet in certain parts of the country is not good, but there is no superficial evidence of lack of food as such. You do not normally see obviously underfed people, nor, outside the main towns, notably Lagos itself, do you see beggars and 'hangers on': even in Lagos there are fewer by far than in, say, Kingston, Jamaica. The boys in the villages shout for 'dash' but this is in fun and without the beggar's whine.

Except in the South-East, the women do not adopt European dress, but their own dress is quite splendid and kept scrupulously clean and fresh looking. In the North the standard of cleanliness is not so high owing to the shortage of water (and the ample supply of dust).

Housing throughout the country is poor looking—mainly of baked mud, roofed in either corrugated iron or thatch. Even Ibadan, the biggest African town, is just a particularly large collection of mud houses. But baked mud is the building material of the country and many Government Rest Houses are of this material, and nice and cool they are. The appearance of the housing, however, is that of extreme poverty and one gets tired of the ever wavy line where one would dearly love to see a straight one. But it is often a matter of appearance only as can be realized when one sees coming out of these houses Market Women of evident substance and boys in clean school uniform.

I have read that, through malnutrition and debilitating disease the people of Nigeria lack stamina. The impression I got, however, was one of activity. Throughout my journey, even in those parts which look pretty blank on the map, there was hardly a mile that was not dotted with people, mainly women-folk, striding purposefully along with their quite extraordinary loads on their heads to and from the market, to and from the well, or to and from the fields, but always on the move. In the Southern Provinces the roads are not dotted with people but crowded. Only by seeing this all along the roads, and such processes as the hand cracking of palm kernels in the villages, can one appreciate the tremendous amount of sheer hard work involved in bringing produce to market: produce not only for export but also for local consumption.

So the impression I got was one of activity and movement, not of lethargy.

They were a people undoubtedly on the move, and the West African Soap Company would have to move, too. We planned for active development of all phases of the business particularly in marketing and in personnel policy.

By far the biggest of the merchants dealing with West Africa was the United Africa Company which, like the Soap Company, was a Unilever subsidiary. But whereas within the Unilever universe the Soap Company was a little star which had not twinkled very brightly, the United Africa Company was a constellation: shining particularly brightly at that time, a large group in itself, managed separately from Unilever up to Board level.

In 1948 the United Africa Company was still mainly a typical merchant company such as had pioneered and developed the worldwide trade of the United Kingdom and Holland from the days of the East India Company. These companies specialized in areas, not in types of produce: they bought anything available in the countries in which they operated and sold anything to those countries that the local people could be persuaded to buy.

Such of these merchant companies as have survived—there are many in different parts of the world—have gradually had to expand their operations into local industrial or commercial enterprises as economic opportunity has offered or nationalist sentiment has encouraged. In this phase of development, which came later in tropical Africa than elsewhere, the Lever interests from which U.A.C. sprang were pioneers. They founded plantations in the Congo and elsewhere. They had soap factories in Nigeria and the Congo. The results during the lean years of the 1920s and '30s did not encourage further moves in this direction at that time, but since the end of World War Two great strides have been made.

In 1948 the United Africa Company was still predominantly a big merchant, owned by Unilever but managed by its own Board, some members of which were also members of the Unilever Board. The West African Soap Company was one of the many overseas companies, mostly originally Lever companies, occupied in manufacturing and selling soap and edible fats and responsible to the Overseas Committee. The overall interests of the United Africa Company were of course of greater importance than those of the small soap company.

The interests of the two however began to diverge seriously when we started to look forward to marketing and personnel development. In marketing we were guided by the policy which had successfully built up the overseas companies, namely to get as close as possible to the ultimate consumer and to the trade that supplied her.

As to the consumer:

We have means of effective advertising to consumers who are discerning in choice, conservative in their habits, and whose standard of life is likely to improve. In these circumstances the policy I recommend for the W.A.S.Co. is the long term development of 'Sunlight' and 'Lifebuoy' as the leading proprietaries of the business.

And on contact with the trade:

A problem closely related to trade margins is our direct contact with the trading community as distinct from the Big Merchants. At the moment we maintain our policy of supplying only those customers who bought from us before the war, which, to all intents and purposes, means that we are restricting the trade to the Big Merchant houses. We can maintain this policy whilst there is an acute shortage of soap and, in fact, we have agreed with U.A.C. that we will do so. The time will come, however, when it will be politic to supply to all potential customers of substance and, indeed, I believe it will be necessary to do so in order to widen our distribution to the full.

It will certainly be a long time before we can contemplate trying to do without the assistance in our distribution of the Big Merchant firms and until that time comes all we can do is to run along their lines of policy trying as far as possible to remove soap from the immediate field of bargaining. This, in my opinion, will be of special importance when we introduce toilet soaps and thus go still further into the proprietary field.

The West African trade was still at the stage where distribution was the dominant factor in selling. You had to get the product down the distribution channel to the village market, and then if it was good and properly priced it would sell. Advertising to the consumer was in its infancy and consisted mainly of posters, which in the circumstances were specially valuable but necessarily had a somewhat limited coverage and life. The big merchants controlled the channels because they were virtually the sole source of the goods and of the credit that helped the flow.

A brand with a strong consumer demand is a good call-bird in the barter/bargaining trading process, and competition in this process tends to reduce the merchant's profit margin on the product concerned. In these basic trading conditions a big merchant is not keen to use the strength of his distributive organization on behalf of such products unless he is the sole agent for the product or by reason of his dominant position has some exclusive price advantage from the manufacturer. If he has such exclusive advantages his competitors would not be likely to support the brand, so either way the distribution channels open to the brand would be limited.

The Lever policy had always been to appeal direct to the consumer by advertising and sell direct to any dealer prepared to buy on the terms published in the price list. So when we contemplated following this policy in Nigeria, to the extent even of selling direct to Nigerian traders, the idea did not appeal strongly to the United Africa Company.

On personnel matters we had obviously generally to follow the lead of the United Africa Company. The Trade Unions, beginning to feel their strength, knew quite well that the two companies were closely allied and that the smaller one would reasonably have to avoid anything which might have repercussions on the other. Further up the scale ideas did begin seriously to diverge (e.g. in connection with young men out from Europe for the first time). To the United Africa Company they were 'first timers' being tried out and learning the business. To the Soap Company they were likely to be skilled soap-makers and other technicians exercising their skill, and also engaged in training Nigerian staff.

Obviously our marketing and personnel policies would take a long time to work out and we could not in the process do anything that would dramatically adversely affect the interests of United Africa Company, but it seemed to me that I should discuss our ideas with the Head of the United Africa Company in Nigeria, the redoubtable A. G. Dawson, in order to explain our policy with a view to avoiding any serious clash.

My private note of the interview ended: '[Mr Dawson] agrees that U.A.C. Rest Houses could do with waste-paper baskets. It was nice to get full agreement on something.'

Having planned a forward marketing policy, I had also to consider what developments would be required in the Apapa soap factory. I had read a book about soap-making and had some knowledge of the main cost factors involved, but my only experience of the inside of a soapworks had been a walk round the visitors' gallery at Port Sunlight when I was a schoolboy. I made a bold approach to the Apapa Factory Manager, Colin Black, who, like all the other members of the management, I had not met till I arrived in Nigeria. I told him that I knew nothing about factories, and could he help me? I could not have been more willingly or better instructed and after a few hot and strenuous days I understood the workings and the problems of the factory and could, with his agreement, make recommendations as to its further development.

The recommendations of my report were accepted and the West African Soap Company, which soon became Lever Brothers Nigeria Limited, was launched on to its development course, which it has since followed through good times and bad. When I made my report total sales were about 10,000 tons, which included substantial quantities for the Gold Coast. When I retired, sales, wholly in Nigeria, were 24,000 tons of soaps and detergents, of which half were in proprietary brands, and some 1,000 tons of margarine. Their total sales value was £6,000,000, and trading profit £1,000,000.

My report so impressed Roger Heyworth, then an Overseas Contact Director, that he passed it to his brother, the Chairman, to read. This no doubt lead to his calling me aside one day and telling me that I should know that the problems of United Africa Company were quite different from those of a company selling proprietary brands, and that the management of that company were capable of dealing with those problems without my assistance.

Toilet Preparations Survey

Shortly after my visit to Nigeria I was closely concerned with a report which was a landmark in Unilever affairs. It dealt with the world-wide trade in toilet preparations: that is to say, toothpaste, hair preparations, perfumery and cosmetics generally.

When the Old Man was building his soap business it was not usual for the household soapmakers to make toilet soap. They frequently made soap chips for the toilet soap trade, but the milling of these chips into toilet soap, during which process the colour and perfume are added, was considered to be a specialist's business. It was in any case comparatively small, toilet soap being a luxury sold through chemists, not grocers. It was however an expanding business and the Old Man made a direct attack on it with Plantol and Velvet Skin soaps. Plantol was 'made entirely from vegetable oils', and advertised on the theme of 'fruit and flowers'. It is worth repeating a comment on the actual advertising made by Sydney Gross who was, next to the Old Man himself, the head marketing man (though not so called) at the time:

> I am sorry to say it is disappointing . . . forcible enough, but not elegant . . . A pamphlet on Toilet Soap needs picturesque hand-ling, something about the tropic climates in which the materials are produced, the care that is exercised in refining the oils, the flowers that are picked by the women of the South on fields full of colour and beauty. That is rather the line that should have been taken, and not a treatise on perspiration, sweat and pores.

Velvet Skin had at one time the theme 'Makes Mummy's skin like mine'.

These soaps were not very successful partly because Lever Brothers lacked an entrée into the chemist distribution channels, which the toilet soap makers had developed for themselves by branching out into the whole field of toilet preparations, cosmetics and perfumery. One of the most prominent operators in this field at the time was Vinolia which the Old Man bought in 1906. Vinolia had an enormous range of products, soundly based for the luxury trade at which it aimed, on really good perfumes and most splendid packaging. At the peak of its toilet soap range was Vinolia Vestal Soap, believed to be used by the Queen, retailing at 15/- (75p) per tablet (bath size) which was cradled in white satin in a gold lettered, hand-made, oval box. The second step down was a mere 12/6 (62½p) per tablet—Otto of Roses, supplies of which certainly did go to the Palace. In this bath soap range, but at a more modest price, was Boracic and Cold Cream Soap which survived certainly in Thailand and South Africa until very recent times, and in my recollection shared with Lifebuoy and Pears Soap the distinction of providing the pervading smell of respectable Edwardian bathrooms.

Vinolia must have been one of the first sellers of toothpaste and its range of cosmetics included many different talcum powders, one of which rejoiced in the name of Bonnie Prince Charlie with suitable tartan décor. There were face powders, creams, etc., which in the price list were supported by a forerunner of the 'film-star' appeal—testimonials from and photographs of reigning beauties of stage and concert platform. I remember Gladys Cooper and Clara Butt. Pomade Hongroise was sold for men's moustaches. There were bath salts, a pine tar shampoo and, the only real survivor, Lypsyl.

So Lever Brothers was in the toilet preparations business. Over the next twenty years other companies in the same business were purchased only one of which had no base in the toilet soap trade— namely the International Icilma Trading Corporation (Chairman, L. H. Hartland-Swann), which during the First World War had made a success of selling reasonably priced creams to the vastly increased market of young women wage-earners, thus helping to found the mass market for toilet preparations, and, though it was not perhaps recognized at the time, sapping the foundations of the traditional practitioners of elegance.

In 1925 Lever Brothers had fifteen companies selling toilet preparations in the U.K., most of them in competition with each other. Ten of them sold tooth cleaning products. Only one has survived as a live name in the business (Gibbs), though the names of Vinolia and Erasmic are still used in some parts of the world, and Atkinson's maintains the Bond Street image in the light perfumery field, though no longer from Bond Street itself. All the other names are fading memories, though I still use as my stud-box a tin which originally contained solidified brilliantine sold by the Crown Perfumery Company Limited, London, Paris and New York (but really Gossages, Widnes). Just after the Second World War the Pepsodent Company was bought in U.S.A. where there was also a temporary flirtation with Harriet Hubbard Ayer which begot a small offshoot in France, since grown to active independence.

Mass marketing of toilet preparations eroded the elegance, and mass marketing of toilet soaps removed the cornerstone of the type of 'toilet company' that Lever Brothers had bought. Although we more than held our own in the toilet soaps with Lux, we failed to keep more than a toehold on the preparations band-wagon, with the result that when things had settled down a few years after the Second World War it was an open question whether Unilever should stay in this business at all.

One day about halfway through 1950 the Chairman, Geoffrey Heyworth, called me in and told me it had been decided to appoint a small committee to make a world survey of the toilet preparations business. Four people had been proposed as members, two of whom I knew well, the other two slightly. What did I think of these men for such a survey? I was gratified to be asked for my opinion and gave it. I was about to leave the room when he said, 'By the way you are to be Chairman of the committee.' This was a surprise, as my experience of the business was limited to the encouragement of others to try to hold together and build upon some incoherent scraps of goodwill that had survived the mass onslaught in some of the less sophisticated markets of the world.

The committee was appointed in June 1950 consisting of: Roger Francis—Thibaud Gibbs, France; Frank Davies—Pepsodent, England; Denzil Budgett-Meakin—Export, U.K.; Paul Fabricius —National Management, Denmark; and Andrew Knox (Chairman)—Export/O.S.C. The terms of reference were given in a letter from Geoffrey Heyworth to all the Companies concerned:

They have been asked to review the whole range of our toilet preparations trade and to make suggestions as to the lines and fields in which contraction or further development is desirable

and to consider whether existing organizational structures are
satisfactory or require modification.

It was emphasized that we should try to gain first hand knowledge of the situation and that we would have to travel widely. We
would, however, have to continue to hold full responsibility for the
jobs we were currently doing. It was expected that our job would
take six or nine months: in fact it took a year, our Report being
dated 23rd June, 1951. The survey was a great success and the
foundations of success were laid at the very beginning in two brief
incidents.

Roger Francis was Managing Director (though that may not have
been his title) of Thibaud Gibbs, Paris, a company then owned
half by the Thibaud family and half by Unilever, through Gibbs. It
had a long and successful record in the toilet preparations business
with which Roger had been associated for many years. There were
few men better known than he was within Unilever and none better
liked. He was a joyous companion and, in Paris especially, a willing
and generous host. Though not the most senior member of the
Unilever toilet preparations management, he would certainly have
been accepted as the doyen, if there had been such a position. He
was greatly respected by all members of the survey committee
including me. At the very beginning of our first meeting he said he
was sure that everyone would and could express their views with the
utmost frankness, but so far as he was concerned the Chairman's
ruling would be final. The others followed him.

We then got down to the two first steps: to agree exactly what
would and would not be comprehended within our survey and to
make a travel programme. In travelling we decided that we would,
so far as possible, 'hunt in couples' but that we would all visit
North America where half the total world trade (excluding Russia
and China) took place.

Visits to North America had always been a difficult and sometimes a contentious matter. Everyone wanted to go there and
unless the floodgates were held firmly our American friends would
have been overwhelmed. As I subsequently learned, when I held
the flood-gates, there is no limit to ingenuity in devising incon-
trovertible reasons for a visit to the U.S.A.

Our travelling plan, covering thirty countries, had to go before the Special Committee as our visits crossed every boundary within the then geographical structure of directional authority and I knew that, just at that time, visits to U.S.A. were a particularly delicate matter. To have a party of five making the visit was certainly a bit of a 'facer'.

It was the only occasion when I felt that I might have to outface Geoffrey Heyworth. He knew that I realized that it was a difficult matter for him, but I knew that he recognized the fact that to agree would do more than anything else to put the stamp of authority on the activities of the survey.

He agreed. I heaved a sigh of relief and we all went forward to the most strenuous and probably the most enjoyable twelve months of our business careers.

Questionnaires from Head Office are not normally greeted with enthusiasm but ours was an exception and we had the maximum possible co-operation from toilet preparations managements throughout the world. The reason for this was simple. Unilever toilet preparation sales were only about a tenth of detergent sales and profits usually less. It was recognized, though never admitted, that toilet preparations were the poor relation of the detergent business, and managements usually hoped to be promoted out of it. Visitors to a country would, of course, show great interest in and enthusiasm for the toilet preparations section of the local business, but it all too frequently happened that these manifestations were programmed for the last afternoon of the final day of the visit.

To have the prospect of visitors from London actually dealing with toilet preparations first electrified the managements concerned and the wide scope of our questionnaires made some of them learn more about their business than they had hitherto dreamed of. We were thus enabled to base our survey on what was probably the first detailed and complete estimate of the total world trade (outside Communist countries) in the products concerned.

Following Roger Francis' *démarche*, our report would be unanimous, and we determined that it would also be clear and definite on every point. We might be judged wrong but we would not be blamed for being indecisive. During our discussions our leading question was, 'Is it Unilever business?' followed by 'If so, how?'

We dealt with about thirty different products in seven categories, each of us undertaking to write the draft of our report on one or two categories. Thus we had seven drafts in five styles. Frank Davies and I spent three days re-writing them so that they would read as a whole and then we all assembled one Saturday morning and carefully edited the whole thing. We were busy from 9.0 a.m. till 8.0 p.m., with a sandwich lunch at a café in the bomb-damaged building by Blackfriars Station. When we had finished we walked to the Savoy and made up for the sandwich lunch.

The following is an extract from our report:

We are in the Toilet Preparations business . . . should we go on? The answer is 'yes', so long as we do so with a clear appreciation of what is, and what is not, our business. The trade goes through distributive channels we understand: the market is susceptible of development by advertising: the technical know-how should not be beyond our grasp.

Although we are in the business, we are in it in a very disjointed way with a heterogeneous collection of products; we have developed no Concern dogma on the matter such as guides us in our main Detergent and Edible business. Admittedly, the Unilever dogma on Detergents and Edibles is unwritten, but there is . . . a profound and widely spread understanding of the business, and an accepted method of approach to its problems. . . . These are founded on tradition, and are continuously being learned and developed by successful experience. In the Toilet Preparations business we lack the tradition of successful experience. Our business needs pulling together and re-enthusing. It needs to be set on a new course the main points of which we have attempted to plot, and to be energized by adequate Research facilities, working to an agreed plan. This can only be done centrally, and to meet the situation we propose the establishment of an Executive created specially for the purpose.

This, we know, strikes across the structure of the Unilever Organization which is based on decentralized initiative with guidance from the centre . . . but we believe that while our International concept for tackling the Toilet Preparations business is being built up we will need a certain amount of what

Carlyle described as Cromwell's method—'compelling them to accept it voluntarily' . . . The function of the Executive would be initiation rather than control: an engine rather than a brake.

The situation requires inspiration and strong leadership from the centre. So led and so inspired, we can, if we put our mind to it, look for a turnover in toilet preparations of £25,000,000 per annum in five years' time, with a profit of £2,500,000.

This should be Unilever business.

Our recommendations were accepted and the report was greeted almost with acclamation. Within a couple of hours of its general circulation, Frank Samuel, Chairman of United Africa Company, who barely knew me, sent for me and said that he knew nothing of the toilet preparations business but that our report was one of the best he had ever read.

It took longer to reach the sales target of £25,000,000 than we forecast and longer still to reach the profit, but there is no doubt that toilet preparations are now firmly established as a growing and profitable section of Unilever.

Ization

When the Old Man started to establish what he called Foreign and Imperial Associated Companies it was natural that key personnel should be sent out from home. Only a few men (including a soap-boiler) were required for countries which were already industrialized, but when it came to countries which we would now refer to as 'developing', a whole range of staff were 'expatriated' for the purpose. Thus, when Lever Brothers (South Africa) was started in Durban in 1911, all necessary staff from factory foreman and clerical 'backbencher' upwards were sent out from Port Sunlight, and I have been told, though I cannot vouch for it, that a gang of expert women soap-wrappers went to teach the African workmen. In 1913, though it is almost impossible to believe it now, twenty-five men went out to staff the small company in Japan, including five foremen, four clerks, one bookkeeper, three fitters—and a soapboiler.

Men sent to South Africa, Australia and New Zealand were expected to settle there and were granted one free return passage with wives and families after ten years.

Men sent to less developed countries, usually tropical, expected to spend the rest of their careers as expatriates with terms of service varying from country to country, leave being normally a sixth of time served abroad. For China it was five years abroad and ten months' leave, India three years and six months' leave. In West Africa, where wives and families did not go, eight to nine months were spent abroad and three to four on leave.

After the initial staffing the usual pattern of staff development was that natives should be trained to take over at all junior levels as the business expanded, and the original staff, mainly young men, would be promoted ahead of them.

The idea that a native could carry responsibility and exercise authority on level terms with expatriates was not one which was readily accepted, and that he might one day be in authority over an expatriate was too shocking even to think about. (I excuse myself for using in this context the word 'native' now debased by colour connotation, by recalling the story of a viceroy who at a viceregal ball greeted an Indian lady friend, 'Oh, Maharanee, you do look marvellous in your native costume.' She replied, 'Thank you, your Excellency, so do you.')

The traditional pattern for developing overseas companies by means of expatriate staff was quite normal and was in no way special to the Lever business, though I believe that the Unilever policy of Indianization, which had its early beginnings in the 1930s, was a pioneer in this field and was certainly the inspiration for what much later became known within Unilever as *ization*.

It may be worth recording however that the first big move towards ization took place in Japan—and for the wrong reason— to save money. The enterprise was not successful and within two years of its establishment Japanese (at less than half the expatriate salary rates) took over all but ten of the original twenty-five expatriate jobs. Even then there remained two foreman, one clerk, one bookkeeper, a fitter and a soap-boiler. It is also worth recording that the total salary bill for the original twenty-five expatriates would not meet half the cost of one expatriate in Japan now.

From the beginning I was a convinced advocate of Indianization. Having dealt with agents of the calibre of C. M. Gobhai, T. T. Krishnamachari and A. Sankar Iyer, I saw no reason why we could not find and train Indians to manage our business and ultimately trust them with full responsibility for its fortunes. I believed that this was a logical and necessary step within the policy of identifying our overseas companies as closely as possible with the countries in which they operated.

My friend Shaw, the first Chairman of Lever Brothers (India) Ltd, was probably not so enthusiastic as I was. After all, he carried the responsibility for the business. However, he made what has been accepted as the first move when he approved the appointment of a young Indian to the advertising department, but definitely for management, in November 1937. I am sure he was encouraged to take this fateful step by the fact that the Indian was not only a U.K. trained chartered accountant but had been trained in the North— at Manchester. The similar appointments which followed stood the business in good stead when the younger expatriates joined the Forces in 1939–40 and the process of Indianization necessarily accelerated.

During the War when the business was expanding rapidly there was considerable recruitment of Indian staff, so that by the end of the war practically the whole of the middle and junior management were Indians and it was generally accepted that this would continue to be so. Moreover it was slowly, though sometimes reluctantly, beginning to be realized that members of the Indian staff were as capable of carrying the responsibility of senior management as some of their expatriate colleagues, and at less cost to the Company as expatriates had long leave and various allowances for children's education at home etc. To begin with, there was a firm belief that salary scales for Indian staff should be lower than those for expatriates, but as Indian members of the staff began to earn promotion to higher jobs, sometimes ahead of their English colleagues, it became obvious that this attitude to salaries could no longer be maintained.

The Independence of India in 1947 gave a further push to Indianization and it was fortunate that by then it had already become a natural process rather than the somewhat forced implementation of an accepted policy. Roger Heyworth, Cecil Pettit and John Hoskyns-Abrahall had brought understanding, clear and open minds to the problem. They, and one or two other expatriates who joined the Indian business after the war, found themselves working naturally with Indian colleagues of high calibre, their minds free from the lingering prejudice of those who had experienced the glories of the Raj and remembered the full dignity of the Bombay Yacht Club in its prime.

In 1939–40 virtually the whole of our management staff of 150 were expatriates. By 1950, of a similar total of management staff, only 50 were expatriates.

I had not been concerned with India after 1935 until I became a member of the Overseas Committee in 1954 when we were under pressure from the Indian Government, not only to put some of the equity of our companies on to the Indian market but also to accelerate and sharpen our Indianization. T. T. Krishnamachari, the Minister of Commerce and Industry, was in a strong position to exert this pressure as he had known the business from the inside, as agent in Madras, in the early stages of its development. He knew that good sound progress had been made but he did not consider that what was being done reflected the great change that India's independence should make in the whole situation.

When I visited India in 1955 the general position had not materially changed since 1950. Total management was 149 with 52 expatriates. However, I did note a difference in proportions as between senior and other management. Of the total 35 senior managers, 25 were expatriates. Of the total of 114 others, only 27 were expatriates. (The slight increase in the total of expatriates was due to the expansion of the business outrunning the pace of recruitment and training of Indians.)

I noted: 'Indianization is however essentially the creation of Indian Managers, not the getting rid of European ones, and steady progress has been made with this, undoubtedly the more difficult part of the operation.'

Such progress had in fact been made that it was possible to foresee by 'an accelerated natural process' a substantial reduction in the total of expatriates.

The real problem lay in deciding and planning 'to build an

Indian business with some European assistance rather than a
European business with Indian assistance.'

As to deciding, I had no doubts:

> Altogether apart from current nationalist sentiment, I believe it
> to be in our long term interests, as well as in accord with declared
> policy, to Indianize in the true meaning of the word, i.e. to the
> uttermost practical extent. India is probably the most favourable
> field for an experiment in imaginative foresight such as this and
> experience in India will help us in tackling similar problems,
> which are bound to arise elsewhere. We must realise however
> that we add to our risk and our responsibilities . . . but we should
> face these in a sincere attempt to teach and encourage our
> Indian management towards ultimate complete self reliance.

By 1966 there were only 6 expatriates in India out of a total
management of 360.

Since rejoining Overseas I had visited many countries, and it
seemed to me that danger lay ahead elsewhere than in India unless
immediate steps were taken both to increase the recruitment and
training of local staff and to widen that training so that it was aim-
ing to fill the highest posts.

In agreement with my colleagues, I put this matter before a
conference of overseas chairmen early in 1956. I believe that this
was the most significant contribution I made to the Overseas
business, perhaps even to Unilever as a whole, and I hope it may be
of interest to see from the following abridgement of my memorandum the sort of argument which could, and indeed had to be put
forward at that time:

> Our world development policy has always been soundly based
> on the belief that our business fares better if it is operated by a
> local Associated Company which can be identified closely with
> the country in which it operates and it has been part of that
> policy that the company should be managed as far as possible by
> nationals of the country concerned.

So ization is not a new policy for us.

But the emergence since the war of many new independent nations imbued with strong nationalist sentiment, but not well endowed with actual or potential management talent, has made it desirable for us to pursue ization more vigorously and perhaps further than we might hitherto have found convenient. And the more recent and more sudden has been the attainment of nationhood the more vociferous and pressing are the nationalist aspirations of the people and governments concerned and we find ourselves in many countries, where we have large and profitable investments, facing the problem of how to match the management and general structure of our companies with the upsurge of nationalist sentiment. The main difficulties as we foresee them are concerned with management.

Although the initiative in the ization process is in the hands of the management of each individual Company the problem is one which cannot be solved by them alone, but only by the Concern as a whole.

EXTENT OF THE PROBLEM

One main problem lies in what are known as under-developed countries where we have 20 operating units and 33 factories. Our total investment is over £30,000,000: and we employ 22,800 people, mostly nationals of the countries concerned.

We have a great deal at stake in these countries and the continued success of our operations therein, indeed almost our continued existence, depends on our willingness and ability not only to take a lead in their economic development but to keep in step with their political advancement.

THE URGENCY

In many countries already permits are required before a foreigner can be allowed in the country for purposes of employment and there are various limitations as to the type of job he can do.

So we are being prodded, and as our experience already demonstrates that the training of local management is necessarily a long process, if it is to be soundly accomplished, it behoves us to regard the matter as one of over-riding urgency lest we find ourselves compelled somewhere or other to break that continuity of sound, efficient and enterprising management which has built our valuable Overseas business.

HOW FAR HAVE WE GOT

		Management in 'Ization' Countries		
	Expatriates	Others	Total	% Expatriate to Total
1950	265	238	503	53
1955	263	550	813	32

It must be realised that the businesses have expanded during the period and while it may appear that not much progress has been made in substituting nationals for expatriate management the great weight of the expansion has been carried by truly 'local' management. When we realize the effort required to train nationals of some of the countries concerned and at the same time to exert the drive necessary to expand our business it cannot be said that our policy of 'ization' has not been forwarded with both vigour and success.

A good deal of the training has been done locally but we certainly could not have gone so far and with such confidence if we had not had the willing assistance of our home companies, both in the U.K. and Holland. As we look forward to the next stage which is to bring locally employed managers into the very highest positions in our business it becomes even more important that they should be 'Unilever' men in the true sense and not merely good local operators; this we believe to be of fundamental importance. The success of our business depends not only on Company managers operating successfully but on their having the capacity to do so successfully as part of Unilever, drawing willingly and without feeling of inferiority upon the fund of knowledge and experience available within the Concern and being equally prepared to contribute willingly and freely to that fund. To put it bluntly, our task is not only, e.g. to Indianize our business in India but we must also Unileverize the Indians who have positions of authority in that business.

We have, in fact, gone fairly far along the road of 'ization' in spite of what the figures may appear to indicate but we have undoubtedly not yet gone far enough to satisfy either the nationalist aspirations of the countries concerned or the management aspirations of the Overseas Committee. In none of the countries concerned have we yet a national who could represent Unilever at Government level in other than a specialised capacity such as e.g. legal matters. By the same token none of the countries concerned is represented here today by a national of that country.

HOW FAR ARE WE GOING

To satisfy nationalist aspiration, which undoubtedly is the spur in this matter if not the guiding reins, we must be prepared to go the whole way. That is, our companies must be effectively managed and seen to be so, by local nationals.

Under this concept, we could foresee a future Overseas Conference at the level of this one being attended by perhaps Indians, Thais, Indonesians, etc.

This, as I say, would be the result of an ization policy which would accord with the aspirations of rising nationalism and I believe that it would be equally in accord with the interests of Unilever.

Of course it depends on the men concerned and we must believe that we will find such men everywhere; but we could not go ahead unless we are assured that men, of whatever nationality and race, who might attain the highest positions in overseas business would be assured of unreserved acceptance at that level by all colleagues everywhere; any reservation on this would eat at the heart of Unilever as it is today. It can be put clearly to you if I ask if you would feel as free and happy as I hope you are here today if amongst our numbers were some of a different race. Alternatively, but most important, would you, subject to any obvious overriding political consideration, be prepared to welcome to your own country the Chairman from a neighbouring country if he were not of European extraction?

If the answer is in the affirmative, as I believe it will be, then I think there can be no doubt but that our business would benefit from the pursuit of the ization policy as far as it will go. Our companies in each individual country would benefit from being managed by nationals who truly know the country, and the business as a whole would have a broader base of original thought, a wider field from which to recruit senior management and a much more truly international aspect.

That more tact, more patience, more spirit would be required to direct and guide a series of businesses so individually managed is also true, but it would be worth it.

HOW ARE WE GOING TO GET THERE

Most of us here have worked in more than one country and I am sure that we would all agree that that experience has been of great value to us.

In fact, I would go so far as to say that it is only by experiencing Unilever in more than one country that one gains a full appreciation of what Unilever really means.

Moreover, I think you would also agree that your own confidence has been materially increased by having had experience of Unilever in more than one country.

And the building up of confidence is the final step in the training of management for ultimate responsibility in any sphere or country.

When we are considering therefore this final step of giving confidence to those nationals who will assume the highest responsibilities in our Overseas companies should we not take a leaf out of our own experience and arrange that they work for a spell in some country other than their own?

I realize that this is not going to be easy to arrange. We are used to training an Indian or a Pakistani in U.K. or an Indonesian in Holland, but what about giving them a job of responsibility there—even temporarily? It might be possible in some 'inside' job but responsibility means authority and one can well see that there would be limits to what could be done. But supposing we think in still wider terms. Would it not be possible to have an Indian Advertising Manager in Thailand for a period— or a Malay accountant in Indonesia? We may not be quite prepared for that at the moment but surely an interchange between Overseas companies would be possible and might serve our ends as well, if not better than trying always to give experience 'at home'.

If we think of these matters and make our plans accordingly there should be no doubt of our capacity to pursue the policy of 'ization' steadily and with full confidence in our ability to develop nationals as the future top management of our business overseas to the great ultimate benefit of Unilever.

The push that this conference gave to ization was fortunately timed as it coincided with the great development in management training which was taking place at that time, and there was no lack of facilities both within and at the command of Unilever. Equally there was no reluctance to welcome men from Overseas on the many courses that were being established, for all levels of management (indeed it became fashionable to add a little colour). Gradually men from companies all over the world were sent not only to U.K. and Holland but to any Unilever company that could offer the training required. Australia opened its courses to men from the Philippines and Malaya. India, with its own big training programmes welcomed men from surrounding countries and from Africa. Senior men on long periods of special training began to be accompanied by their wives, a step forward which I had not forecast but certainly encouraged, and one might find a Belgian heading a seminar in India or an Indian chairman of a conference in England.

Total Overseas Management of Unilever Companies in Developing Countries.

	Expatriates	Others	Total	% Expatriates
(a) Companies in operation in 1955:				
1955	263	550	813	32
1960	182	1,093	1,275	14
1966	102	1,622	1,724	6
(b) All companies:				
1966	201	2,394	2,595	8

During the ten years following the launch of ization in 1955 some new overseas companies were started and they followed the standard practice of having more expatriates to begin with than they would have when they got going: hence the split in the comparative figures above.

So ization became a natural process, not an astonishment, because the men who came to the top in their own countries were known all over the world. It was not 'a Ghanaian' who became Chairman of Lever Brothers (Ghana) Ltd., it was Myles Hagan. I felt that ization had been successful when in 1961 the young man whose appointment my friend Shaw had blessed in 1937, Prakash Tandon, was appointed Chairman of Hindustan Lever Limited.

9

Travel

I have travelled a lot and although I kept a record of most of my longer journeys I did not usually record mileage. However, a reasonable estimate would be that I have travelled 1,000,000 miles: I have a certificate from B.O.A.C. that I did 250,000 miles on their aircraft. A million miles is not an exceptional figure in these days of commuting by air across the Atlantic and North America. An Australian businessman can also put up a big mileage in the course of his normal work. Travel has lost its glamour and excitement and it is no longer 'a better thing to travel hopefully than to arrive'. The great thing now is to get there.

Some of my travel was in the leisurely days of ship and train and a good deal more in the early developing days of air travel when you certainly had to travel hopefully and were profoundly thankful to arrive.

My first journey abroad was the one already mentioned with the Old Man to the Continent. It may be of interest to recall the itinerary, which was certainly not leisurely—travelling seven nights out of sixteen.

1924	12th August	Dep.	Liverpool Street	8.30 p.m.
	13th ,,	Dep.	Hook of Holland	7.13 a.m.
		Arr.	Hamburg	6.5 p.m.
	14th ,,	Dep.	Hamburg	4.15 p.m.
	,,	Arr.	Berlin	9.4 p.m.
	15th ,,	Dep.	Berlin	10.47 p.m.
	16th ,,	Arr.	Danzig	8.8 a.m.
	17th ,,	Dep.	Danzig	11.28 a.m.
	,,	Arr.	Stettin	7.8 p.m.
	18th ,,	Dep.	Stettin	7.16 p.m.

1924	„	Arr.	Berlin	9.34 p.m.
19th	„	Dep.	Berlin	6.25 p.m.
20th	„	Arr.	Copenhagen	6.11 a.m.
	„	Dep.	Copenhagen	7.20 p.m.
			Malmö	10.7 p.m.
21st	„	Arr.	Nyköping	7.10 a.m.
	„	Dep.	Nyköping	4.46 p.m.
		Arr.	Stockholm	6.50 p.m.
22nd	„	Dep.	Stockholm	9.56 a.m.
	„	Arr.	Christiania	10.37 p.m.
24th	„	Motor to	Fredrikstad	
25th	„	Dep.	Fredrikstad	8.04 p.m.
	„	Arr.	Christiania	10.9 p.m.
		Dep.	Christiania	11.0 p.m.
26th	„	Arr.	Bergen	11.0 a.m.
	„	Dep.	Bergen	12.0 noon
27th	„	Arr.	Newcastle	5.0 p.m.
		Dep.	Newcastle	10.53 p.m.
28th	„	Arr.	King's Cross	5.40 a.m.

It is not worth while to give full details of the mailing list, which gave me some trouble, but I doubt whether the Post Office today could give a better service, in spite of air mail, than this:

Last posting time from New Bridge Street Post Office, London			for delivery at the hotel in:		
1215	13th	August	Hamburg	afternoon	14th
1800	13th	August	Berlin	afternoon	15th
1215	15th	August	Danzig	morning	17th

My second journey was more leisurely, full of excitement, though of quite a different kind, and I suppose could reasonably be said to have had an element of glamour. This was my first of many visits to India, in 1927. H. R. Greenhalgh told me to visit all the main ports twice because, he said, you get to know a place better by doing so. He was right and I well remember that on my return to Bombay after the first round I felt almost that I was returning home, though anything less like home than the Taj Mahal Hotel in 1927 is hard to imagine. When I first arrived there and went along the dismal and dark stone floored gallery to my bedroom I felt as if I was being led to my prison cell. The public rooms and general amenities were spartan and ugly too but have been greatly improved since; though, when I was last there, I still felt the threatening gloom of the gothic wooden-arched bedroom galleries.

It would be easy to describe travelling in India at that time in such a way as to make it seem extremely uncomfortable. It was of course hot, sometimes very hot, and there was no air-conditioning. In a place like Madras, with high humidity, you had to get used to being, if not soaked to the skin, at least soaked from the skin outwards all day. After a bath you applied talcum powder liberally to enable you to get your singlet on. Papers either flew off the desk in the wind from the ceiling fan or stuck to your damp arm. At night you had to choose between feeling cool in a draught with the fan on, or hot and wet with it off. You had to get used to flies of all sorts, mosquitoes, ants, beetles and lizards. In trains, in spite of the triple windows—glass, mosquito netting, sun shutters— you were hot and, after the usual journey of two nights and a day, indescribably dirty. On my first morning in Bombay I bought a copy of *The Times of India* and my eye was caught, and so was my breath, by a list of the number of cases of smallpox, leprosy, cholera, etc., that had been reported during the previous week.

But 'the getting used to' took a shorter time than one would have expected, particularly as there was work to do and something to occupy the mind, and thereafter travel in India was made very agreeably comfortable by the ministrations of a travelling 'boy'— an Indian servant especially experienced in looking after men wishing to travel in India, Burma and Ceylon. These servants were usually from Madras, spoke and wrote English and seemed also to know all the languages required for travel in the area they covered. They were at the top of the servant hierarchy and were undisputed masters of hotel staff, station coolies and garry drivers. My boy, James, who must have been some years older than me, was typical, and certainly smoothed the way for me in a strange environment. He soon got to know my requirements and my likes and dislikes, to all of which he attended with cheerful regularity. He was butler and valet when we were in hotels and courier when we travelled. He paid all laundry, and bought general domestic supplies such as tooth-paste, soap for washing underwear and socks (which he did himself), oranges, matches, and cigarettes. He arranged and paid for all garry hire to transport luggage to and from stations and any excess expenses on the railway. He no doubt made a 'turn' on these expenses but that was unofficially recognized and there is no doubt that what he charged me was less than I would have myself had to pay. He was completely trustworthy and guarded my interests at all times. He woke me in the morning with freshly squeezed orange juice and hot water and laid out my clothes for the day. If I wanted breakfast in the bedroom he ensured that the waiter brought it at the proper time. Even if I told him I was not in for lunch, and happened to come back unexpectedly to the hotel, he met me in the corridor walking to my room. When I got back to the room in the evening he produced tea within a few moments and in due course ran a bath for me to exactly the temperature I liked. While I had my bath he laid out clean underclothing and my dress suit and shirt. (You dressed for dinner except on Sunday.) At first he wanted to help me to dress by holding my trouser legs out and doing up my shoes but I drew the line at that.

When we moved, I gave him the tickets. He did the packing, transported the luggage to the station or dock and had all necessities duly laid out in the carriage or cabin when I arrived. At the other end he did the same thing in reverse and I found everything laid out in the bedroom of the next hotel exactly as they had been arranged in the last one.

I was not merely served, I was cherished, and I have never travelled so care free as I did in India in the 1920s and '30s.

James' wages were Rs.60 per month (£4.50), plus accommodation. I remember asking what was covered by the item on the Taj Mahal Hotel bill 'Garages and outhouses, 4 annas (about 1½p) per day'. It was servant's quarters.

My itinerary and mileage (which on this very special occasion I did record) were as follows:

	Miles
London/Marseilles	700
Marseilles/Bombay	4,567
Bombay/Calcutta	1,223
Calcutta/Madras	1,032
Madras/Calicut	413
Calicut/Cochin	120
Backwaters	100
Quilon/Dhanushkodi	314
Ferry to Talamanaar	22
Talamanaar/Colombo	209
Colombo/Kandy return	150
Colombo/Madras	687
Madras/Bombay	794
Bombay/Karachi	450
Karachi/Delhi	906
Delhi/Agra	122
Agra/Calcutta	760
Calcutta/Rangoon	780
Rangoon/Madras	1,004
Madras/Colombo	687
Colombo/Marseilles	5,047 (including visit to Cairo)
Marseilles/London	700
	20,787

My expenses within India, Burma and Ceylon:

Fares (including James')	Rs. 1,414
Hotels and meals	1,992
Taxi/garry/rickshaw	157
Sundry expenses, including roll of bedding needed for train travel	577
James' wages and gratuity	248
Total:	Rs. 4,388 = £3·67 per day

This was for first class travel and the best hotels available.

Train fares were less than 1p per mile for me and less than ¼p a mile for James.

The railways were largely staffed by Anglo-Indians, but engine-drivers were frequently ex-soldiers. It was impressive to see the majestic figure of one such, in spotless white dungarees and topee, strolling with unhurried dignity along the platform, a few moments before the train was due to start, in order to take command of the engine, already prepared and attended by a gang of Indian subordinates.

I am sure you get to know a place better by working in it than by visiting it as a tourist even if you do see fewer of the 'sights', and you see a lot more from a train than from the air. My job took me to shops and market places, docks, warehouses and factories, and travelling by train you see both country and village life. Travelling slowly in a little motor boat through the backwaters of Malabar provided a continuous panorama of life in an area of tropical vegetation. Crossing the Deccan by train, I glimpsed the patient and never-ending toil required to squeeze sustenance from a parched and exhausted soil.

In fact you saw a great deal of Indian life from the train. Even express trains did not go very fast and stopped frequently at stations which were obviously much more a centre of community life than they are now in U.K. I travelled a lot by train, fortunately often with my friend and colleague, W. G. J. Shaw, who was a master of all reasonable means of ensuring maximum possible comfort in travel and hotels. He admitted that his outlook was somewhat selfish and summed it up in the well known slogan of the then main theatre ticket agency in London: 'You want the best seats, we have them'.

The trains had no corridors and first class accommodation on long distance stock was either a two-berth with one above the other placed across the compartment, as normally in sleeping cars, or a four-berth. These four-berth compartments were 6 ft. wide and 15 ft. long with three berths 'seat high' and one upper berth. The berths were just benches thinly upholstered—you provided your own bedding. There was a small toilet compartment smelling of disinfectant but not looking very clean which could be used with a liberal supply of Milton. There was room to walk about and if, as was usual when travelling with Shaw, we had a four-berth to ourselves there was a feeling of spaciousness which seemed to give a slight element of comfort to what was a hot, long, dirty and sweaty journey. The doors were bolted quite simply on the inside by two strong 'back-yard gate' bolts unaffected by any physical or vocal attack from the outside. There were ceiling fans which usually worked, always noisily.

'Spreading yourself' and, hopefully, remaining undisturbed, were the main comfort factors. The interest was the observation of village life as you travelled along and taking a walk at the stations, which were noisy scenes of great animation both day and night. Officials loudly calling for instant obedience from everyone under them. Excited passengers looking for their relations or for room somewhere on the train. Itinerant vendors calling out their wares and, if you were at the end of the train away from the main buzz, a gathering of children hopefully slapping their stomachs and calling for baksheesh.

It was frequently very hot indeed in the middle of the day and Shaw's method of dealing with this was to shut all and every type of window thus keeping out the sun, the heat and some of the sandy dust, and to get his servant to bring in a bucket of ice at every stop. This was put in the middle of the floor with a fan playing on it, and occasionally we sat on it to get the satisfaction of at least one part of the body feeling cool.

The inside bolts were particularly useful during the night when boarding passengers frequently tried to enter the compartment, usually having mistaken the number of the compartment booked for them, or just in the hope that we would let them in. We once withstood a considerable siege. The railways had an arrangement by which if you were travelling on the Frontier Mail but wanted to get off in Delhi, where the train arrived very early in the morning, your coach would be detached to enable you to continue your rest till a more appropriate time. We decided to test this. The coach was certainly detached and shunted far from the station, but the noise and the bumps and the starting and stopping that this caused would have awakened the dead. However, we lay low till about 5.00 a.m. when there was some noisy discussion outside probably about what was to be done with a coach standing by itself in a siding. The deputation withdrew and returned in due course with higher authority tentatively knocking on our door. No answer. Knocking became more insistent, but still no answer, so the debate became louder till the party withdrew for reinforcements, which apparently included a ladder on which someone mounted to the roof on which he hammered with some strength. This was too much for us so we shouted something like 'What do you want?'

Reply: 'Sir, your destination has come.'

A GLIMPSE AT BURMA

Early in the morning, sailing up the river to Rangoon, I was delighted to see painted in large letters on some tanks along the river bank BURMAH OIL COMPANY, SCOTLAND, and a few moments later, on some big godown, THE IRRAWADDY FLOTILLA COMPANY, SCOTLAND. Nearer in were the golden pinnacles of the pagodas, but Rangoon was not a Burmese city. The businessmen were mainly Scottish, the traders Chinese and the coolies and servants Indian. Some brightly clad, cheerful Burmese women smoked big cigars as they tended their cloth stalls in the market: there were Buddhist priests in saffron-colour robes with their begging bowls, but I do not remember meeting a Burmese man.

One happy memory of a Chinese dealer. He was an old man with a few long white hairs for his beard. I was young, and he looked very venerable. In the course of our opening courtesies I told him it was my birthday. He smiled and called up to the balcony above his shop something which sounded to me like 'Ho, Ho, Ho', but with a different emphasis on each 'Ho'.

In a few minutes someone came down from the balcony with a large silver tray set out daintily for tea with beautiful china—and some preserved ginger. This was set on the old man's desk and we smiled at each other as we took what was one of the most refreshing cups of tea I have ever had.

And at Ceylon

Journeying from South India it was a great refreshment and delight to get to Ceylon.

The ferry from Dhanushkodi reached Talaimannar in the evening and the night train to Colombo awaited. On the first occasion, what a surprise—and on future occasions what a relief—to be ushered into a real sleeping-car with separate sleeping compartments, all prepared with clean white sheets and a smiling attendant in smart uniform, instead of the dusty, if spacious, empty austerity of the Indian trains. Admittedly one was welcomed also by the loudest and most continuous chorus of frogs I have ever heard, but it was not long before that was left behind and for-gotten in the comfort of feeling clean. This feeling was reinforced on looking out of the window in the morning: everything green and fresh looking, sparkling in the sun, and the country people evi-dently living in less arduous and more agreeable conditions than in India, and looking more seemly and more cheerful in consequence.

This atmosphere of apparent cheerfulness was not belied by subsequent experience of Colombo and some travel about the Island. To a visitor at that time, it was a cheerful and happy place to visit—and there were a lot of visitors, especially to Colombo. All the main mail boats on the routes between Europe and the East and Australia stopped a day in Colombo, so there was an almost continuous succession of 'trippers' anxious to make the most of a day ashore in the middle of their voyage, and, it seemed, also to make the best of their tropical wardrobe. You used to dress up to go ashore not dress down. The 'tourist rubbish' industry had not developed to its present all-pervading flood of pseudo-folk artistry, and with low customs duties into Ceylon, there was a large selection of mostly genuine silks, lace, carvings, and especially jewellery; some of the jewellery being made from local gems and semi-precious stones, notably sapphires, rubies, zircons and moon-stones. All these things tempted those going to Europe on leave and those from Europe in search of novelty.

An expedition ashore in Colombo was worth it anyway, curios or not. There were no docks so the steamers lay at anchor in the harbour and you went ashore in a launch. Then followed a rick-shaw ride along the sea-front with the waves of the Indian Ocean only a few yards away, and lunch on the verandah of the Galle Face Hotel with dignified Cingalese waiters wearing sarongs that looked like long skirts, a jacket, and a large circular comb in their hair. Or if you were energetic, you swim in the sea at Mount Lavinia only a mile or two down the coast. It was hot and humid, but with a breeze and the sea to look at, it did not seem so if you were just on a day's outing. Working in Colombo was hot and sticky but with so many people about in holiday attire and mood it was difficult not to feel light-hearted.

And I was light-hearted when I woke up early one morning to see the P. & O. R.M.S. *Cathay* on the horizon steaming towards the harbour. I was going to board her later in the day to start my voyage home.

I visited India (Burma and Ceylon) four more times, in 1930–35, going twice further east to the Dutch East Indies, Siam and Malaya. On one of these further expeditions, Sidney van den Bergh took me to Bali—'The Paradise Island of the East'. After the initial shock of seeing Balinese women both old and young in 'topless' attire, I remember most vividly the dancing of some extremely well trained small boys who 'danced' with their fingers, arms and eyes, their fingers and their eyes twinkling and darting to the music. They were enchanting.

At the end of 1933 I was in India just finishing off my job and preparing for my journey home when I received cabled instructions that I was to fly to Batavia. Neither I nor any of my colleagues had ever flown, so it was a somewhat exciting instruction. K.L.M. was one of the pioneers of long distance air travel and had already developed a twice weekly service described as 'Amsterdam—Batavia V.V.' (It took me many years to find out that V.V. stood for vice versa) and claimed to be the longest regular air route in the world.

It was something to be facing a journey of 2,600 miles as a first flight.

The aeroplane was a three-engined Fokker with two pilots, a mechanic, and a wireless operator, and seating for five passengers, who, as there was no barrier between them and the crew, were treated as 'part of the outfit'.

The crew took the plane right through from Amsterdam to Batavia and considered it a point of honour to arrive on time if at all possible. Our flight had been delayed in Naples and I joined it in Calcutta on the last stage of a thirty-six-hour spell of continuous flying, except for refuelling, from Baghdad to Akyab on the coast of Burma. I did not know this when I joined the flight: all I knew was that it was late in Calcutta, giving me some hours of waiting. It felt like being in a dentist's ante-room.

But when the call came there was little ceremony. When I arrived at the aerodrome the plane was already there, by the hand-operated petrol pump, the crew and two passengers standing nearby and looking somewhat the worse for wear having had no

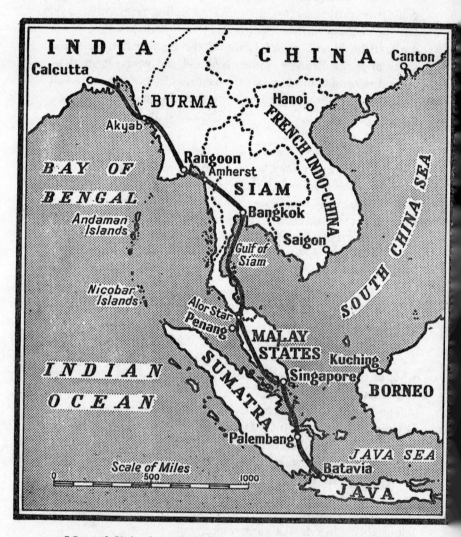

Map of flight from Calcutta to Batavia, 2,640 miles, 1934.

shaves for a couple of days. I was weighed with my luggage and then all aboard. We taxi-ed to the end of the aerodrome, turned to face the long stretch for the lift: each engine in turn raced and the ailerons and rudder tested—then full speed, brakes released and we were off.

The following excerpts from my account of the flight give contrasts with modern flying conditions:

As we flew past the hangar I had another wave from those seeing me off and suddenly found myself looking right down on them—we were turning on our tracks and I was for a second or two almost horizontal, the earth below from my window and the sky above from the other. The roar of the engine makes it impossible to talk except by putting your mouth to the ear of the person you want to address. There is also considerable pressure on the ear drum when either mounting or descending with the result that when we came down from our 3,000-ft I thought my ears and glands leading to them were going to burst. About 30 or 40 miles from Akyab we decended to about 70 feet above the sea and flew just along the coast following the actual coast line in and out. It was exciting to see the trees that looked almost opposite me passing quickly by and below us to see the fishermen waving up to us and the children, goats and cows scurrying away. It was something like being on a switchback railway. Suddenly we turned a corner and there was Akyab Bay—we mounted up to see the aerodrome and the wind vane, circled round again with the earth on one side and the sky on the other—flatten out—the engines stop roaring and for one instant you seem to have stopped altogether, then a swoop down, almost touching the trees,—a slight impact and we are down (after three hours flying).

We were met by the KLM Agent and, while the mechanic and the wireless operator starting overhauling the engines and re-fuelling, the pilots and the passengers went to the Agent's bungalow where we had a family tea party with the Agent, his wife and children, overlooking a lawn, a vegetable garden and the bay. Later, those who are not already asleep had dinner with the Agent and everybody was in bed by 9.00 p.m.

We were wakened at 2.30 a.m. and even in the tropics that can be chilly and cheerless especially if you have to shave in cold water with the assistance of a trembling oil lamp and a broken mirror. After some tea we sallied forth to the aerodrome where all was quiet beneath the pale light of the moon.

Some shivering coolies were despatched to light flares along the 'runway' and these yellow dots of light coming to life one after the other made the scene somewhat eerie. In due course all the flares were lit in a big L, the long stroke being the length along which we could run and we had to clear the short stroke. The engines were started—a roar, and, from each exhaust, a mass of flame about two feet long like a large blow lamp. You do not see it in daylight. The taxi to the end of the 'runway', test engines and we charge down the line of flares into the darkness.

All the way to Rangoon the pilots and the wireless operator were checking the course and now and then they gave us the thumbs up sign and a cheery grin to let us know that all was going according to plan. It was with our consent that we were flying by night, the regulations being that normal (daylight only) timing must be observed when carrying passengers.

Leaving Rangoon I was interested to see again the Burmah Oil Company, Scotland, oil tanks.

As we approached the mountains into Siam I stood between the pilots, looking round the 'half of the world' that could be seen from the 'bay window'. Immediately below me was the 'drift' observation hole—a circular hole on the floor about a foot in diameter with two parallel pieces of metal down the centre. Looking through this with the eyes half closed the ground seems to be passing in a series of parallel lines and the difference between these imaginary lines and the metal lines down the centre was the measure of the drift.

We only stayed half-an-hour on Siamese soil and for this privilege I had paid 7/6d [37½p]—a dear walk on the grass which is all I had in Siam.

Our mechanic now turned himself into Chief Steward and extracted from his store cupboard some Dutch 'bread biscuits'— like large rusks—and cheese—they were quite good, as we were hungry. To drink we had 'tea' made by leaving a tea bag for five minutes in some hot water from a thermos flask filled in Jodhpur two days previously. This served with tinned milk in a carton cup can be highly recommended to those who are thirsty and have no alternative.

En route from Bangkok for Alor Star the pilot had promised us elephants, and elephants we surely had. He circled round till he saw a herd and then came down to within what seemed to be a few yards of them: a huge one in front and followed by others in descending order of size.

Landed in Alor Star 4.30 p.m., 1230 miles in eleven flying hours . . . the following morning the pilot came round to make sure we were all up at 4.45 a.m.

Flying over land in daylight the pilot picks out landmarks from a large map on his knee and tries to follow either a road, or better still, a railway. Over Malaya we struck bad weather conditions for the first time. Clouds hung heavily over the ground and the further south we went the thicker they got till at last we 'lost' the road we had been following and were almost enveloped in mist and heavy rain, and we were 'lost' too. Circling round looking for a landmark: here a glimpse of the ground, there a glimpse of the sky. Suddenly there loomed up along side us (or so it seemed to me) the side of a hill and at this the pilot decided that the only way for safety was the sea. So right turn and away out of our normal course till we reached the sea coast where the mist was less thick. By closely following the coast we eventually 'found' Singapore and its Military Aerodrome in the midst of a rain storm which had already lasted thirty-six hours. The Officers who invited us to coffee at the R.A.F. Club told us we had been lucky to be able to land . . . one of the passengers had left the plane at Rangoon and the others left in Singapore so I rejoined the plane as the sole passenger.

The bad weather continued and both pilots were on the go together till we were well clear of the mist when one of them left his seat to come to tell me that we were across the Equator. As it was my first time I got a handshake. We flew so low above the water on this stretch that the sea looked the same as it looks from the deck of a ship and the little islands glided past us, dull and forbidding in the absence of the sun.

On the last leg from Palembang to Batavia I sat in the reserve pilot's seat and, having been instructed in the theory, I was interested to watch the practice and actually to do the job myself for a tense twenty minutes. My job was to aim from the coast of Sumatra to two islands, known as 'The two brothers'. I did not mind when I saw the nose of the plane going up a bit but I fair hated to see it dropping down. The consequence was that I had unconsciously climbed 500 feet. Keeping level, the hand control, was difficult; steering (a straight course!) with the feet was easy. The pilot amusingly demonstrated my faults to me after I had finished my 'solo flight'.

At 4.15 p.m. we sighted Java and were soon circling round and sweeping down to the end of an exciting, interesting and pleasant flight.

(Note: Depart Calcutta Thursday noon; arrive Batavia Saturday evening).

My first overseas travel after the war was again to the East— Malaya in 1946—but thereafter I travelled further afield.

> 'How much a dunce that has been sent to roam
> Excels a dunce that has been kept at home.'

Certainly by all the reading I might have done at home about the economics, politics and history of the countries I visited I could not have gained just that mental picture, that appreciation of the 'atmosphere' of the place which was necessary for my job, particularly for dealing with the people from the countries concerned. I knew the circumstances in which they were working, and had some idea of the stresses to which they were subject, whether climatic, social, political or economic. And if you have visited a place it stands on its own in your mind—you cannot lump it even with a close neighbour. I think I could still get at least a pass mark in answer to the sort of question we used to get in history examinations, 'Compare and contrast' about any two of the countries I visited.

But I am not setting myself any such questions. I am writing about travel, and what I really did was to travel through and experience the metamorphosis which has taken place in travel.

When I first went to India it was an event: now it is hardly an incident. The weekly departure from Victoria of the P. & O. Special was a big occasion. The daily departure from Heathrow of twenty flights to the East is just routine, and there is little satisfaction or glamour in seeing people off when all they do is to go through a departure door to sit down and have a cup of coffee.

Travelling by boat the more luggage you had the more important you were and you had to muster one or two to be labelled 'Baggage not wanted on voyage.' My requirements were modest, being only four suitcases plus certain hand baggage. Admittedly they were the biggest suitcases available but my experienced friend Shaw had warned me against trunks, especially the splendid cabin trunks, then popular, which opened out like miniature wardrobes. Trunks were all right for residents in India but not for travellers. 'One suitcase—one coolie' was quite understood and accepted, no matter the weight of the suitcase, but trunks lead to arguments and bargaining: and cabin trunks looked fine, but there were very few cabins big enough to enable them to be used as advertised. One of my my suitcases was heavy as it carried everything required to enable me to set up an 'office' in my bedroom. Typewriter, code books, stationery, files, dictionary, reference books, pin tray, pencils, and, of course, a paper weight.

My clothing consisted of three tropical suits; one semi-tropical suit; one European suit (cold weather); two evening suits (one tropical); tennis flannels and white jersey; shorts; sports jacket, pullovers, etc.; about fifteen shirts of various types: ten sets of underwear; topee in special tin container; pyjamas, stockings, socks, shoes, handkerchiefs, etc.

Though I was no great player of games I took also a tennis racket and golf clubs.

Air travel made nonsense of this sort of thing and there came instead the struggle to keep within the permitted weight. How many shirts? Could you do with two pairs of shoes? Would a dinner jacket be required? Would it be cold in the evening? How many thin suits?

Drip-dry shirts, nylon underwear and socks, the decline in 'black ties' and the habit of wearing light suits everywhere in air conditioned offices and central-heated houses have virtually eliminated this weight problem and now it is easier to pack for an overseas visit than for a few days' golf in Scotland.

I certainly flew my way up through most of the main aeroplanes that have been used in international flying. After the three-engined Fokker, I crossed India in an Imperial Airways Heracles: an enormous aircraft providing about ten seats beautifully if somewhat elaborately upholstered in red leather, reminiscent of the smokeroom of a London club. Certainly the crew made it abundantly clear that the passengers were unwelcome guests in the club!

In the Caribbean in 1947 I was introduced to the planes I subsequently used all over the world—the DC3 and DC4—which did more than any other type of aircraft to pioneer air travel and give it its essential reputation for safety. I daresay some of them are still active on the more remote routes. Unfortunately at the time the U.K. could only produce converted Halifax and York bombers, known as Speedbirds, but ultimately produced the first jet—the original Comet—and what I thought was the best of the propeller planes—the Britannia. Meantime there were Constellations, Super Constellations, Stratocruisers, Argonauts, Convairs, DC6 and DC7.

I have also yawned (and smoked) my way through the delays, uncertainties, irritations and frustrations which seemed inescapable when, after the war, the number of flights and the number of passengers far outstripped the communications facilities and the number of trained staff available for handling the logistics.

On the Malay journey in 1946 I went and returned by Sunderland Flying Boat. This was comparatively dignified and comfortable travel. The theory was that you slept each night on terra firma, if a houseboat on the Nile could be so described, but, if this failed, bunks were arranged, so far as possible, from transformed seats in the cabins. Those who did not get one of these were accommodated on mattresses and bedding laid out on the floor of a sort of loft between the ceiling of the cabin and the top of the aeroplane. The accommodation was spacious with a sort of lobby amidships where you could take a stride or two and, leaning on a bar, look out, as you can do in a corridor train. Flying off the water and descending on to it was a more obvious thrill than in a land plane, and as there was no competing traffic we got V.I.P. treatment so far as the primitive facilities allowed. We departed from Poole and landed at Marseilles, Augusta, Cairo, Basrah (or nearby, and I remember being nearly overcome with heat as we chugged our way out to the plane in an open motorboat), Karachi, somewhere near Jaipur, up river from Calcutta, Rangoon, Bangkok. We were late in both directions with no information available either in Singapore or in London as to where we were or when we would arrive. Our manager in Singapore had no anxieties on the matter and had to be hurried off the golf course after we had landed, but my wife was not very happy when I was 'lost' for thirty-six hours on the return journey. Actually we were stuck in Marseilles after two unsuccessful attempts to rise off the water.

I will not attempt to recall all my flights since then. They were not particularly remarkable in their own era. The delays and uncertainties were typical and were the more wearisome because they seemed usually to occur in the early morning or through the night. Some typical examples, from my diaries, may give the jet flyer some idea of what it was like when passenger air travel was growing up.

1947 New York to San Juan, Puerto Rico

An early start as usual with air travel. We were wakened at 4.30 a.m. and as I was in America I thought that everything from there on would be looked after smoothly by an efficient Air Service but I was disappointed. The New York Air Terminal has not even got a soda fountain, and is dingy and dirty and has hard seats. As we were up so early we thought we might have been given coffee to cheer us on our way, but when we asked, we were directed to a near-by cafe which happens to keep open all night—Childs by name. So we went across the deserted street and had bacon and eggs and coffee. We then went back to the Air Terminal at about 6.00 a.m. and after waiting another twenty minutes we were ushered into a bus for the air field, for which we had to pay the fare of $1.15.

At the air field there was again a complete lack of organisation. We just followed our noses, without any directions whatsoever and after extricating ourselves from a bunch of passengers

inward from Vienna we found a counter which seemed interested
in us. Our flight had been cancelled, we were told, though we
were not told the reason. But it did not seem to make any
difference for we were to depart at the stated time for our flight
and go by the same route. We slowly passed from one counter
to another, baggage, tickets, exit visa, etc., till we reached the
Immigration Counter. There we were told to wait again which
we did on some more very hard seats. Finally at 7.30 our flight
was called without the Immigration Officer having turned up at
all. It appeared that this did not matter and we were put on the
plane—a Skymaster seating, uncomfortably close together, 54
people. All the seats were taken so it was a crush, and as I had
beside me a particularly large woman, my seat and arm rests were
somewhat overflowed.

However it was an uneventful and smooth flight of some $8\frac{1}{2}$
hours, flying right over Bermuda at about 12.30 p.m. and
arriving San Juan, Puerto Rico, at 4.15 p.m.

As usual with the Air Service the people at the receiving end
only had a hazy notion of when we were to arrive, so none of our
Agents met us, even although it took fully an hour to clear us
through the Customs.

As our flight had been cancelled, the Hotel had let our rooms
to someone else so we had to be squashed together in a dungeon
of a room on the ground floor, but there is hope that we may get
better accommodation tomorrow.

By the time we had had a bath, one of our Agents had made
up on us and took us to a roof garden somewhere for dinner.

Havana, Cuba to Balboa, Panama
13th February   Depart Hotel 10.30 p.m.
14th February   1.00 a.m. Still enjoying the impersonal discomfort of the Air Terminal, as the flight I am to join is late,
to an unpredictable extent—we were due out at 12.01 a.m. The
Cuban Customs had kindly examined my baggage and turned
my orderly packing upside down. Why it should be necessary
to examine luggage for an outward flight I do not know but you
have just to suffer the buffets of fate in these matters. Regulations are endless: I have already parted with twenty copies of

my passport photograph since leaving New York less than three
weeks ago.

At last at 1.30 a.m. I found myself in a nearly empty plane.

Marida (Mexico)	arr.	4.45 a.m.
Marida (Mexico)	dep.	5.15 a.m.
Guatemala City	arr.	8.00 a.m.
Change planes dep. an hour later which is		
still 8.00 a.m. after putting the clock back		
an hour.		
San Salvador	arr.	8.50 a.m.
San Salvador	dep.	9.05 a.m.
Tegusigalpa	arr.	10.00 a.m.
Tegusigalpa	dep.	10.30 a.m.
Managua	arr.	11.20 a.m.
Managua	dep.	11.30 a.m.
San José	arr.	1.00 p.m.

Since dinner sixteen hours ago I have had only

1 cup coffee and sweet bun
1 cup soup and sweet bun

so I was not very happy to be told on arrival at the Grau Hotel in
San José, Costa Rica, that I was too late for lunch.

15th February dep. Hotel 11.30 a.m. and it was lucky I did so
for when I got to the air field I found my booking was not
recorded. Fortunately the flight was late, as usual, as it took
an hour of patient negotiations to get my booking sorted out.

San José	dep.	2.00 p.m.
David (Panama)	arr.	3.15 p.m.
David (Panama)	dep.	3.40 p.m.
Balboa	arr.	5.10 p.m.

This was the quickest, in fact the only flight available for this
journey.

Seeing off some colleagues bound from Trinidad to New York
In the evening the usual enquiries began to be made about
how 'El Presidente' service, making its way up from Brazil, was
getting on. The news was rather depressing: 'It had not yet left

Belim'. There were various calculations made by the experts as to how long it took to get from Belim and what the chances were of making up time, but forecasting the times of air travel is as chancy as forecasting the weather. In due course definite news came that passengers were to report at 2.15 a.m. It was a pretty silent party that left the hotel at 1.30 a.m. for seventeen miles along the Churchill/Roosevelt highway to the air field. The plane came in from the south at 2.00 a.m. and things looked quite hopeful till it was announced that there would be a two hours delay. No reason was given but it gradually became known that one of the tyres had burst and this knowledge seemed to satisfy the hardened air travellers who had experienced this before. However, passengers and those attending them were in pretty low spirits when Pan American said they would transport all present to their Guest House near by. And what a surprise! Comfortable, clean and cool: and a hot, well served breakfast far above the standards of the Queen's Park Hotel to which I have become inured. Spirits drooped a bit thereafter but at last at 5.00 a.m. the passengers got on board, the plane sailed away leaving me in a deserted airport. All Pan American staff and all others, except a cat, had disappeared.

Early in 1948 I flew to Lagos in a type of plane which fortunately was not in service very long.

I went from Airways Terminal at Victoria to Heathrow by bus. There were eight adults in the party and two babies, one of whom very soon made its presence heard if not felt.

Heathrow is hardly palatial. It consists of a dejected series of huts, a couple of runways and evidence of much further Public Works in the shape of mounds of earth, holes and other disfigurements.

We were promptly marshalled through our various formalities by B.O.A.C. and joined the plane at 12.45 p.m. The plane had the high sounding name of 'Halton Speedbird' but in fact it was a converted Halifax bomber with extremely confined space for passengers. I had leg room but no space for moving sideways in my seat. A big person would be very uncomfortable indeed. Also

9 Packing Sunlight Soap in the factory at Port Sunlight, about 1925.

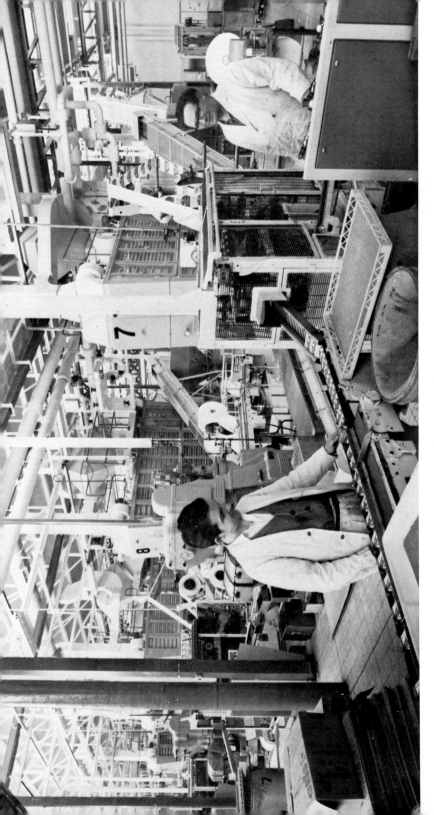

10 Port Sunlight: toilet soap being packed in the 1960s.

11a In September 1973 a meeting of retired directors took place at Noordwijk aan Zee in the Netherlands. *Seated left to right:* the late Frits Tempel; James van den Bergh; Noud Caron; David Orr (present chairman of Unilever Limited); Andrew Knox; Sidney van den Bergh; Willy Faure; the late Geoffrey Heyworth. *Left to right, second row:* Rudi Jurgens and Evart Hofman. *Standing left to right:* Robert Siddons; Johan van Moorsel; John Mann; Guus Blaauw; John Stubbs; Frederick Pedler; Maup van Hengel; John Hoskyns-Abrahall; Hans Nagel.

11b In the modernisation of Port Sunlight village during the 1960s, one of the new closes was named after the author's father. Andrew Knox and his wife are seen here with Bruce Rumgay, then a director of U.M.L. Limited, which administers the village.

12a and b Lever House and Unilever House. Lever House was De Keyser's Royal Hotel, set up by Polydore de Keyser in 1874 to cater for passengers using the continental services to and from Blackfriars Station nearby, the terminus of the London, Chatham and Dover Railway. The hotel building was bought by Lever Brothers in 1921 and converted. Unilever House, built to replace it, was opened in 1932. 'The design,' says a contemporary Press report, 'is quite a free classical treatment showing that although the company possesses the qualities of quiet and dignity which the classic symbolises, it is the free use of these rather than the literal enslavement to tradition that is symbolised.'

little space for coats, hand baggage, etc., which had to be draped round your feet, though I felt it cold enough to wear my coat.

We had been promised lunch on board and were in lively expectation when we got above the clouds but it did not begin to appear till 3.00 p.m. and we reached the coffee by 5.00 p.m. This was followed by some tepid tea just before we came down at 8.00 p.m. in Castel Benito (Tripoli) where we waited two hours. The aerodrome consisted of a very large hangar, empty except for a small enclave for passenger accommodation in one corner, and after some refreshment and a wash and brush up I occupied my time very agreeably walking up and down the dimly lit hangar. We were not allowed outside, but the big sliding doors were open and it was reasonably cool.

We joined the plane again at 10.00 p.m. and I was able to discard my overcoat in favour of a light rug and slept fairly well till 4.00 a.m. when we were awakened with a cup of tea by a rather more energetic steward who had joined us in Castel Benito, to prepare us for Kano where we arrived at 5.40 a.m. We left Kano at 7.30 a.m. and, flying above the clouds, we saw nothing till the corrugated iron roofs of Lagos where we arrived just after 10.00 a.m. almost exactly on time! It had been a smooth and uneventful journey and I concluded that as a means of getting from place to place, flying is effective—but it can hardly be called 'travelling'. Anyway, I am in Lagos in less than twenty-four hours since leaving the Terminal in London. It seemed impossible that we had come 3,400 miles.

My first flight across the Atlantic seemed at the time to be, if I may use the word, a landmark in my flying experience, and I think that my wife and I shared a slight but unmentioned apprehension. I flew from London to Jamaica in February 1951.

On arrival at the Airport the main thing was that the flight was 'on' and also on time, but when I was through Customs and in the Departure Lounge at 4.00 p.m., we were informed that there was to be an hour's delay.

My heart sank a bit (if indeed there was any room for it to sink any lower) because one delay on air travel often leads to another. I took a cup of tea to cheer me on my way and noticed as usual that it is impossible for an airways canteen in the British Commonwealth to let you have a cup of tea which is not slopped over into the saucer. However, it was tea.

The delay was only the hour as announced and we were duly called forward at 5.30 p.m. by which time it was dark. The plane was pretty full, mostly of people going on holiday to Bermuda or Nassau, but I had a good seat by a window at the back of the plane. We were off at 5.30 p.m. and were soon above the clouds with nothing to see but a star. My next door neighbour was fortunately of the silent type so I was able to keep my own counsel, and I did so by wondering what on earth made me take these long trips away from home!

However, I was cheered up by quite a good dinner at 7.30 p.m. to 8.15 p.m., and dinner included some pleasant wine which induced an equally pleasant doze afterwards.

Even in my doze I began to realise, in due course, that we were coming down a bit. There was some movement—not exactly bumps, but just an occasional jerk. Also my ears began to hurt so I looked below for the lights of Lisbon. There they were below me at about 10.15 p.m. and we were running along the runway at 10.20 p.m.

B.O.A.C. lost interest in us as soon as we landed and we had to follow our noses to find the lounge and restaurant, at the Airport. The restaurant was very full, very cramped, and did not give the impression of being very clean. However, we were offered a free cup of coffee. Anything else had to be paid for in dollars. Pounds were no good! So I was not tempted to sample the local port and just wandered about what must be one of the most uncomfortable, cheerless and directionless airports I have ever struck. Just endless benches and formidable-looking but disinterested and dirty policemen and Customs officials dotted about the place in bored idleness.

I was not sorry to be called on to the plane at 11.30 p.m. and to see, soon after, the lights of Lisbon fading away below.

There was nothing for it but to try to sleep, and I was fortunate in that my neighbour had departed at Lisbon, and no new passenger took his place, so I was able to remove the arm-rest between the seats and thus have rather more lateral scope for movement. The trouble with aeroplane seats is that you can usually only have variations on one position, i.e. lying on your back more or less sitting up, and there are no foot rests to help smaller people like me. With the seat next to me vacant I could do the sitting up position and more or less lie on one side or the other. So I bunched my feet up as best I could, being surprised that it was still cold enough to need a blanket, and I dozed off again.

Awoke, stiff, at 3.25 a.m. to find that we were in the Azores. We were told that we could have 'supper' there and were then abandoned to the tender care of the local waiters. What we actually got looked more like breakfast to me, being bacon and eggs and coffee. In any case you don't feel much like eating at that time of the night, so I had a cup of coffee.

We were off again at 5.00 a.m. and, after such a long journey already accomplished, it was disheartening to be told that it was nine hours to Bermuda. Nine hours is a long time even on two seats, particularly when it is all over water. So I read a bit and then dozed off once again, to be awakened really properly by daylight and some general movement within the plane (to and from the toilet) at 10.00 a.m. So it had been a long 'night'—from 5.00 p.m. last night in London till 10.00 a.m. this morning somewhere high over the Atlantic. I had got through it not badly. Some reading, some dozeing, some dreaming and some sleep. But a good deal of stiffness of the neck and knees!

Looking round my fellow passengers, I was amazed at the contrast. One woman had spent the night with something that looked like a mudpack on her face, and had not yet removed it— she looked awful. Another had not only straightened her hair and 're-done' her face, but had changed from an afternoon to a morning frock! I thought that was real courage and the sight almost, but not quite, encouraged me to queue up for my turn at the inadequately small and cramped facilities for shaving.

So with a cottonwool sky below us and a matchless blue above, the Captain of R.M.A. Berwick sent round a notice saying we were at a height of 18,000 ft., travelling at 265 m.p.h. and giving us the latest news of the Test Match!

It was beginning to get warm too, but not hot and I still did not feel burdened by my winter woollies.

At 11.00 a.m. (still my time) we had a breakfast and at 1.10 p.m. I saw Bermuda and we were down a few minutes afterwards.

I had safely flown the Atlantic!

As Bermuda is an expensive U.S. holiday resort I expected to find an appropriate Airport but it was the usual few scattered wooden huts with H. & C. facilities, but only C. available, and of somewhat doubtful cleanliness. I shaved with difficulty and was disappointed to find that there was no tea to be had, only some poor coffee.

I flew on to Jamaica via Nassau, arriving Jamaica just after midnight.

Then an hour's dismal discomfort while my temperature was taken and I passed the Health Authorities, Immigration, Customs, who all carefully examined the forms I had filled in on the aircraft giving such interesting information as the date of my vaccination certificate, the number of my passport and where I had spent each of the last fourteen nights. Our Jamaican manager met me when I finally got through, after 1.00 a.m. I was almost speechless and not much interested in the fact that it was only 8.00 p.m. yesterday in Jamaica.

I cared even less about the time of day at the end of the longest and most exhausting flight I ever had. I flew home from Hong Kong in 1953, a journey which took fifty-two and a half 'elapsed hours'. My arrival in Hong Kong by air had not been propitious. I had travelled through the night from Singapore by Cathay Pacific, not a 'registered' air line at the time, and some of my friends had pointed this out to me and had also told me what a bad place Hong Kong was for fog and how frequently landing was made difficult through bad visiblity. I remembered all this when instead of landing at 7.00 a.m., as promised earlier by the pilot, we began to zoom round in the clouds for much longer than it would normally take to come down. There was a particular 'close' sort of noise when you circle in a fog and it can not be ignored. We did this for about an hour which is unnerving to say the least of it, but eventually we shot through the clouds on to the runway. I was told later that we would have gone on to Manila if we had not had a mad Australian pilot with a girl friend in Hong Kong.

I was not in a very steady mood when a few days later I had to experience the same thing, so to speak, in reverse, on the day of my departure for London. In the morning I was informed that B.O.A.C. hoped the flight would be on time but the plane had not yet arrived from Tokyo. Then the clouds descended and so did my spirits. When we got to the airport we were told that the plane was circling overhead waiting for a break in the clouds. Oh! If only I could get safely out of Hong Kong!

Actually we got off in the afternoon and the following is my account of the flight:

I am writing this on the last hop of this long flight, between Rome and London—Dawn is just streaking across the sky.

It has certainly seemed a long and wearying trip. Unfortunately I lost my diary in Bangkok. So what with that and my watch broken I have lacked both the facilities and I am afraid the spirit to make any detailed record of the flight.

It is especially wearying because after, say, a five hour flight you find that the clocks have been put back, so five weary hours in the plane have only 'got rid of' four hours 'time', and this repeated six or seven times so benumbs you that in the end you not only don't know the time of day, but you are not even sure of the day!

And I am heartily sick of 'light refreshments'.

It was hot and well after dark when we arrived in Bangkok. Friends kindly came to the airport to see me—they were hurrying off back to a cocktail party and that sounded attractive.

It must have been pretty late when we arrived in Rangoon and there were more friends to welcome me. They had been to a cocktail party! And were completely immaculate and cool-looking in evening dress, which made me feel even more scruffy than I probably was, but at least I was more in keeping than they were with the dark dismal dispiriting surroundings of Rangoon Transit Passenger accommodation.

In Karachi we landed at an R.A.F. station instead of the Civil

Airport. This meant 'light refreshments' instead of breakfast, and a great disappointment. The hostess was good enough to tell us before we left the aircraft that there were no facilities for showers at the R.A.F. station. It would have been more truthful if she had merely said 'There are no facilities'! We were there two hours.

Bahrain and Basra were not notable for much. 'Light refreshments' of course. Bahrain was pretty deserted and no one took any interest in us except the inevitable Immigration Authorities.

The Airport Hotel at Basra is fairly new and seemed to be something of a social centre on a Sunday afternoon. There was a children's tea party going on in the Hotel garden and the well groomed (European) fathers and mothers were able to look with due distaste upon the scruffy 'Transit passengers'. The waiters did not make the mistake of trying to make the light refreshments seem more attractive by willing cheerfulness and even the lavatory woman failed to smile—knowing full well that we were British and therefore penniless in any currency which might interest her.

In Beirut, however, we were served most expeditiously and courteously with quite a good dinner. For the first time on the trip we felt the cold and it was pleasant to start off quickly with some hot soup and have the whole meal really served well. It was a very long way, or so it seemed, from Beirut to Rome. The plane was absolutely full so there was not much room to move—even I had someone in the next seat, though B.O.A.C. had kindly avoided that up till then. So it was a long 'night' as we started and ended the eight hour flight in darkness.

'Light refreshments' in Rome; but at least beautifully served if it was 3 a.m. and now I get the Captain's Flight Report:

Our position 05.30 G.M.T.—Genoa
Height above sea level 18,500 ft. Ground speed 240 m.p.h.
Due London Airport 08.30 hours.
That is good enough for me! But what day is it?

I found in all this flying that I could stand up to about eight hours in one hop and a total flight of about thirty hours. After these times my nerves began to give way, probably through tired-

ness, and I jumped, internally at every perceptible movement of
the plane or change in engine hum. So when my wife first joined
me for a journey overseas (to Australia in 1955) we planned to
break the journey by a stay for three nights in Bangkok.

PLAN OCTOBER		*ACTUAL OCTOBER*
Thursday, 13th		
	G.M.T.	
Depart London Airport	20.00	Depart London 20.25
		Arrive back London 21.30 being turned back over France with engine trouble
Friday, 14th		
Rome		02.00 arrive Selsdon Park Hotel
Cairo		10.00 depart Selsdon Park Hotel
Karachi		12.15 depart London Airport
		15.30 Rome
		21.30 Cairo
Saturday, 15th		
Calcutta		4.00 Breakfast on plane
Bangkok 03.25		06.30 Karachi
		12.45 Calcutta
		18.00 Bangkok
		(1.00 a.m. on 16th local time)
		To keep in touch with local times we had had lunch, tea, dinner, breakfast, lunch, dinner in twenty-four hours.

LOCAL TIMES

Tuesday, 18th October		
Bangkok/Singapore		Bangkok/Singapore
Wednesday, 19th October		
Depart Singapore	8.00 a.m.	Still in Singapore ⎤ Connecting
Djakarta		Still in Singapore ⎰ plane from
		⎱ London late
Thursday, 20th October		Still in Singapore ⎦
Perth		
Sydney due	7.00 a.m.	
Friday, 21st October		Depart Singapore 2.30 p.m. local time
		Djakarta
Saturday, 22nd October		Arrive Perth 1.30 a.m.
		Arrive Sydney 12.40 p.m.
3 nights in Bangkok		1 night in Selsdon Park
		2 nights in Bangkok
		3 nights in Singapore

$54\frac{1}{2}$ hours late on schedule and a total 'elapsed time' of
220 hours—9 days and 4 hours.

In spite of spending more time 'resting' on the journey than we had expected, we arrived more tired than we would have been if we had been on schedule. It is somewhat deflating to start on a long journey and have to turn back and it is certainly very tiring to wait about in uncertainty as to when you are to start on the next stage and we had this both in London and Singapore. And the last straw was when on the final hop to Australia, we and our luggage were decanted on to a cold and wet Perth Airport at 1.30 a.m. and after a more than normal amount of form filling, put through medical inspection, customs, immigration and currency control. Even a cup of tea did not wash away our bewildered tiredness.

We returned from New Zealand via the Pacific and in spite of spending a few daylight hours for a rest in Honolulu and having sleeping berths for the two flights at night Fiji/Honolulu, Honolulu/San Francisco we arrived in Vancouver forty-one hours after leaving Auckland completely exhausted, and I was sorry I had not been stricter on my thirty hours maximum, especially as we had to go on to Toronto the day following our arrival in Vancouver.

However, the jet planes were not far off. I had already made one brief flight on the first Comet in 1953 and although jet flying certainly reduces the 'elapsed hours' it adds to the fatigue which I am sure results from the rapid change in time on westward and eastward journeys. I only hope that this will be recognized by those who may soon, on the Concorde, arrive in London before they left New York.

Perhaps I might conclude by the following record of a journey over the Pole to Japan in 1963.

TIMING
MY TIME   LOCAL TIME
5.00 p.m. Sunday
Depart Amsterdam   17.00 hours = 5.00 p.m. Sunday 17th
                          9.00 hours
                          _____
                          26.00 hours
Deduct difference   11.00 hours
                          _____
2.00 a.m. Monday   15.00 hours = 3.00 p.m. Sunday, 17th
In Anchorage   1.00 hours
                          _____

3.00 a.m. Monday		
Depart Anchorage	16.00 hours	= 4.00 p.m. Sunday 17th
Flight time to Dateline	1.00 hours	
	17.00 hours	= 5.00 p.m. Sunday 17th
Cross Dateline ADD	24.00 hours	
	17.00 hours	= 5.00 p.m. Monday, 18th
Flight time from		
Dateline to Tokyo	6.30 hours	
	23.30 hours	
Deduct time difference	5.00 hours	
Anchorage/Tokyo		
10.30 a.m. Monday	18.30 hours	= 6.30 p.m. Monday, 18th
Total elapsed time	17.30 hours	

Therefore by my watch it was 10.30 a.m. when I arrived Tokyo. But I had *added* twenty-four hours, and *deducted* sixteen hours. So I had added a net eight hours; hence the time in Tokyo on arrival was (as shown above) 18.30 hours = 6.30 p.m.

All this is hard on your watch but it is even harder on your stomach, and sleeping apparatus. Up to 9.30 p.m. my time was all right, dinner and go to sleep (in bright sunlight) but then the hammering starts.

Keeping to my time:

    1.0 a.m. Cocktails and supper
    3.0 a.m. to 4.0 a.m. Anchorage—light refreshments
    4.0 a.m. on plane—full breakfast
    7.30 a.m. on plane—coffee and sandwiches
    8.30 a.m. on plane—cocktails and lunch
    10.30 a.m. arrive Tokyo in the dark

I found that I could stand the strains of flying better than what to me were the miseries of long distance motoring. Experience taught me that a motor journey said to take 'a couple of hours' meant fully three; one of 'three or four' meant six—and so on. If you know a journey well it certainly seems shorter than if you don't, and I have found that a motor journey through country that you don't know at all seems endless—and most of it usually indescribably dull. Hour after endless hour, either suffocatingly hot or in a draught, with the destination seeming to recede like a mirage. Your companion, usually your host, points out the land-marks, the significance of which you do not understand, and draws attention to the beauties of the scenery. This latter was apt to depress me, particularly because if there was a hill in sight I was sure to be told that it was reminiscent of Scotland. I was brought up to believe that Scotland is the most beautiful place in the world and, like other beliefs in which I was brought up, I have stuck to it. Doing so has saved me from the bother of having to enthuse over other scenery but has caused me distress when I have been called upon, through politeness, to agree that the 'Blue Mountains' in various parts of the world are like Scotland. I drew the line when asked to pass judgment on the mountains of Ruanda-Urundi in the middle of darkest Africa, but that was probably because the hotel in Usumbura was particularly depressing and I had been frightened when, turning round to see the man standing next to me, I found myself looking at his hip—he was a Watusi.

You also have the more immediate hazard of concluding within the first few moments of the drive that your host, or his chauffeur, is a bad driver. This is especially difficult if he happens to be given to driving on precipitous mountain roads with one hand on the steering wheel while he points to the surrounding beauties with the other.

My worst motoring experience, though the motoring as such could not be blamed for it, was a safari from Nairobi to spend two nights 'camping' in the Tsavo National Park. I was past the age when I felt I was adequately dressed in shorts and a shirt, so I was (to me) comfortably dressed in a thin tropical suit. About the middle of the morning I overheard one of the members of the party at the back of the shooting brake saying to another, 'It must be getting hot—he's taken off his tie.'

All went well until we entered the park after several hours' driving, then—desolation. I am sure the driver lost his way and we drove for miles along narrow tracks through barren, broken country strewn with the fossilized remains of trees looking like the crumbling skeletons of prehistoric monsters. An occasional frightened little deer darted across our tracks and, amidst almost unanimous excitement, we once caught sight of a herd of zebra on the skyline. Otherwise nothing moved, except the dust from our wheels. In a park of one hundred square miles I got what seemed to me to be claustrophobia and I told the leader of the party to get me out of the place as quick as he could. I had to stay the night in the 'camp' which was really a sort of resthouse, though an air of verisimilitude was given to the proceedings by the fact that the beer could only be cooled by putting the containers into a near-by stream. The following morning I saw the peak of Kilimanjaro above the clouds and somehow that relieved the claustrophobic feeling. However, after breakfast I departed, leaving the remainder of the party to the excitement of seeing a lion, or whatever it was they thought they saw. When, after getting through the gate of the park, I saw a couple of Africans walking along the road I heaved a sigh of relief and said to myself, 'Civilization at last.'

Sailing was a much more civilized method of travel and enjoyable so long as the sea was reasonably calm and you were a reasonably good sailor and did not make an attempt to do any work. Unfortunately sailing is no longer travel, it has become cruising which is a different thing altogether.

Certainly the fortnight from Marseilles to Bombay could be passed very pleasantly. A games committee would create itself the first morning after leaving Marseilles but you did not need to participate in the competitions they arranged: after the first rush you could usually find a deck-quoits or even a deck-tennis court free for a friendly game. As competitions developed you were subject to being interrupted in whatever else you were doing to be asked if you were Mr Jones. If you denied this, you would probably be pressed by a further question: 'Are you sure you are not down to play bullboard at 11.15?' You could walk round the deck as often as you liked. A swimming pool was usually rigged up when it got warmer. The smoke-room bar was open a good deal of the day, light music for pre-lunch drinks, and afternoon tea in the lounge and dancing and such games as Bingo after dinner. You could also sit and read, or talk, or sleep all day. The cabins were comfortable, the service excellent and cheerful, the food over-abundant.

My approach to the problem was to establish a sort of routine: walk round the deck after breakfast, then read or write letters for a couple of hours or so; wander round, watch deck games, talk to people till lunch; read or doze p.m.; walk round the deck about 6.0 p.m.—then bath, change, dinner, and if possible, dance. I sat usually in the lounge which was generally empty except when the library was open. To sit on the deck in comfort one had to be a regular, establishing a proprietary right to the desired space by a combination of a good tip to the deck steward and occupying the space regularly. A single man did not stand much chance in this against a married couple or, better still, an established group. In any case the deck was frequently hot and the glare from the sea made reading difficult.

The daily round was interestingly broken by passing through the Straits of Bonifacio, looking for the smoke from the volcano on Stromboli and passing through the Straits of Messina. Sometimes there was a call in Malta where it seemed that half the British Fleet lay at anchor.

Then there was Port Said where the first thing you saw after passing the de Lesseps statue at the end of the breakwater was a sign 'DEWARS WHISKY'. When the ship was tied up you were also welcomed by the shouts of hordes of touts and vendors of all sorts on the quay at one side of the ship, and from small bobbing boats on the other. If one of them caught the eye of a lady she was addressed loudly as Mrs Cornwallis-West; if a man, as Harry Lauder. These people were not allowed on board but the gully-gully man was. He was a genial, large, voluminously robed Egyptian who conjured marvellously with live chicks, to the huge amusement of all his audience, especially the children.

Going ashore you had to walk purposefully if you wished to evade the attentions of the hawkers intent on selling you 'amber beads'—or, more confidentially, 'dirty postcard'. Of course you made for the well known emporium of Simon Artz, the only shop where you did not bargain and which supplied important items such as 'Bombay bowlers', a popular shape of topee, cotton shirts, in addition to the full range of 'tourist rubbish'.

Port Said was an exciting, but not a pleasant place.

Then on to the best part of the journey—the Canal. It was only about 120 ft wide in places and 32 ft deep, so ships had to go very slowly to minimise the wash—You just glided along with the banks close on each side and hardly even a beat from the engines. At night it was particularly impressive. A searchlight on the ship lit up the way ahead, otherwise darkness except here and there on the bank the orange glint of a village fire. Silent except for an occasional shout from a lascar giving an instruction. The sky above was lit by a brighter moon and a myriad more stars than there seem to be in northern skies: the heavens, as they must have been seen by the shepherds as they watched their flocks by night. An unforgettable memory and I think we will leave the ship there.

But I have always liked train travelling best, especially the Night Scot, northward bound—if you can book a sleeper.

10

Overseas Committee: 1952–1968

In 1952 I was appointed to the Board of Unilever and at the same time became a part-time 'Overseas Contact Director'. In 1954 I became a full time member of what was then again known as the Overseas Committee. I was Chairman of that Committee from 1957 till I retired in 1968.

In some ways the appointment to the Board was unexciting, as it made no difference to my work nor the authority I had for doing it. I continued as Chairman of Unilever Export Limited and as part-time member of Contact Directors, and I don't think either my immediate colleagues or the members of the Special Committee listened to me more attentively because I was a Director. And I did not notice any particular signs of deference amongst my valued friends in the service divisions. The service in the directors' dining room was perhaps more stately than with the managers, but the company was considerably less entertaining. The custom was that the lower, more junior, end of the long table read their newspapers, as they could not hear any conversation that might be going on round the Chairman at the top. So lunch was good, comfortable, but also quick, and you could be back in your office in half an hour without giving offence. There was no alcohol.

When I was called into his room by the Chairman to be told I was to be nominated a Director, I was completely taken by surprise. I suppose I just had not thought about it and certainly did not expect it. I was told by my friend Marguerite Shearer of the Personnel Division, that I must have been the only interested party not to expect it as I had been top of the betting. To ensure secrecy till an announcement was made I went to an outside call box to ring up my wife. It was a great day for us both.

Inside the boardroom I had access to a great deal of information about the whole operations of the Company and I found this most fascinating. Of course outside Unilever House it was something to be a Director of Unilever, the tenth (or was it the seventeenth) biggest company in the world. I had no need to bask any longer in the reflected glory of my brother in the University of St Andrews.

There had been no nominated Chairman of Overseas Contact Directors and the re-creation of the post for the Overseas Committee, and my appointment to it, was at the behest of my fellow members of the Committee: A. D. Bonham-Carter, G. D. A. Klijnstra, R. H. Siddons. I was surprised by this too and felt greatly honoured: there were few if any jobs in Unilever as fascinating and completely satisfying and I never wished for any other.

During the ten years after I became Chairman there were ten changes in membership of the Committee. I enjoyed working with all my colleagues but so many changes were a strain in a world-wide organization where so much depended on mutual confidence.

One of my colleagues, new to the Committee, had evidently come from a job where he was supported by a great deal more 'staff work' than we had. Items on our weekly agenda were not usually supported by memoranda of explanation—members were expected to know what was going on. The absence of data frustrated my new colleague to such an extent that, half way through the meeting he said somewhat exasperatedly, 'How does the Overseas Committee work?' I answered, 'Amicably.' It could also be said that it worked personally. Not many people were involved, there was a long and well-established pattern of work which proceeded with the minimum of fuss and a maximum of mutual understanding and confidence.

The key of the operation was that all incoming and copies of all outgoing mail went to the Secretary whose duty it was to circulate correspondence on matters of note to all members of the Committee, and also to see that any department or person outside the

Committee received copies of anything that might interest them if such had not already been sent direct. By long tradition and practised attention to it, this system actually worked, thus insuring that, although each member 'looked after' his own specified countries, joint responsibility for the whole could be maintained. If anyone was in doubt about something in the circulation pad he could either go and see his colleagues about it immediately, or, more usually, just note the correspondence concerned 'Agenda please' and the matter would be raised at the next weekly meeting of the Committee.

The division of the countries for administration purposes amongst the members usually appeared haphazard to new members, and I was asked why the division should not be on a geographical basis—one member taking the Western Hemisphere, one Africa, etc. I was always against this as it seemed to me that a geographical division would lead to the members becoming 'specialists' on their area. They might lose interest in the rest of the world, or begin to think that they knew better how to tackle the problems of their countries than their colleagues—and even than their Chairman! More importantly, I think it might have tended to make the people from the areas feel that they were within the confines of an administrative group, whereas one of my main objectives in encouraging visits from overseas was that the visitors should have every opportunity and encouragement to meet people from as many countries as possible. Another advantage of the apparently haphazard division was that, when a new member joined the Committee, adjustments to the division could be made so that continuing members might be relieved of a country which they were perhaps beginning to find a bit tedious.

The advantage usually claimed for the area method of division was that it would ease the travel burden, as many countries could be visited on one journey. In my experience it is not a good thing anyway to visit many countries on one journey. It is very exhausting if you are doing the job properly, and the more countries you visit the more indistinct does the impression on your mind become of those at the beginning of the itinerary. The main purpose of a visit by a member of the Overseas Committee, it seemed to me, should be to gain or update an impression of the country, of the Company and its staff. Brief visits to deal with problems should either be left to others, or the problems dealt with by a visit by the Chairman of the Company concerned to the Overseas Committee. On this basis a member need not normally visit an Overseas Company more than once in two years: the visit should be long enough to see the whole operation, to join current discussions on outstanding problems, rather to see the staff in action than to solve the problems, and thus to gain a lasting impression of the business and how and by whom it was being run.

There is no harm in making an impression too so long as it can be an encouraging one.

'In depth' visits such as these were, I believed, more valuable to the Overseas Committee, and probably also to the Companies, than frequent 'in and out' visits. They are fundamental to the furtherance of human relationships which I regard as more important than marketing, technical or other such decisions. Specialists can deal with marketing and technical matters, but human relationships depend on line management.

On a visit it was important to get and keep as close to the Company as possible, almost becoming part of it, and anything coming from London needing attention was an interruption to this process. I arranged that I should not be so interrupted except for matters of outstanding importance and urgency. I suggested that my colleagues should adopt the same system, leaving me in their absence to deal with matters concerning other countries within their administrative sphere. This worked well and was particularly valuable in view of the many changes in membership of the Committee, enabling new members to be free to travel widely on first joining the Committee.

I was able to act as 'back stop' in this way partly because, having been so long associated with Overseas, I knew most of the senior staff and the history of the companies and had visited them, many more than once. It did involve me in a great deal of reading even though long experience gave me an instinct for finding what was important to me in a report or even in a bundle of reports. I did not find précis very satisfactory. Most business problems and situations have a key factor and I suppose only experience gives the perception required to recognize them.

It was a good thing for the Committee that it had Ron Fortune as Secretary. He took over from Charles Cole in 1954 and between them they covered a span of forty-five years. Two incumbents only of a key position, depending so much on *people*, was a most valuable continuity. The Secretary was really the Manager of the Committee with authority over its staff and absolute responsibility for its whole operation including, where necessary, prodding its members (and their secretaries—a much more delicate operation) if they showed signs of straying from accepted practices.

In addition to following Charles Cole's precepts in administration, Fortune made a notable personal contribution to the Overseas operation. He devised methods by which it was possible to pay salaries to both expatriate and local personnel all over the world in conditions of vastly different and frequently changing costs of living, exchange rates, taxation and finance regulations, such salaries (in local currency) to be credibly related to the standard management sterling salary structure which gradually emerged from the earnest endeavours of the Personnel Division. It was not always easy to convince the Special Committee at the annual salary review that an astronomical figure in some obscure and rapidly inflating currency was equivalent to only £5,000 p.a., but Fortune never failed. His greatest master stroke was when the rate of exchange he was using for a certain conversion was challenged as not being the rate quoted in *The Financial Times*. He blandly said, 'We don't use those rates,' and his questioner was dumbfounded. He also dealt gently, firmly and privately with people who, on appointment to a job overseas, wished to take with them, at the firm's expense, not only their wife and family and motorcar, but their grandmother and grand-piano too.

During the late fifties and early sixties there was a great increase in the number of people coming from overseas companies for training. For most of them it was their first visit to Europe, frequently the first time they had left their native countries. Gradually these trainees began to be accompanied by their wives, some of whom were frightened by the strangeness of the circumstances in which they found themselves. There was an accelerated flow also of people coming for discussions.

It soon became obvious that these visitors needed a good deal of help to enable them to make the most of their opportunities and, in some cases, even to avoid failure through shyness or panic.

We needed someone with great patience, a sympathetic attitude towards younger people, experienced in dealing with different sorts of people and a wide knowledge of the business. I thought of my old friend Denzil Budgett-Meakin who had worked for a short time in France and for many years in India. By nature he was an enthusiast, especially for new projects, and I was delighted and relieved when he said he would like the job which, though never so described, was really that of being 'uncle' to all men (and their wives) who came from overseas for training. It was not an easy job, especially in the early stages, when many arrived with only a hazy idea of what they would be doing, others with exaggerated ideas of what could be accomplished in the time available, and some with just exaggerated ideas. Denzil could deal with them all. He 'talked their problems out' even if it took hours.

We were fortunate also in having Miss Long who rapidly established herself as secretary to all coming for discussions at whatever level, and Miss Braddy who was guide, philosopher and friend to the frightened, and other, wives. For a time, till airways staff was provided for the purpose, she spent many days and sleepless nights meeting children either arriving at or departing from London Airport and seeing them safely on their way.

It was 1955 before I was able to take my wife with me on an overseas visit and it was a great experience for us, enlivened by the company of my colleague Robert Siddons and his wife Elisabeth. We visited Australia and New Zealand, going round the world in the process. The visit was, of course, much more enjoyable than it would otherwise have been, but also much more valuable, because I found that I got to know people better and more quickly than I had previously been able to do. I had met the wives of managers on previous overseas visits, but doing so did not normally make me feel that I knew the husbands any better. The wife always seemed to be on the embarrassed edge of the conversation, unless she was particularly gushing, in which case the poor husband was on the edge. In either case the meeting tended rather to freeze the ice than break it. It was altogether different when my wife was with me, and we came away from Australia and New Zealand feeling that we had made some friends and certainly with a clearer picture of who was who than I would have had on my own.

This alerted me to the importance of wives in the special circumstances of overseas operations wherein one must establish and maintain a feeling of close personal relationship even though contacts are infrequent.

From then onwards I worked towards a more generous outlook on the subject of wives accompanying their husbands on business visits, and this coincided with very necessary moves towards more liberal travel arrangements for the wives and children of expatriates in tropical countries, eventually ensuring that they could be together either at home or abroad for all school holidays.

These last few pages may give the impression that the Overseas Committee was a sort of superior welfare organization. I certainly believed that it was our duty to ensure that overseas managements were conscious of a close bond between themselves and the Committee, that the Committee understood their circumstances and problems, was alert to their successes and supported them in their difficulties; and I know we succeeded in this.

I also believed it important that overseas management should feel that they were part of a coherent and identifiable section of the Unilever business, and not just working in geographical isolation. Two overseas conferences created this feeling, which has subsequently been maintained by the greatly increased number and variety of special conferences, training seminars and other gatherings where people from all over the world meet together.

It was also our duty to play our part overseas in the development of the Unilever business and I think we did this too.

In the 1920s and 1930s most countries in which we were interested were under British, Dutch or United States control, and had both firm governments and stable currencies. There were rumblings here and there of eventual independence but there seemed no reason to suppose that this would interrupt the steady, if slow, progress in the development and welfare of the peoples concerned, which was the declared purpose of sovereign rule. So, when a project for establishing an overseas venture was examined, only two questions had to be asked: has export established a stable trade? is it cheaper to manufacture locally than to export?

With the exception of Argentine, which was very much *Anglo-Argentine*, a negative answer to the first question had steered us clear of Central and South America where political and economic conditions were not quite so reliable as elsewhere (and where postage stamps, as I remember, though beautiful, were scorned by schoolboy philatelists because of their continual flood of commemorative issues. Are such issues perhaps a sign of an unstable currency?). It was the purchase of the Atkinson perfumery business that had given us a small toe-hold in Uruguay, Chile and Brazil.

After the Second World War there was a vast change in the situation. The calm certainties of currency and political stability on which I was brought up disappeared. The protection of the sterling area faded away as red gradually receded from the map of the world—at least as printed in England—and instability followed in the wake of a widespread but untutored rush for political independence.

The certainties had gone, but so had stagnation. Vast numbers of the peoples of the world were not only finding it possible but were being encouraged and taught to aspire to something more than the simple wants of a primitive and constricted existence. The radio told them of something different and they wanted it. A consumer boom was borne along on the 'free world' wave of Aid, Independence and Inflation: the 'Coca-Cola Revolution'.

We would have lacked the essential element of our calling—enterprise—if we had not gone out to meet this surge of demand for the everyday products which Unilever sells.

We encountered unexpected problems and difficulties. We had disappointments and surprises, and hard but valuable experience in all phases of international business.

Almost overnight we had to replace our Dutch management when the Dutch East Indies suddenly became Indonesia. Subsequently the British contingent had to withdraw and we looked on helplessly as our Indonesian staff struggled to keep the Company going under ever more difficult conditions. It was due to the success of their struggles that it eventually became possible to rebuild the Company.

A factory built in Rahim Yar Khan as a reasonable step in the expansion of the Indian business was in quite the wrong place from which to serve the newly created Pakistan.

When the Central African Federation was formed, uniting what are now Zambia, Malawi and Rhodesia, the future seemed to smile as broadly and confidently as did Sir Roy Welensky himself, and we had some good years.

We made a big investment in Brazil with our eyes open to inflation.

It is difficult to have confidence from the outside, looking in on a country where inflation is blatant ... and economic policy is based on the assured hope that something will turn up—in time even if only just. Deus é Brasileiro (God is a Brazilian). But there is a vigour and a growth inside the country which is remarkable. More and more people are being drawn up to the standard of living which makes them potential customers for modern consumer goods and facilities for modern marketing are rapidly developing.... It is more difficult to break even with inflation than on the profit and loss account and it will take longer.

Subsequent hair-raising experience taught us the truth of this latter reflection, but I think present members of the Overseas Committee will agree that it has been worth it.

When I retired, in 1968, the total sales of the Overseas Companies had grown to £300 million. Even allowing for inflation the Overseas business could reasonably be said to be four times its size in 1946 and it had grown both geographically and in the range of products sold.

Geographical expansion doubled the number of Overseas Companies by the following additions: Japan; Malaya; Ceylon; Pakistan; Turkey; Rhodesia (blocked); Zambia; Malawi; Kenya; Ghana; Morocco; Chile; Peru; Colombia; Venezuela; Trinidad; Salvador, and Mexico.

China had disappeared and Burma, Egypt, Iraq and Newfoundland appeared and disappeared.

Development in scope was largely in margarine and edible fats, but also in ice cream and toilet preparations. One could say that all this development constituted a valuable spread of the risk; another could say that it represented a dangerous increase in the risk, and both voices were heard.

Not every project met with success and there were political, economic and financial problems as difficult to foresee as to cope with. Modern accounting techniques designed to expose the truth are salutary and necessary, but are more apt to cast shadow than brightness, gloom rather than hope, and doubts arose as to whether investment in the less sophisticated countries met with an adequate reward. I remember some that didn't and some that triumphantly did, but I recall the latter more often.

On the whole, the swings and roundabouts of the years produced not unsatisfactory profits from our enterprise. I never had any doubt but that Unilever was strengthened by the widespread, strange and often rigorous experience resulting from that enterprise, and that some able young men were given the inestimable advantage of learning the hard way.

11

Reflections

—————•———————

Unilever

In the days of the Old Man the business was already international, and since the formation of Unilever it has developed into a truly multinational concern. Multinational investments, multinational customers, multinational staff, multinational shareholders and multinational opportunities. One might add multinational problems, multinational risks and recently, multinational opprobrium.

I was told by a man quite outside Unilever that someone from inside had said that, at the time of my retirement, I knew more about Unilever than anyone else. In some ways that may have been true because I had been at the centre, at the heart, of the business for nearly fifty years and had been in working contact with every chairman and many of the directors over that period. So perhaps I may be permitted to write something about what I know to have been the motives, the aims and the policy of the Company.

People of my generation who 'went into business' had been brought up in the belief that it was 'a good thing' to build up a business and thus create wealth, and that if you participated honestly and energetically in the process some of the wealth might come your way. I am not going to try to pass a moral or a philosophical judgment on that belief, though in the retrospect of my own career it seems to have been a reasonably sound one. What I suggest is that people should be judged on the basis of the beliefs and standards of their own generation.

I am proud of the Unilever enterprise both nationally and internationally. Throughout, it has been built for the future and not just for the present. Investment has been long term, policy has been long term: it has been inspired by honesty of purpose and carried through with honesty of endeavour.

There is greed, selfishness, malice, envy and dishonesty in all walks of life, and I do not think that more exist in business than in other occupations except on the basis of the answer to the child's riddle, 'Why do white sheep eat more than black sheep?' 'Because there are more of them.' There must be many more people occupied in business of one sort and another than in most other ways of making a living. Certainly greed, selfishness and dishonesty are more readily manifest in business than elsewhere, but in view of the vast amount of the world's commerce which is conducted on credit, that is, trust, I do not think there is any basis for the idea that seems to have gained ground in recent years that a business can normally be expected to be motivated by greed and activated by dishonesty.

The business of Unilever consists very largely in supplying the ordinary things in the everyday life of a housewife, wherever she lives, and development has stemmed from improvements in quality and performance of some of the basic products and the invention of new ones. There is no doubt that housewives, and indeed whole families, have benefitted from these improvements and inventions, be they soap powder instead of bar soap, soft margarine instead of stiff butter, fish fingers instead of unfilleted fish. There is equally no doubt that these innovations were not devised for philanthropic reasons—it was hoped that profit would accrue, thus enabling the business to survive in bad times and grow in good. And that was believed to be 'a good thing'.

I have no doubt that in the case of Unilever, and probably many other international companies, it has been a good thing not only because, through early export enterprise, people were taught to use products which helped to lift them from the squalor of a primitive existence but also because as overseas companies began to be established in countries with little or no experience of sophisticated industry they brought with them, and trained their local staff in the technologies, the skills, and the humanities of the parent company.

This process, developed by 'ization' to which I have already referred, has led to the training of local staff and it has given them the inestimable advantage of continuing contacts with colleagues not only in the United Kingdom and Holland but in many other parts of the world which are securely based on mutual understanding, respect and confidence. Helping 'developing countries' needs not only money: it needs skill, patience and understanding. To put it bluntly it needs money, skill and love, and the greatest of these is love.

Unilever's dealings with Governments have always been above board. If we could not get into a country through the front door we did not go through the back and, once in, we built to stay and played the game by the rules even when they became onerous. The basic policy was that Companies were supported financially till they were profitable and, if prospects were then good, profits were left in the Company to provide for development. It must have been ten or fifteen years before the Indian Company (which was profitable and expanding) paid a dividend, and I remember in the '30s when cash was by no means plentiful that 'Boston' (the Lever Company in U.S.A.) was allowed to retain its substantial cash flow to push ahead with successful development—much to the disgust of some of the home directors who considered that they could have used some of it to advantage. Exchange control and other regulations, widespread throughout the world since the war, have changed all that and now every remittance, whether in or out, is a matter of cautious, prudent, individual decision against an uncertain background of ever-changing currency values. It has had to become firmly established that 'Cash belongs to Father'.

Since I retired, and I am glad it is since I retired, I have read in the papers about *multinationals*, writ large. These companies apparently 'bestride the narrow world like a Colossus,' hell-bent on frustrating the eager plans of the bureaucrats and operating 'beyond control'.

Recalling my last twenty years in business this idea makes me laugh (or cry) because I do not think there was a country without some sort of controls—silly, reasonable, stringent, damaging or lethal. Against this rising flood it was no good telling the tide to recede. What you did was to put your seat back a bit, and if by moving back you eventually found yourself pushed out of the country altogether, which did happen, you withdrew with such politeness as could be mustered, more in sorrow than in anger, because valuable human links had been broken.

If it is 'a good thing' to sell more soap, to make available throughout the free world sewing machines, corrugated iron, kerosene, medicine, bicycles, radio sets and so on, and if it is a good thing that peoples of different countries be brought to work together in international companies instead of to quarrel at international conferences, then the free world would be a less 'good thing' now than it would have been without the multinationals.

I am sure most managements try to make a reasonable place for themselves in the countries in which they have investments, but if there are companies which arrogantly trample on the susceptibilities of the weak, I am sorry for them. Unilever does not.

The amalgamation of Margarine Unie with Lever Brothers Limited which created Unilever took place at a time of worldwide economic depression which added to the strains of bringing together two large businesses staffed by men of different nationality with strong attachment to the individual companies in which they had been 'brought up' and with somewhat different business philosophies. Only determined and strong leadership could have achieved success in these conditions, but such leadership was not lacking.

Francis D'Arcy Cooper was the first Chairman of Unilever, jointly with the Earl of Bessborough, and with the second Viscount Leverhulme as Governor—but we knew who was boss. D'Arcy Cooper led the Company through the '30s which were a hard slog for everyone with nothing much to show to the outside world in the way of sparkling results.

In May 1930 Unilever issued in the United Kingdom 2,000,000 ordinary shares of £1 each at £3 per share.

The price of these shares on the London Stock Exchange during the remainder of that year was High 76s 3d (just over £3·81), Low 31s 3d (just over £1·55). During the next ten years prices fluctuated, reaching a High of 46s 9d (just over £2·33) in 1937 and a Low of 15s 0d (75p) in 1940. The smallest spread in any one year was in 1934 with High 26s 6d (£1·32½) and Low 17s 10½d (just under 90p).

There was 'rationalization' (reductions in staff numbers) which was dealt with fairly, firmly, quickly and as generously as circumstances allowed, but there was never any doubt within the Company about ultimate success and by the late '30s the Company was securely based on the sound morale of the staff and the sound reserves in the balance sheet.

D'Arcy Cooper died, before he was sixty, in 1941. Geoffrey Heyworth, aged forty-seven, succeeded him as Chairman. He followed his predecessor in a distaste for personal aggrandisement and fulsomeness of speech and in his belief in straightforward and honest dealing. He was not much of a talker but he was great at plain speaking. He knew every stone of the foundations laid by D'Arcy Cooper and he was the architect of the superstructure built over the next eighteen years.

In 1945 there was nothing like the sudden burst of euphoric optimism which, all too briefly, marked the end of the First World War in 1919. People during the First lived under the heavy cloud of the casualty lists but were not otherwise seriously oppressed except by poor food. In the Second there were few who did not feel the strain of anxiety, austerity, restriction and uncertainty, and when the end came there was little puff and less cash left for celebration. But there was relief and a justified hope of better things to come. Something worth working for. So people came flooding back from the Forces and other forms of National Service and Unilever was ready to put them to work in a business poised for expansion.

Geoffrey Heyworth reduced the Special Committee to three members: himself, Sir Herbert Davis and Paul Rykens. They formed a triumvirate of great distinction and strength and established the Committee firmly at the head of the business. All three knew the business, though from different aspects, and they had different attributes. Geoffrey Heyworth looked forward to new methods of marketing, new methods of management development, new accounting methods and practices, new product fields to enter. He set a fresh pattern for chairmen's annual meeting speeches, dealing with subjects of general business interest such as research, management, and transport. Herbert Davis was a shrewd man of business with long experience of oil milling involving day-to-day decisions on raw material purchasing and oil selling prices. He was Controller of Oils and Fats in the Ministry of Supply during the Second World War. He had an acutely penetrating mind and could and did delve deep by questioning to find the weak spot in any project or any man he doubted. If you convinced him that you knew what you were talking about, and it was not easy, you were home and dry. Paul Rykens, for Margarine Union, and John McDowell, for Lever Brothers, were responsible for the detailed negotiations which set up the twin Unilever Companies, N.V. and Limited. This was an extremely complex matter and it is a tribute to their negotiating skill, their foresight and their ingenuity, that the agreements under which the two companies work as one have stood the test of forty years of vastly changing circumstances. Paul Rykens could see and find his way through any difficulty, no matter how complex and delicate.

It is not of any significance but it is interesting to note in passing that Geoffrey Heyworth was a Lever man, Herbert Davis was from Jurgens and Paul Rykens from Van den Berghs—the three main family companies linked in Unilever.

Responsibility for running the day-to-day business was placed clearly upon those at the head of the operating units, be they company chairmen, national managers, or (overseas) group heads.

Highly qualified specialist divisions were established at the centre to advise, guide and help the operating units; these were independent of the main line of command and answered direct to the Special Committee: Marketing Advisory Division; Technical Division; Personnel Division; Financial Group; and, later, Organization Division.

Research was also centralized and greatly expanded after the war. Centralization was probably the only way of building it up quickly and the Company owes a great deal to Ernest Woodroofe (later Sir Ernest, Chairman of the Company 1970–74) for having done the job so well.

Unilever's food interests were greatly extended in the 1940s. In 1943 Unilever bought from General Foods a 75 per cent interest in the Birds Eye deep freeze business outside the U.S.A., and in the same year acquired full control of Batchelors, a Yorkshire business specializing, at that time, in processed peas. In September 1946

Unilever bought a controlling interest in Lipton's, U.S.A., who had a large share of the tea trade in the States.

Geoffrey Heyworth's greatest contribution, however, was the impetus he gave to management training. His convinced interest in this was demonstrated by his giving practical shape to the project for the establishment of a national industrial Staff College and his Chairmanship in 1945 of the first to be established—the Administrative Staff College at Henley-on-Thames. It was not long before Unilever people from all over the world were attending anything from a course at Harvard Business School to a seminar for supervisors (hitherto known as foremen), and this built up the inner strength of the company, which can only come from its management and staff.

The results from these dispositions and Geoffrey Heyworth's leadership over the eighteen years of his chairmanship can be simply shown as follows:

	1942	1959
	£	
Sales	300,000,000	1,300,000,000
Consolidated net profit	6,000,000	60,000,000

People

D'Arcy Cooper once said that there was an element of luck in all careers and it lay in the chance of whom you happened to meet. He said that his luck was to meet the Old Man.

He was talking to about 130 Unilever managers, members and guests of a private luncheon club. I was present, but I am indebted to my friend George Kirkpatrick for the following account (written by him at the time for the *Port Sunlight News*) of the story that D'Arcy Cooper told:

Probably because his father was an accountant before him, he began business by entering accountancy; he was not specially drawn to that profession, indeed he disliked arithmetic! The first piece of advice given to him by a fellow-clerk was that if he were ever sent out on audit (and the clerk didn't seem to think there was any great likelihood of it) he should keep clear of Port Sunlight, as they made them work overtime there on Saturdays. That advice he followed faithfully for over eleven years; he never even saw Port Sunlight. But the objection did not apply to the Continental audits. There was never any urgency about them, and they had the great advantage to a young man of allowing him to see the world at somebody else's expense.

Mr. Cooper then recounted the history of an unusual and individual investigation which he was sent to undertake in Germany, after he had become a junior partner. There was a business in Dusseldorf which Lever's wanted to buy. When he returned to London his senior partner said, as usual, that 'I had been a long while away and he could not think what I had been doing. Sir William Lever was in a great hurry, and I had better take the report round myself in case he wanted to ask any questions. I thought that here was a chance of telling the great man not only the financial position but also what I thought of the personnel and of the future of the business' (with which Sir William was in negotiation).

'I was shown into his room at Sunlight Wharf,' Mr. Cooper continued. 'I said, "I have brought the report on the so-and-so business.' The only reply was, 'Thank you, put it down there, good morning.' I was in and out in fifteen seconds.

A few weeks later, when I was in Bristol, I received a telephone call to report to London at once and go over to Dusseldorf that night, as Sir William was there, and the Germans had said that all my figures were wrong. This made me furious, and when I arrived next morning and found McDowell waiting for me at the station, saying that I was to come at once to see Sir William and Dr. Seiglin, I replied that I was going to have a bath and a shave first, and it would give them time to think over an apology to me.

When I went into the room I found there not only Sir William Lever and Dr. Seiglin, but also Dr. Seiglin's staff and a few professors from various universities who had been called in to assist with the accounts.'

During the ensuing argument Mr. Cooper waited until he could catch Dr. Seiglin's eye. When he did, it seemed suddenly to dawn on the doctor that perhaps it was not wise to let his fellow-countrymen know too much about a business, the peculiar working of which was known only to himself and Mr. Cooper. He withdrew with his compatriots for a private discussion. While he was out of the room, Sir William expressed himself strongly about Mr. Cooper's figures.

On returning, Dr. Seiglin 'told Sir William that he was satisfied that my figures were entirely right, that I knew more about his business in three weeks than his staff knew in thirty years, and he was prepared to sign the agreement forthwith. In the train that night, returning with Sir William Lever, I was his "blue-eyed boy".'

About eleven years later the light blue eyes which had frightened Dr Seiglin must also have outfaced the light blue eyes of the Old Man himself, probably for the first time in his life, but that did not diminish the mutual respect and affection which existed between the two men.

Affection shone through D'Arcy Cooper's remark on the day after the Old Man's death: 'He's probably now arguing with St Peter about the architecture of the gates.'

A day or two later when he was addressing members of the staff there was a catch in his voice as he said: 'His precepts will be our guide.'

Some years later, at the unveiling of the memorial to the Old Man, in Port Sunlight, Cooper said:

To those outside the business who may ask what testimony is required when the village, the factory and the Art Gallery stand as everlasting memorials to the greatness of his intellect and the fertility of his imagination, we reply that we who worked with him . . . desire to place on record some permanent sign of our affection and respect . . .

In the five and a half years that have passed since we laid Lord Leverhulme to rest in the Church of the village I do not think that we have been false to the traditions that he laid down and I believe that they will be maintained in the future as in the past.

He rescued the Old Man when he was floundering in the flood of depression which so soon and so devastatingly swept away the euphoria of optimism and confidence that had exploded on the world at the end of the war to end wars.

After the Old Man's death he carried Lever Brothers Limited through to firm ground and subsequently laid firm foundations for Unilever.

As Charles Wilson in the History records:

'. . . if an author of the era of good feeling had to be named the title would fall to Francis D'Arcy Cooper. The power of his orderly yet imaginative mind, and above all his blunt honesty of purpose, were gradually recognised by everybody. Refusing obstinately to admit that distinctions of nationality on business origins had any validity, Cooper proceeded to cut clean across the old boundaries between Jurgens' and Van den Bergh's and between Dutch and English. He fought tenaciously, and eventually with success, for the principle that posts should be filled and responsibility shouldered by those best qualified, irrespective of previous affiliations or the imagined rights of the disinherited.'

He was a man's man, direct of speech, even blunt, and fearing no one. If there was a hard thing to be done, and there were many, he did not hesitate. But my contacts with him support what the Old Man is reported in the *History* to have said about him. He was 'one of the type of men that I consider most resemble a warm fire and people naturally seem to come up to him for warmth'. I have mentioned his general kindness to me when I was much the junior of the party on the Old Man's last visit to the Continent but there was one act of special kindness. On the morning in Danzig when the Old Man sent me back to bed with a flea in my ear and a dose of salts Cooper, just before lunch, climbed up several flights of stairs to my room to see how I was. I was better so he said I needed some fresh air and took me a walk round the park.

A couple of years later, when I was looking after the Lever exports to India, the profit for a certain quarter was down on the previous year. The day after I had reported this I was summoned to the Chairman's room. My heart sank. When I got in, Cooper said, 'I want to congratulate you, Knox. I see that your last quarter's results were below the previous year but that you had estimated they would be. If everyone estimated as well as that, my job would be a lot easier. Thank you.'

Very early in his Chairmanship, on a New Year's Day, the staff in Lever House were electrified by a circular passed round about noon saying that the Chairman had decided to go home after lunch and suggested that the staff might like to do the same.

Shortly after the Unilever amalgamation he saw two Dutch colleagues in the corridor smoking cigars. He drew their attention to the fact that smoking was not allowed in the office. The colleagues said of course they knew that, but they were directors. The no smoking rule was cancelled the next day.

My last story I got from Barnish who told me that he went into Cooper's office one morning (presumably in his usual breezy manner) and said 'Cooper, I am sure you will be interested to know that this morning I complete thirty-five years service with the Concern.' Cooper looked up and said, 'If I were you, Barnish, I would keep quiet about that.'

Two of his Board colleagues paid written tribute to him. The second Lord Leverhulme and H. R. Greenhalgh: both had known him for over twenty-five years:

> D'Arcy Cooper possessed a great personal charm, a bright and courageous outlook. Of ready wit, fearless and outspoken, one felt at once that nothing but plain and straightforward dealing would succeed with him. He was ruthless with deceit or wrongdoing (Greenhalgh).

and

> His honesty and fairness of mind were, I consider, the secret of his personal ascendency and influence. Men trusted his judgment and knew that they would get a direct answer . . . It was the honesty which faced facts and it was the source of that remarkable courage which we all so admired.
>
> In private life he was the best of company, an ideal host and companion in the shooting field, a resolute opponent but a

tolerant partner on the golf course,* while at the bridge table he found a form of mental recreation for which he was naturally suited (Leverhulme).

D'Arcy Cooper was a great man and I was fortunate to have known him.

I was also most fortunate to meet J. Laurence Heyworth so early in my life, not only for the way he helped me to grow up and encouraged me towards self-confidence but also because through him, also early in life, I met his two younger brothers, Geoffrey and Roger. All three became Directors of Unilever. Both Laurence and Geoffrey took a lot of getting to know and it was well to start the process early. They were not 'stand-offish', but seemed to be exceptionally self-contained and their somewhat grudging and muffled monosyllables could be disconcerting, even frightening, to those who did not know them. They both 'came up the hard way' in the business, knew it thoroughly and were devoted to it.

Laurence was the quietest of the three. It was said that during the first war he refused a Commission on the grounds that the bridge was better in the sergeants' mess, but could call the roll by heart, knowing the name and number of all the men under him. He worked quietly and effectively on the overseas side of the business throughout his career.

I have recorded Geoffrey's great work for Unilever. He also did much valuable public service and strove to improve the links between Industry and Government and between universities and the world of business as a whole. He was Chairman of the Leverhulme Trust Fund for nearly thirty years during which its income greatly increased. The Fund was established under the Will of the first Viscount Leverhulme partly for the encouragement of education and scholarship. Under Heyworth's guidance the Fund gave support to new ventures in scholarship rather than established studies and gave considerable encouragement to the establishment

* Charles Cole, who was there at the time, recalls that Cooper did not express himself very tolerantly when his partner, Leverhulme, took seventeen at the 16th hole at Littlestone in an inter-company golf match known as the Dash Cup. Cooper also enjoyed poker which he played only with his equals.

of links between universities, especially links over national
boundaries.

Heyworth was created Baronet in 1948 and Baron in 1955, this
being one of the few hereditary peerages of recent years. He was
honoured by the Queen of the Netherlands and held many academic
appointments and honorary degrees. All these honours did not
disturb his natural modesty which was described perfectly in *The
Times* obituary: 'Affectation, arrogance, pedantry and conscious
charm were all alike utterly foreign to him.' I remember a poignant
moment when he was showing me the title deeds of his peerage
and said, 'Nobody to carry it on'. He had three brothers and a
sister and none of the family had any children.

He had a great interest in sport but not of the hunting, shooting
and fishing variety. Being brought up in Scotland, he was an
enthusiastic golfer throughout his life though arthritis prevented
him from playing in the latter years. He never missed an important
Rugby occasion at Twickenham and, when possible, followed the
Calcutta Cup to Murrayfield. He was interested in and therefore
knowledgeable about other games, was a good swimmer and particularly enjoyed driving a big car, both of which forms of exercise
gave him special satisfaction after arthritis restricted his movement.
His highest praise was 'satisfactory'. My mother's was 'correct'.

After retirement he devoted his energies and liveliness of mind
to furthering the interests of education and the social sciences, but
his heart remained close to Unilever and he greatly enjoyed reminis-
cing about the old days. He gave me encouragement to continue
the writing of these notes when he read my first draft and as I write
this revision I record with sorrow and a deep sense of loss his death
on 15th June, 1974, at the age of seventy-nine. My contemporaries
in Unilever and I mourn the passing of a great leader and an understanding and affectionate friend. Our hearts go out to Lois who
supported him through very nearly fifty years of married life with
a modesty which matched his and a graciousness all her own.

Roger Heyworth was quite different from his brothers. He had
a powerful mind (Oxford, First Class, P.P.E.) and acquired a wide
and detailed knowledge of the business like his brothers. But he
was more voluble than they were in the expression of his thought
and ideas. He had an openness and easiness of manner that made

him approachable. He was on Christian name terms with his colleagues whether junior or senior long before this became the fashion.

I met him, I think, even a day or two before he joined the Lever
business, straight from Oxford. We were near contemporaries and
although we did not work closely together for many years we
became friends. He worked on the Continent and then in the East.
He was captured, along with Mr Arthur Hartog, by the Japanese
when they overran China, but fortunately released on a civilian
exchange. His sudden death while on a visit to Ceylon in 1954 was
a great loss to the business. It was more than that. It was a profound shock and caused deep and lasting sorrow to all with whom
he had worked, for the simple reason that he was beloved. That is a
strange word to use for a business colleague but no other will serve.

Looking back, I think I was generally fortunate in those I met
and those with whom I worked throughout my career, but I
specially recall the ten years connected with India with gratitude
to John Hansard for his friendship and for the absolute confidence
he placed not only in my work but in my judgment. Also to Bill
Shaw who, though older in age and experience than me, never
questioned my leadership nor withheld his dedicated and complete
co-operation.

Of course there were one or two people through the years with
whom I did not get on very well, but I was fortunate or wily
enough to separate myself from them before serious damage was
done to either party.

A further good fortune was that my career was in an era when
the importance of people in a business was increasingly recognized;
that I was in a Company that was expanding and which recognized
that successful management depends more on the calibre, capacity
and personality of the men concerned than upon any trick of
organizational structure: indeed that the atmosphere within an
organization is more important than its form.

Thoughts on Management

A manager's job used to be to do what he was told and see that
the other people did likewise. This authoritarian concept dies hard

in family businesses and must have been all-pervading in the early days of the Old Man's business experience, but force of circumstances, if nothing else, would have driven him away from it as his business grew, first geographically and then through what is now called 'diversification'. He could not give day-to-day instructions to a man looking after a business in Australia or developing plantations in the depth of the Congo forests. He could and did give general directions. He could, he wished to, and he did leave people to get on with the job but he kept a keen and watchful eye on every detail of the business he had built up. He was alert to criticise and reprove and even more ready to praise, but he no longer handled day-to-day business. He did not propound any theory of management based on this practical experience, but this experience none the less was the base from which the successful development of management for Lever Brothers Limited and subsequently Unilever grew.

The fundamental difference between the old concept of management and the new is that, under the old, authority and responsibility were firmly centralized whereas now they are both effectively delegated. The change from one to the other has been gradual and has not followed any predetermined or even accepted pattern. Like Topsy it 'just growed', the exigencies of the situation having been met as they have arisen with greater reference to the man available for the job than to any theory of management other than the conviction that if responsibility is delegated, authority must go with it. The problem of providing competent and effective management for a rapidly growing and diversifying business was a practical one and, to the inestimable advantage of the business, it was solved mainly by giving men already in the Company a chance rather than by recruitment of specialists from outside. As an old Scottish farmer said, 'Better a guid coo than a coo of a guid kind.' There were many successes, some brilliant, but few failures. The operation was made possible by the fact that amongst the flood of people returning from the Services in 1945 some had had experience of management before the war and most were keen to take a chance.

This was fine for the immediate circumstances but it had become clear that much greater attention would have to be given to management training for the future, and indeed training for management has subsequently become a growth industry on its own.

In the early days that I remember there was quite serious opposition to the idea of training, as distinct from learning by doing. You were trained by doing a job—and if you did one well you might get a better one. In other words, the only way up was 'the hard way'. Billy Barnish certainly came up that way and seriously believed that it was the only proper way, to the extent that he told my father that, though the Staff Training College at Port Sunlight might be a useful social amenity, it was of no value to the business.

The Old Man gave my brother a pretty good idea of what he thought of university men for business, as I have already recounted. About the same time in a letter to my father he wrote:

From a business point of view, I am not at all attracted by the average University Professor. For instance, I gave an address at the Liverpool University some years ago, in which I used the illustration of Edison asking the man who had taken the highest mathematical prizes in a certain University to tell him the holding capacity of a glass electric light bulb. He worked it out and Edison declared he was wrong. He worked it out a second time; Edison still declared he was wrong. These two calculations had taken the man, I think, some eight hours. Edison took the electric light bulb, cut round the pointed end with a plumber's diamond, tapped it and it fell off. He filled the bulb with water, measured the water in a graduated beaker and read out the contents—all in the surprising space of two minutes. A University man present, after my speech was over, criticised this method and stated as an objection to it that you wasted an electric light bulb. The absolute blindness of the business principle shown by this objection rather shocked me for if the University Professor's time for eight hours has not got a value above 1/6d, and he would waste eight hours to save 1/6d, then that type of outlook and that type of man would be no good in business.

My brother accompanied the Old Man, as his Secretary, on his last visit to the Congo. During the visit the Old Man wrote once or twice to my parents and my brother, who typed the letters, must have got a bit tired of comparisons between his disadvantage of being a University man compared with the advantages he would have had had he been apprenticed to a grocer, even though it was all obviously intended to be taken light-heartedly. My brother would not have known at the time that the Old Man had written in a handwritten letter to my parents: 'You know my preconceived prejudices against University men—Well it seems to me that Malcolm has set himself to reverse these old opinions of mine and he looks like succeeding.'

Incidentally, the Old Man's experience as a grocer's apprentice must have been particularly successful because at age twenty-one he had a salary of £800 p.a., which in 1872 must have been a good salary even for a 'journeyman' grocer!

The Old Man was in fact a great supporter of education and scholarship. He left no legacy of prejudice against helping people through education and training and he left also the first means of staff training established within the business, namely, the Staff Training College at Port Sunlight to which I have already referred.

When the College started in 1917 all junior employees spent one day a week there for the first two years of employment. Students from the works (usually aged 14–16) had classes for English, arithmetic, hygiene, geography and civics; from the office (16–18), English, arithmetic, commerce, book-keeping, shorthand and typing. There were special arrangements for apprentices which supplemented, or helped them with, their night-school work, but also included English, commercial arithmetic, elementary accountancy and freehand drawing. All students had one period of physical training.

Later the College developed into a general educational and cultural institution available to all employees, and offering a wide range of subjects including not only bookkeeping, commercial correspondence and languages, but economics and 'personality'.

A lot of the teaching was done by works and office staff and, while some of it was specific to the pupil's job, the basic concept was the encouragement of continued learning first of all by those who had just left school, and subsequently more generally. I have already recorded testimony of its success.

The idea that the hard way is the only way was generally held throughout the business. Not all young people relished the idea of attending the S.T.C. even though it was in the Firm's time. When the management trainee scheme for university graduates was started in 1927 there was doubt about its value. This may have stemmed partly from not unnatural jealousy of university trainees but arose also from a genuine belief that a two years' course at management level could be no substitute for ten years experience up to that level.

Even when management courses started in the 1950s there was a certain initial scepticism about them among those who thought they knew their jobs. (The position is quite different now—you don't rate unless you have been to at least two courses.)

I admit that I was no exception to the general rule about 'the hard way'.

I went to night school with reluctance and not for very long. I was doubtful about the trainee scheme but it did not bother me when I found that trainees did not generally come overseas. As to courses, I certainly never went on one, mainly because I had to travel a great deal at the time they were really getting going, but I certainly helped by 'lecturing' when called upon to do so. I did, however, maintain a front of some scepticism as a brake on the over-enthusiastic, and it may be apt to quote a rhyme I wrote (with apologies to Henry King) for my retirement party.

> The chief defect of Knox of late
> Is being rather out of date.
> He will not give the respect he ought
> To everything that we are taught
> About the modern business tools
> When we attend post-graduate schools
> At last his colleagues tried to force
> Him on to a Computer Course.
> But in reply he firmly said
> 'I think I'll take "lump sum" instead'

(Taking the 'lump sum' was the current euphemism for accepting early retirement.)

When considering management courses one should differentiate between those run by the Company and those run by the Administrative Staff College, business schools, etc.

As to Company courses, I have been astonished to come across a copy of a letter I wrote in 1943 to Hansard then on the United Kingdom side of the business. I really must quote from it because it describes well what I believe has been, and is, the supreme justification for the cost and the enormous amount of effort which has subsequently been put into the courses, conferences and seminars held at what is known throughout the Unilever world as 'Four Acres' (a residential training centre at Kingston-upon-Thames).

One aspect of the organisation of the Ordnance Filling Factories has interested me particularly, though it is outside my immediate scope, and that is the matter of training. This is largely technical training whether it be in Filling technicalities or Administrative routine. But some of the senior management at R.O.F's [Royal Ordnance Factories] have grasped the wider possibilities of such training, and it is this which has attracted my attention.

These possibilities lie in the field of staff morale, esprit de corps, employee goodwill, or whatever name you care to give to what used to be known as 'the Co-partnership spirit' in Lever Brothers.

Whether the training schemes in the R.O.F's have been consciously used to engender morale or not I do not know, but I believe that they have had that effect and could certainly be shaped and used to that end.

In Lever Brothers in the past we have not needed to bother much about esprit de corps: it has been there. I am old-fashioned, or sentimental, enough to believe that the foundations laid in this sphere by the Old Man have stood the firm in as good stead as his more directly commercial enterprise. The foundations have subsequently been well built upon by an enlightened and human staff and labour policy.

But can we rely only upon these for the future? Individual units of our firm are already so big that the influence of personality can not be brought to bear directly on all the staff concerned in them, and when we consider the firm as a whole I think we must realise that some substitute must be found for the personal touch if we are to avoid the degeneration of our esprit de corps into a negative or passive loyalty.

With these thoughts in mind I suggest the establishment, either on a temporary or permanent basis, of a Training School for staff of all grades: for all who are likely to take leading places in whatever section of the firm they may be placed. If this could be made a residential school we would bring together for a short time men who would be going to widely separated posts of duty, and this would help to build our esprit de corps. I have frequently been struck by the lack of knowledge of our business as a whole possessed by many senior members of our staff. A wider knowledge need not necessarily contribute directly to a better performance of a given job, but it should contribute substantially to an understanding of and enthusiasm for the firm.

As a permanent establishment it would be almost a Management Training Centre where men due for or worthy of promotion could be taught the full implication of their new responsibility, and where they would have the opportunity to mix with and become known to at least some of the senior members of the firm. In this way they could be brought to feel that they were more closely associated with the firm as a whole than they would do were their contacts to remain only those of their immediate sphere.

We don't want to grow into a series of separate, almost antagonistic concerns. We must engender the spirit of unity even in the diversity of our interests, if those interests are to work for and not against the common good.

The staffing of such a Training Centre would admittedly not be easy. On the technical training side it might not be difficult: a matter of providing the men with the necessary experience and ability to impart their knowledge. But on the 'morale' side it would be hopeless if the thing got into the hands of professional 'trainers' or even professional 'Staff Managers'. The policy of the firm could only be interpreted by those responsible for it, i.e. the Directors and senior staff, and to make a success of it the 'highest levels' would have to be prepared to devote the time necessary to take part in the activities of the Centre.

To add to the duties and ties of the Directors and senior staff is a serious matter, but I believe that the training, choosing and placing of management staff is one of the most important jobs in any organisation, and it becomes increasingly important the bigger the organisation. Surely it is worth the effort to do it well.

It never occurred to me when I wrote my letter that within ten years I would be one of those called upon to co-operate in courses at Four Acres, and finding it worth the effort to do it well.

I am sure that what I wrote had no influence on, nor connection with, the establishment of Four Acres. I am equally sure that the basic purpose of those who started management courses was to pass on to others the benefit of their own specialized knowledge and experience.

The first residential courses I remember were on Advertising, run by the late Jack Beausire at the Mandeville Hotel, Marylebone. Jack had had wide and long experience of all the elements of marketing and I am sure his pupils gained greatly from his instruction and that of others he could muster to his aid. But if the records of Unilever management were searched through twice, nobody would have been found who had such a gift for ready but real friendship as Jack. The warmth of his spirit flowed out naturally and generously, overcoming shyness and reserve and creating an atmosphere of trust and confidence. He could not help but build goodwill, and he set the pattern for subsequent courses, the first problem for which was to find a good leader. Thus was established the tradition which I am sure has made a major contribution towards the continued strength of the morale within the business.

I am not so enthusiastic about courses outside the Company and indeed I think that business schools have grown so fast that they have outgrown their strength. In saying this I realize that I am in the exceptionally privileged position of having been at the centre of a large international business that has, by tradition, been as open to new ideas from the outside as it has been generous with its own. I have been kept abreast, at least until five years ago when I retired, of the developments of business technology, if that is the right name for it, and if in some cases I have not grasped the full detail I have learned what it was all about and the jargon which I have often found to be all you really need to know when dealing with experts. Moreover I have operated from the bottom to the top of a diverse business which, whatever else it may be, is exceptionally well managed, and always has been.

Here I wish to pay tribute to the very backbone of good management: those responsible for accounts, finance, taxation, statistics and legal matters. Inspired and encouraged by successive chairmen, the men (and recently a woman, Miss Graham, Assistant Chief Accountant) dealing with these matters have made and continue to make a vital contribution to the strength of the whole management structure of Unilever. Accounting procedures were ahead of the times (I was taught inflation accountancy in the late fifties), finance was handled with skill, foresight and prudence, taxation with vigour, statistics with accuracy and unfailing regularity, legal matters with absence of fuss. Those concerned were experts, some of national repute; but they never tried to 'blind you with science'. They were always ready to help with advice, explanation and suggestions and ensured that the flow of information to those concerned with the day-to-day business of the Company should be accurate, comprehensive and presented in such manner as to be easily comprehended.

It is invidious, I know, to mention names, but through the years the following have been great names: Frank Bower; Joost de Blank; Frank Walker; Harold Odling; Gerard Norton; 'Brockie' (S. R. Brockbank); and more recently and with particular reference to 'Overseas': Evert Hofman; Arie Haak; Gerald van Loo; Bert Aylmer; Eric Nortcliffe; Morris Stubbs; Dick Smith and Sydney Stone.

Somewhat to my surprise I have come to appreciate in recent years that this state of affairs is not so general within industry as I had assumed it to be. I have heard a business consultant extol the advantages of making forward estimates of sales and profits as if this was a fine new idea, and I have been doing it practically from

my cradle. It is obvious from the Press that there are companies
that have no proper control over important elements of expenditure nor any clear idea of their cash flow. On the other hand I have
seen with utter amazement the enormous sheets of figures that the
booking clerk at our local station has to complete week by week,
and also a couple of supervisors or auditors spending days with
him going through these figures. I wonder if the Railways Board
makes any use of this massive detailed daily record, and if they
have any idea how much it costs to ensure that, as my friend told
me, he got a tick-off, in his first year, when on the total receipts of
£80,000 for the thousands of tickets he had issued he was 7/8d
out.

Obviously there is need for management education, but the
academic approach to the subject has tended to make it appear
more scientific than it really is and may divert students' attention
from the fact that business is largely made up of a lot of jolly hard
work. I find it difficult to realize that so many new sciences have to
be applied to problems that I have been so ignorant as to suppose
could be solved by common sense and simple arithmetic.

People should undoubtedly be taught how to use the tools
available to them, even if only to understand when they are not
necessary. The great danger of the eruption of management
systems, operational research, computers, calculators etc. that has
burst upon the business world in the last twenty years is that young
people have been led to believe, firstly, that they must use all this
paraphernalia of psuedo-scientific technique, and secondly, that if
they do so they can't be wrong.

People who already have experience of business can undoubtedly
gain from attending business schools. They learn new techniques
but have the experience to enable them to judge how applicable
these may be to their own working situation. More importantly, in
my view, is that it gives them the chance to rub up against people
from other spheres of activity and to realize, according to their
temperament, that their fellow students are as good as they or that
they are as good as their fellow students.

As Chairman of the Overseas Committee I was responsible for
'administrative contacts' with North America. This brought me
into contact with those who went on courses at the Harvard Busi-

ness School. I used to ask them if and how they had benefited. I got a standard answer which I thought was somewhat negative: 'It was very stimulating.'

A graduate going straight to a post graduate business school with no practical experience is likely to meet with disillusion when he gets into business. He may find that there is little of the intellectual stimulus he may have been encouraged to expect and his techniques may have little relevance to the daily job in hand.

In glancing through a recently published book 'concerned with the use of modern management tools at the strategic level' I noticed that the sixth item in the recipe of 'How to Plan' was 'Decide what tasks have to be done to exploit the options chosen' The seventh was 'Give somebody these tasks'.

It is better if those who are going to do the deciding have been a 'somebody' first.

From the time when I was a 'somebody' till I retired I was close to or part of the decision-making process. It seems to me that the essential element in the process is determination, and management tools don't provide that. They may guide and encourage determination but I think they could also misguide and discourage. If a man makes a bad decision he cannot claim in mitigation that the model pointed firmly in that direction. If he does, he condemns himself: he did not make a decision at all, he merely signed a cheque which someone else vouched for. When making a decision in business, the results of which affect other people, it must be made on the basis of your own knowledge and experience and on data of which you are a master. In the end it is your assessment that should support your determination not that of someone else.

If the Overseas Committee, when I was Chairman, had been faced with one of these spider's-web-like diagrams setting out in frightening detail the estimated results from following every one of the options open to us in a certain situation, I think I would have been reminded of what the Duke of Wellington said during the Peninsular Wars about a certain section of his army which he did not like the look of: 'I don't know what effect these men will have on the enemy, but by God they terrify me.'

The management tool which is most apt to discourage determination and hence decisiveness is research, or as it is sometimes

now called 're-search'. (This is perhaps a better name for some of
what now masquerades as research which is simply the assembly
of facts already known.) Market research can become an opiate
tending to lull the minds of marketing people into a belief that
they are necessarily doing something active if they are having
something researched. It is much easier to research than make up
your mind and it usually takes longer so that you can thereby miss
the bus and let the competitor get his blow in first. The essential
elements of successful marketing are ideas, imagination and initiative, and from what I remember of the earnest dullness of market
research reports they are not a likely source of these. (When the
Old Man established his first Advertising Department he called it
I.C.A.—ideas, copy and art—and he knew which should come
first.)

I do not mean to de-bunk modern management tools. I am sure
they are as valuable in current conditions as were the Systems of
the '20s. If they make modern managements think, they will do a
good job. If they encourage modern managements to leave the
thinking to others (the specialists) they will do harm. In using the
specialist one had better also reflect with the writer of Ecclesias-
ticus: 'A man's mind is sometime wont to tell him more than seven
watchmen that sit above in an high tower.'

The real job of a manager, whether he is modern or not, is to
manage and that usually means or involves managing people, a
job that should not be delegated or left to the personnel officer, the
personnel manager or even the personnel division. When the Old
Man first created what would now be called either staff or personnel
department he called it the Service Department, and this is not a
bad title for a function which is essentially one of service. Service
to and for members of the staff and managers but not the link
between them.

Personnel Division in Unilever was set up to advise and assist
the Board on the appointment of senior managers and on matters of
general staff policy; also to give guidance and advice to Companies
everywhere on staff policies and on labour relations, all aspects of
industrial medicine, training, recruitment and remuneration.
These functions had to be undertaken discreetly, gently, but also
firmly, and the activities of the Division were not the object of

universal, unanimous and continuous approbation. No man in charge of an individual business likes to lose an outstandingly good member of his staff even though it may be for the good of the business as a whole and of the man concerned. But it has to happen, otherwise exceptional men will arrive at the top of the business not only knowing only one small section of it but knowing nothing at all of the others, and that would severely weaken the Board as the main cohesive element in the Company.

At the other end of the scale, managers had to operate within the salary scales and policies set for the whole Company, and I confess that I was glad that when this began to operate I was no longer immediately responsible for any staff, except perhaps my secretary, as I would have found the regulations awkward. Rises were no longer to be considered as annual but given only for exceptional service, but the annual report was to be shown to and discussed with the member of the staff concerned. I was informed that the latter was the general wish of the staff, but I never heard that they too did not like annual rises. I was perhaps fortunate (but not by any means exceptional) in that, after my initial decrease in the early '20s, I think I got a rise every year (except during the war) until I became a Director and the vision of my having a set interview with my various bosses to discuss their view of my work quite shatters me. Just before I retired I was able to look at my file and was interested to see that my boss, quite early in my career, had written that I had 'great strength of mind'. That had never occurred to me and certainly if I had been told so when I was young I would either have lost my nerve or got swollen-headed, either of which would have been disastrous. A boss should be able, and be encouraged, to make his views on a subordinate's work quite clear to him during the normal course of business and even a small confirmation of a good opinion at the end of the year is quite nice.

No matter how careful the recruitment and training no boss at whatever level can expect to have other than an average staff. Some will be above average, some below. He has to see that, combined, they do better than average and he can only do this in his own way.

Generous and far-seeing staff policies are certainly an element in staff morale, but they are not the mainspring which lies in the sustainment of direct personal relationships, a process which can only start from the top. Unilever has been fortunate in that successive chairmen have devoted thought, time and effort to ensuring that the cohesive force generated by such relationships should remain strong and not be baffled by barriers of unnecessary protocol.

The chairmen of Limited and N.V., either together as members of the Special Committee or separately, would normally, during a year, meet hundreds of senior managers, which general category included chairmen and directors of all operating companies, large or small, and senior members of the Head Office Services. The Special Committee had regular meetings with all services and all members of the Unilever Board. There were no hard and fast rules about who attended these meetings: you took with you anyone you thought could contribute to the discussions. On any major project the Chairman and a couple of Directors of the operating company concerned would certainly expect to accompany their immediate boss on the Unilever Board to the Special Committee meeting at which a decision was to be made on the project. It was usual for the Overseas Committee to take to a Special Committee meeting any overseas chairman who was on a visit to Unilever House even if only to give a brief review of the position in the country from which he came.

Once a year the Chairman of Limited in London and the Chairman of N.V. in Rotterdam gave a review of the whole business to a meeting of senior managers (popularly known as the O Be Joyful). The reviews were full and frank 'mentioning the virtues, it is true, but dwelling on the vices too', and in the process giving guidance as to the aims of the Company for the ensuing year. At the dinner which followed the seating plan was devised to bring together people from different parts of the business. Some of them may have met before at management conferences or even have worked together in previous jobs, but whether this was so or not they met at the O Be Joyful as colleagues, not strangers.

Members of the Board, including the Special Committee, were assiduous in giving support to conferences, courses, seminars, etc. at all main centres and I used particularly to enjoy being the 'Aunt

Sally' at management courses when, towards the end of the course, an hour or two was devoted to question time. All members of the course could ask any question they liked about Unilever. It was not too serious an exercise and I sometimes found that it was more difficult to satisfy a persistent questioner in the bar after the meeting than when he had to pose his questions, and suffer the answers, in public.

So far as I was able to judge, and certainly overseas, this belief in the importance of maintaining direct human relationships as part of the everyday job of management ran throughout the business. The ethos of Unilever was cohesion and therein lay its strength.

I realize that the whole basis of staff relations has changed in recent years. Loyalty to one's employer is being gradually replaced by solidarity against him. Up and coming young people seem to feel that they don't rate till they have had two or three different jobs. A 'temp' is queen of the secretaries. Leisure is equated with happiness and work with misery. I don't think that leisure necessarily leads to happiness—it is more likely to lead to boredom; but I am not much of a judge on this as I have never had a lot of leisure. Nor have I really wanted it as I have never been any good at games (I am beaten before I start, even at Snakes and Ladders) and I never took up fretwork or any other hobby.

I do believe, however, that if people find work to do which gives them a sense of achievement, and some personal recognition of that achievement, within a community with an honest aim that they can understand, they have one great element of happiness in their lives.

It will, I know, require increasing effort and perhaps effort of a different kind to maintain the cohesion within Unilever which I believe to have been the mainspring not just of the morale but of the very spirit of the Company which meant so much to my generation.

I am grateful that I spent my working life in an organization which did give that element of happiness to thousands of people not just in the U.K. and Holland but in all parts of the world and of every colour and culture.

If, in writing this, I have paid some tribute to those who built

this great and spirited organization and given a smile of encouragement to those now running it, I am satisfied.

> And in his final speech he told
> Of everything he'd learned of old
> And said 'This message I will leave behind.
> Hard work, good sense, a lively mind,
> Are all the Company requires.'
> With that the happy man retires.

Index

Pettit, Cecil, 164
Philippines, 131
Plantol toilet soap, 155
Political expenses, 75
Port Said, 204
Port Sunlight, 1–15
  amenities, 5
  housing, 61
  isolation, 8–9
  Lady Lever Art Gallery, 45
  recreation ground, 11–12
  renovating houses, 14–15
  village council and committees, 6
  village shop accounts (1896), 6–7
  workers' standard of living, 7–8
Port Sunlight Monthly Journal, 6
Price's Candle Company, 90
Pricing policy, 88–9
  in India, 104
Profit-sharing, *see* Co-partnership scheme
Progress, 60
Property assets, 73

Quin, Ned, 39, 142

Rangoon, 179
Rationing, 125
Registrars Department, 80
Reid, Lionel, 23
Research, 221, 239–40
Residential training courses, 234–6
Retailers' sales returns, 122
Rhodesia, 131, 214
Richman, George, 125
Rigby, Bill, 107
Rinso, 31
  advertising appropriation (1938), 122
  sales, 123
Roberts, Sir Frank, 23
Roberts, H. George, 23
Robinson, C. S., 129
Rotterdam, 140, 141–2
Royal Ordnance Factories, 125–9, 234
Rushworth, Geoffrey, 132
Rykens, Paul, 220–1

S.P.D. Limited, 67
Salaman, E. V., 23–4
Salaries, 60–1
  'Chairman's List', 60–1
  for overseas staff, 210
Salesmen
  comparative results (1939), 121
  overseas, 22–3
Samoa, 49–50
Samuel, Frank, 161
Sandwich Islands, 47–9
Sanitas Limited, 21, 22
Sankyar Iyer, A., 163
Savonneries Lever Frères, 29, 31
Scott, W. P., 115
Sea travel, 203–5
Seddon, Fred H., 6
Shanghai, 90
Share prices, 219
Shaw, W. G. J., 93, 107, 177, 229
  appointment of Indian staff, 163
  Chairman of Lever Brothers (India) Limited, 109
  Manager in India and Ceylon, 107
Shearer, Marguerite, 206
Siam, *see* Thai Industries Limited; Thailand
Siddons, Robert H., 207, 211
Siddons, Elizabeth, 211
Singapore, 143–4, 185
  regional office established, 106
Smith, Dick, 237
Soap flakes, 68
  see also Lux Soap Flakes
Soaps
  blue mottled, 87, 88
  constituents, 84
  wartime distribution, 134
  see also Sunlight Soap
Social occasions, 60
South Africa, 131
  sales (1938), 131
  sales (1946), 132
  soap market, 89
South America, 213
Sparklets Syphons, 21, 22
Special Committee, 80–1, 220, 242
Spry, 123